Keeping the Harvest

Preserving Your Fruits, Vegetables & Herbs

Keeping the Harvest

Preserving Your Fruits, Vegetables & Herbs

Nancy Chioffi & Gretchen Mead
Revised by Linda M. Thompson

A DOWN-TO-EARTH BOOK
STOREY PUBLISHING

STOREY COMMUNICATIONS, INC.
POWNAL, VERMONT 05261

Cover design by Carol Jessop

Text design and production by Andrea Gray

Interior illustrations pp. 16, 19, 24, 25, 37, 46, 60, 89, 95, 160, 167 by Alison Kolesar; pp. 157, 166 by Elayne Sears; pp. 5, 110, 111 by Charles Cook; pp. 14, 17, 34, 36, 92, 93 by Doug Merrilles

Illustrations pp. 33 and 35 courtesy of U.S. Department of Agriculture

Indexed by Kathleen D. Bagioni

Copyright © 1991 by Storey Communications, Inc.

Printed in the United States by Capital City Press
Eighth Printing, August 1994

Library of Congress Cataloging-in-Publication Data

Chioffi, Nancy, 1942-
   Keeping the harvest : preserving your fruits, vegetables & herbs/
Nancy Chioffi and Gretchen Mead. — [New ed.] / rev. and updated by
Linda M. Thompson.
       p.   cm. — (A Down-to-earth book)
    Includes index.
     ISBN 0-88266-650-9
       1. Vegetables—Preservation. 2. Vegetables—Storage. 3. Fruit—
Preservation. 4. Fruit—Storage. I. Mead, Gretchen.
II. Thompson, Linda M. III. Title. IV. Series.
TX612.V4C45 1991
641.4—dc20   90-50413
                                                          CIP

Contents

List of Charts

Preface

In the fast-paced world we live in, it would appear that preserving and storing food in the home is an activity that few of us have time for. It is also true that fresh produce is available in more quantity and variety year round than it used to be. Why preserve food at home then? We are living in a world that is rapidly being depleted of natural resources and where taking responsibility for ourselves and our families seems to be taking a back seat to our jobs, careers, and lives in general. No wonder that many of us feel a bit "out of control" at times! Having a garden is noted these days as a way to reduce the stress in our everyday lives, and the number of gardens is increasing, not decreasing. Putting food by is a way of saving some of that homegrown goodness and bringing it out when you are unable to provide your own fresh produce. Even though fresh produce has become more available in stores, the quality is not as good as when it is picked at home in its natural growing season. Just a few days in transit causes supposedly "fresh" produce to lose significant amounts of all-important nutrients. Home-preserved produce does lose some of its nutrition in processing and storage, but there is no question of its freshness at the outset.

Putting food by is a method of self-guided quality control. You control the freshness of the original food, and you add no chemicals or preservatives in the processing, something that is not always true in the commercial preserving procedure. It can also be a family experience from which all can benefit. All members, except maybe the very young, can learn about human and family dynamics by a cooperative process in which each member has a job to do. It allows all members to learn to take responsibility for themselves as well as for the family as a group.

As important as taking responsibility for ourselves and our families is, today we also need very much to take responsibility for our planet. Recycling efforts are underway in more and more communities, and we can expect this to be the way of the next century and beyond. Home preserving allows us to recycle continually. Jars can be reused from year to year, and if they are properly cared for they will last indefinitely. Even the heavy-duty freezer bags with the zip-type closures can be washed thoroughly, rinsed, and dried for use again (providing there are no holes or leaks in them).

A revolution of sorts has occurred in the average American kitchen since this book was first written. Time-saving devices abound, from automated coffee makers that turn themselves on in the morning, to all kinds of equipment formerly available only to the professional or to institutional kitchens, such as heavy-duty mixers. Two appliances now available and affordable have become mainstays in many kitchens—the food processor and the microwave oven. These two appliances are very useful in the preserving kitchen. The food processor makes the preparation of purées and sauces infinitely easier than ever before; it can save tremendous amounts of time and relieve the tedium involved in hand chopping, slicing, and shredding of fruits and vegetables for preserving. Any place in this book that the instructions include the use of a blender, you can substitute a food processor. The microwave oven, boasting ownership in about 70 percent of American households, can also be a timesaver in a number of ways. See page 24 in the freezing chapter for instructions on how to blanch vegetables in a microwave, and page 101 for a discussion of the usefulness of the microwave oven in the quick drying of fresh herbs — a job that no longer has to take hours, days, or weeks to complete, but can be done in a matter of minutes.

This edition has been completely revised to reflect the current standards considered safe by the United States Department of Agriculture (USDA). It is a book for beginners and veterans alike, as so many things have changed in the past few years. It is my hope that you will have as much fun using this book as I have had working on it. Above all, enjoy!

Special thanks for this edition should go to Dr. Valerie Chamberlain at the University of Vermont, Dr. Gertrude Armbruster at Cornell University, Karen Schneider at Addison County Extension Service, and to Bill, Rhiannon, and Rory for living with me through this project.

Linda M. Thompson

PART I

Methods of Preserving

CHAPTER 1

Planning Ahead

A friend of ours, in her first summer of serious gardening and preserving, planted her green beans in May despite frost warnings and the wet clayey soil so typical of this part of New England. She was feeling very proud of herself because her neighbor — a more experienced gardener — had yet to put a bean in the ground by the first of June. But her pride turned to vexation when in the heat of August she found herself trapped by a hot stove, blanching bushels of beans. And her neighbor? She was at the beach while the hot sun was maturing her later beans, to be preserved in early September when the kids had returned to school and the weather was cooler. The moral of this story is to plan ahead!

WHEN TO PLANT

If you have ever stayed up until 2 A.M. on a hot summer night cutting and freezing corn, or been turned down by the neighbors when offering them just one more bushel of extra cucumbers, you understand why good garden planning is essential. With a little forethought you can control the time of maturity and the quantity of vegetables in your garden and provide just enough fruits and vegetables for in-season eating and winter storage. Your plantings should be made so that you are not left with gaps when there are no vegetables to eat or preserve, and so that you are not overwhelmed later with more than you can possibly handle.

Your enjoyment of preserving will depend on how well you plan the seasonal progression of your produce. Some crops do best in certain types of weather. Spinach and peas, for example, prefer the cold of spring, while tomatoes and melons thrive in the hot summer sun. You will have to follow nature's guide for these: plant them when they will grow best, and harvest when ripe.

Another factor in your garden-planting schedule should be what plants you might want to have mature at the same time. For example, to make dill pickles the dill should be ripening at the same time the cucumbers are reaching the various sizes good for dills (from tiny gherkins to 6-inch spears). So make several successive plantings of dill, a few feet of row at a time, starting in early spring for summer salad use, and continuing every couple of weeks to the middle of July. Dill can be frozen at its best stage for pickling (just before the flowers open) and used when needed; or the seeds can be dried when it matures. But the most distinctive dill flavor in pickles results when the dill flowers are picked fresh from the garden.

Harvesting can start with rhubarb and asparagus in May and continue into November with Chinese cabbage and parsnips. Depending on the climate, some vegetables can winter over in the garden for year-round harvest. Stagger the planting of vegetables to maximize yield and minimize preserving bottlenecks during the summer months.

HOW MUCH TO GROW

The table on page 6 will help you decide how much of each vegetable to plant for preserving. For summer use you can make additional plantings. With the vegetables that mature quickly you can plant small quantities of the earliest varieties to mature toward the beginning of the season for table use. Later, plant a larger storage crop to ripen near the end of the summer or early fall. For example, depending on your climate, you could put in a few onion sets for summer eating as soon as the ground can be worked. The rest should be planted so as not to ripen before they can be stored for winter; if you try to store onions during the warm weather of late summer or early fall, they will rot in or out of the ground. But if you hope to get storage onions from seed, they should be planted as early as possible, as it takes almost four months for them to reach adequate size.

Cabbage is another example. In the spring, set out only a few plants of the early varieties for your summer cole slaw needs. Wait until early summer to plant the later varieties that you plan to store. Otherwise they will ripen long before the harvest season and you will have cabbages that are choice targets for cabbage worms cracking in the sun. The later, longer-growing varieties of most vegetables are usually the strongest *and* have the best flavor and storage qualities.

The vegetable planning chart, page 6, shows how much of each vegetable you can harvest from 100-foot rows, and how much seed is needed to plant those rows. It also shows how many quarts of canned or frozen vegetables you can expect per pound or bushel of produce. This table should be helpful whether you grow your own or buy in bulk.

The "days to maturity" column of the vegetable chart will help you plan when to plant each type of vegetable for winter use. Decide when you want to *harvest* the crop, and, using the number of days to maturity, count backwards. For example, you may be planning a vacation in August and want a crop such as beans to ripen either before or after that

**FROST-HARDY
VEGETABLES**

All root crops
Kale
Broccoli
Lettuce
Brussels sprouts
Parsley
Cabbage
Spinach
Cauliflower
Swiss chard
Celery

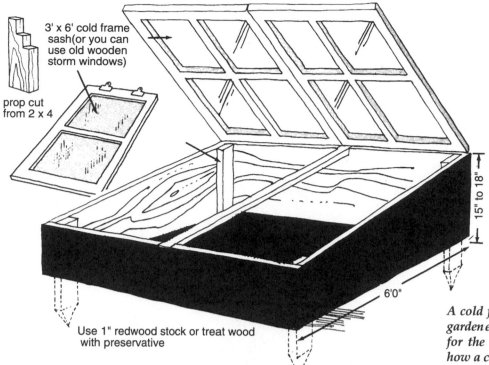

3' x 6' cold frame sash(or you can use old wooden storm windows)

prop cut from 2 x 4

15" to 18"

6'0"

Use 1" redwood stock or treat wood with preservative

A cold frame can help you start your garden earlier for tasty fresh vegetables for the table. These diagrams show how a cold frame is made.

time. So that the beans will not mature while you're gone, you can plant them in several batches, one to ripen a week or two before you leave, another a week or two after. Some varieties mature in about 50 days. If you are going to be away August 8-15, you could plant one batch before June 10, which should ripen by the last week in July. The next planting could be three weeks later (July 1) in order to mature around August 24. Both plantings will continue to produce beans if they are kept picked.

Successive plantings can be made all summer, so long as the last planting will mature before the first frost. Use the average annual fall frost date for your area for calculating the growing season of non-hardy vegetables such as beans, squash, and tomatoes. Hardy varieties — cabbage, broccoli, Swiss chard, etc. — can withstand many light frosts. The box on page 4 indicates which vegetables can survive the cold.

WHEN TO PICK

Of all the lessons we have learned from our garden, the most important has been that *when a crop is ripe it should be picked and eaten or preserved as soon as possible*. Otherwise, you will have overripe, poor-quality vegetables and fruit that won't be improved by preserving. What is second-best fresh is third-rate processed.

If you've ever grown zucchini, for example, you know what we mean. These summer squashes are most tender and delicious when 6 to 8 inches long. If you pick them all at that size, your plants will continue to produce until frost. However, if you turn your back on the plants for even a few days, you will have overgrown, tough-skinned monsters that must be peeled and the seeds and soft core removed before they can be

Vegetable Planning Chart
100-Foot Single-Row Planting

VEGETABLE VARIETY	EARLIEST PLANTING TIME* 1	2	3	4	DAYS TO MATURITY	SEEDS OR PLANTS NEEDED	YIELD PICKED	YIELD CANNED OR FROZEN	VITAMIN CONTENT
Asparagus	R				After 2 yrs.	65 1-yr. old crowns	30# spears	10 qts.	B_1,C
Beans, dry			S		65-100	2#	varies		B_1,B_2,E_1 protein
Beans, lima-bush				S	65-80	¾#	64# in hull	13-16 qts.	B_1,B_2,C
Beans, lima-pole				S	80-95	½#	2 bushels		B_6,niacin
Beans, snap, green & wax-bush			S		50-60	¾#	(60#) 2 bushels	30-40 qts.	B_1,B_2,C
Beans, snap, green & wax-pole		S			60-70	¾#	(60#) 2 bushels		B_1,B_2,C
Beets		S			50-65	1 oz.	(104#) 2 bushels	30-52 qts.	A,B_2,B_6,C (tops)
Broccoli	T				50-80	65 plants	60#	20-30 qts.	A,B_1,B_2,C
Brussels sprouts	T				65-75	65 plants	varies		B_1,B_2,C
Cabbage	T				60-90	65 plants	65 heads +		B_6,C,raw
Cantaloupe			S	T	75-100	1 pkt.	60 melons		A,C
Carrots		S			55-80	½ oz.	(100#) 2 bushels	34-50 qts.	A
Cauliflower	T				65-80	50-70 plants	50-70 heads		B_1,C
Celery	T				100-150	200 plants	200 bunches		E
Chard, Swiss		S			45-55	2 oz.	(54#) + 3 bushels	18-27 qts.	A, B_2,C
Collards		T			65-85	65 plants	(54#) + 3 bushels	18-27 qts.	A,B_1,B_2, C, niacin
Corn			S		60-95	1#	6-8 doz. ears	4-6 qts.	B_1,niacin, E
Cucumber			S		50-70	1 pkt.	1½ bushels	30-50 qts. pickles	C
Eggplant				T	80-90	50 plants	100 eggplants		
Okra				S	50-55	2 oz.	1000 pods		B_1,B_2,B_6, C, niacin
Onions	S sets T				85-200 35 + 35 +	½ oz. 8-10# 400 plants	200-400 scallions & onions or green tops 4 ½ bushels		A,C

VEGETABLE VARIETY	EARLIEST PLANTING TIME* 1	2	3	4	DAYS TO MATURITY	SEEDS OR PLANTS NEEDED	YIELD PICKED	YIELD CANNED OR FROZEN	VITAMIN CONTENT
Parsley		S			50 +	1 pkt.	varies		A,B$_1$,B$_2$, C,niacin
Parsnip		S			120-150	1 oz.	75-100#		B$_1$
Peas, green	S				50-80	1#	2 bushels (60# in pods)	12-16 qts.	B$_1$,B$_2$,C,E niacin
Peppers				T	60-100	50 plants	4 bushels		A (red),C
Potatoes	eyes				100-120	10# seed potatoes	3 bushels	60 qts.	B$_1$,B$_6$,C, niacin
Pumpkin				S	100-120	1 pkt.	300#	100-200 qts. 50#=15 qts. or 1½-3# =1 qt.	A
Rhubarb	R				1 yr.	8-10 plants	varies		
Spinach	S				40-50	1 oz.	3 bushels	18-27 qts.	A,B$_1$,B$_2$,C, iron
Squash, summer and zucchini			S		75-80	1 oz.	135 squash	100 qts. 2-4#=1 qt.	C, niacin
Squash, winter				S	85-100	1 oz.	400#	130-250 qts.	A,C
Strawberries	T				1 yr.	60-100 plants	varies		C
Sweet potatoes				T	120-150	75-100	80#	30 qts.	A,B$_1$,B$_6$, C,E
Tomatoes				T	55-90	40-60 plants	3 bushels (160#)	45-60 qts.	A,C,E
Turnip (& rutabaga)	S				40-60	½ oz.	100#		A,B$_1$,B$_2$, B$_6$,C,E (greens), C (root)

*Earliest Planting Time Key:

(1) as soon as the ground can be worked in the spring, 20-40 days before last average annual frost
(2) early, 10-30 days before last frost
(3) on average date of last frost
(4) when soil is warm; 10-20 days after last frost

Symbols: R = Root
            S = Seed
            T = Transplants
            # = Pound

used. At the same time, there will be fewer tender little squash since the plant has now produced its seeds. That's the primary purpose of most annual plants — to produce seeds for the next generation. When this has been accomplished, the plant ceases producing fruit. We don't mean to imply that large zucchini are useless; on the contrary, the thick flesh can be cut into cubes and used to form the base of many casseroles. In addition, zucchini can be substituted for ripe cukes in pickle-making. However, wait until the end of the growing season before letting the zucchini grow.

It is important to remember to pick all your vegetables when just ripe so that you will have a continuing harvest; let them go by a few days and you will have fewer, less appetizing vegetables. Knowing this, you may want to put in fewer plants, encouraging maximum production from your rows and preserving in small quantities over several weeks. If your plants ripen all at once, many may go by because you cannot concentrate enough time on preserving in such large quantity. This is particularly true in the case of summer squash, cucumbers, spinach, beans, broccoli, and asparagus. It is not so true with plants that set only a certain number of fruit, such as corn and the root crops — you'll get only one carrot or turnip per seed no matter what you do.

In the case of vine crops like pumpkins, winter squash, and melons, you may even want to discourage vine growth so more energy will be devoted to fewer large fruit. If so, pinch off the fuzzy ball at the end of the vine. This stops the plant from spreading. Also pick off some of the blossoms. This will limit the number of fruit and thereby encourage the growth of a few bigger ones. Mammoth pumpkins weighing 100-200 pounds are grown in this way. Only one fruit per vine is allowed to ripen, and that one is coaxed with fertilizer or even "milk-fed" to grow enormous.

Size, however, is not usually an important goal with the vegetables you plan to keep for winter use. Giant tomatoes make attractive slices on the summer table, but they have to be cut up to fit into a mason jar. The smaller varieties are more practical. Green and yellow wax beans are best when pencil thin (not yet knobby with maturing beans), crisp and tender when snapped. Extra-large carrots and beets may impress the neighbors, but they tend to be tough and tasteless. For fresh eating and for storage, the smaller "table size" vegetables are preferred.

HOW TO PRESERVE

There are many methods of storing and preserving foods. Common storage, or "root cellaring," is the simplest method. If you live in an area with a cool or cold climate, you can store many vegetables for several months in a cold cellar or any space with the appropriate atmosphere. This method requires no preparation and can be used for onions, carrots, beets, potatoes, winter squash, pumpkins, cabbage, and fruits such as apples. Dried seeds, such as beans and split peas, and grains require only darkness and a cool, dry spot protected from the three M's — *mold*, *moisture*, and *mice*. (See Chapter 8.)

☙ KEEP IT FRESH

To achieve the very best in quality in your canning or freezing, pick garden produce at the last minute, when you're all ready to process it. Corn is perhaps the most critical item. Even if it's stored at 40°F., in one day half its sweetness will have turned into starch. If you can't get to the processing at once, chill the foods immediately to as close to 32°F. as you can get them. Strawberries, for instance, *respire* (lose quality) ten times as fast at 40° as they do at 32°. Even apples sitting for one day in 70° heat lose as much life as they would at 32°F. in a week.

Take along a pre-chilled cooler if you go shopping for garden-fresh produce at a farm market. Then it won't lose so much on the hot ride home. Best of all, if you can, have the water boiling on the stove before you go out to the corn patch to pick.

Other methods include freezing, canning, pickling, fermenting, drying, and making jams and jellies. Freezing is the easiest and can be used for almost any fruit or vegetable. There is little loss of nutrients compared with other methods, but it does involve the most expensive equipment and the continuing use of electricity. Canning by boiling-water bath is the tried-and-true method to preserve high-acid foods like fruits and pickled vegetables; pressure canning is necessary for the majority of other vegetables, such as beans, peas, corn, and beets, which are "low acid." Low-acid foods also can be preserved by freezing, drying, fermenting, or pickling. Choosing a preserving technique will depend on the equipment you have available or can afford to buy. Equipment such as jars, freezer containers, and a pressure canner should be purchased well in advance of the season while they are still plentiful. It can be downright discouraging in August to be faced with a bushel of tomatoes rotting on the porch because the stores have run out of canning-jar lids. Whether you are a gardener or not, you can never be over-prepared for the summer deluge of local and homegrown produce. In the following chapters you will find the information necessary for each method. A discussion of the effects of the different methods on the nutrients in the foods is also included.

If you do not have a garden, you can pick produce at local farms and orchards, buy specials at supermarkets, or check roadside stands for good, fresh foods. It is also possible to buy in bulk from food cooperatives and farm-supply stores. Wild berries, fruits, "edible weeds," and asparagus are yours for the picking in some areas, the property owner permitting.

Unless they are kept cold and moist, vegetables will lose taste and nutrients within a few hours once picked. If you buy or pick vegetables in bulk and then find that you are unable to process them right away, we recommend that they be washed quickly in cold water, drained, put in large plastic bags, and kept in the refrigerator. Do not cut or peel them, as this hastens the loss of nutrients. Stored in this manner they should be good for one or two days, and in the case of root crops and cabbage, considerably longer. But for good quality, preserve your vegetables as soon after picking as possible.

Most fruits will keep for a while, but if they are ripe they should be kept cold until you can use them. Raspberries and other soft fruits that deteriorate rapidly must be handled gently and briefly and preserved immediately.

Preserving foods actually starts in early January with the arrival of seed catalogues. Study them carefully. Many new hybrids are designated as especially good for canning or freezing. You may wish to choose a few new varieties each year. Sometimes you will hit on a family favorite, or at least increase your knowledge for next year. But be realistic. Take into account your family's likes and dislikes. It is easy to get carried away with the glossy pictures. If your family will not eat a certain vegetable, you will have wasted your time and garden space by planting it. Save your garden plan from year to year. If you also record the varieties and how well each did, you will be spared from making the same mistakes and be at least partially assured of the same successes.

✿ HINTS

A few hints that apply to all aspects of preserving:

1. Plan to have the right kind and amount of equipment ready before you start. You will need to have on hand enough jars and lids for canning, bags or containers for freezing. You will find lists of other necessary equipment for each preserving method in later chapters.

2. Always label your canned and frozen foods with the date, product, variety, and method or recipe used. The date is important because food should be eaten within one year of processing to insure good quality. And unless you can see through the container, you'll also want to specify the contents. Nothing is more frustrating than opening dozens of food containers in a freezer in order to find the right box. Labeling the variety also will help you avoid planting an unpopular vegetable again next year. If in the spring you are faced with dozens of containers of frozen summer squash, you will realize it's not a family favorite.

3. Also note the recipes used for pickles and relishes and vegetable combinations so you can repeat your successes next year.

Some good vegetable combinations that you might want to grow for preserving together are tiny peas and onions, corn and limas (succotash), tomatoes and celery, and zucchini and eggplant. For bread-and-butter pickles, you will need onions and cucumbers; for relishes, red and green peppers and onions are needed together. Sweet red peppers are mature green peppers; in order to have red and green at the same time, allow all the peppers on a few of your plants to mature to the red stage while picking green peppers as needed from other plants.

NUTRITIONAL EFFECTS OF FOOD PROCESSING

One important consideration in deciding which methods of home food preservation to use is the effect each method has on the nutrients in the food. There is evidence that the greatest losses in vitamins and minerals often result from the way the food is prepared. Water-soluble vitamins, such as vitamin B_1, riboflavin, and niacin, tend to be lost by "leaching" or dissolving in cooking water. Losses of the fat-soluble vitamins (A, D, E, and K) and vitamin C, on the other hand, are more likely to occur during heating and storage in the presence of air.

Here are some of the known nutritional losses from each type of food processing:

Blanching. Blanching before freezing or drying foods inactivates the enzymes that would otherwise gradually destroy the color, flavor, and some nutrients of the food during storage. Blanching in boiling water will eliminate more nutrients than blanching with steam. For example, steaming spinach will cause the loss of up to 10 percent of vitamins B_1, B_2, and C and niacin, while blanching in boiling water for 2 to 5 minutes can cause losses of up to 35 percent of these vitamins. Minerals are not destroyed by the heat, but they may be lost by leaching into water. Blanching by microwave causes even less loss of nutrients than steaming.

Canning. Most vitamins, except riboflavin and niacin, break down when heated, so losses during the heat processing for canning can be expected. Riboflavin will break down when exposed to light, which is one reason for storing canned foods in the dark.

Foods that form a dense pack in the canning jar, such as greens and strained pumpkin, and require a long processing time in order for the heat to reach the center of the mass, will lose more of their vitamin content than will the more liquid vegetables, such as tomatoes.

The water-soluble vitamins in canned foods will become evenly distributed throughout the solids and liquids in the jar soon after canning. Since liquid may make up about one-third of the contents, one-third of these vitamins will be lost unless the liquid is consumed with the solids or is used in soups and gravies.

The storage temperature of canned goods makes a difference in long-term retention of some nutrients. At cold temperatures (below 65°F.) very little loss occurs. Thiamine is preserved at 65°F., but at 80°F. for one year there may be losses of 15 percent in canned fruits and 25 percent in canned vegetables. Storage of canned tomato juice at 80°F. for a year can result in the loss of 25 percent of vitamin C and 10 percent of vitamin A.

Drying. The process of drying preserves a percentage of most vitamins except those lost during blanching. However, during a long period of storage, major losses of vitamins A, C, and E may occur in foods dried at home because they are stored in the presence of oxygen. Commercially dried foods that are vacuum packed or packed in nitrogen will retain more of their vitamins over a long period of time.

Freezing. Freezing does not significantly destroy any vitamins except vitamin E and pyridoxine (B$_6$). Processing losses that occur are primarily the result of blanching the vegetables before freezing. Frozen foods will retain most of their nutrients if kept at a constant temperature of 0°F. or less. At temperatures above 15°F. the easily oxidizable vitamins will be gradually lost. For example, half of the original vitamin C in asparagus, peas, and lima beans will be lost during storage at 15°F. for

🌱 OUR BEST METHODS

The following list contains our recommendations of the best methods of preserving each vegetable and fruit, balancing nutrition, flavor, convenience — and personal prejudice!

Vegetables

Asparagus: freeze
Beans, dry: dry on vine and store in airtight containers
Beans, lima-bush: freeze
Beans, lima-pole: freeze
Beans, snap, green, and wax-bush: freeze
Beans, snap, green, and wax-pole: freeze
Beets: root cellar, in sand or sawdust
Broccoli: freeze
Brussels sprouts: freeze, or leave in garden and keep eating (we've had as late as Christmas)
Cabbage: sauerkraut, or wrapped in newspaper in *cold* storage

Carrots: root cellar in sand or sawdust
Cauliflower: freeze
Celery: root cellar
Chard, Swiss: eat from garden all season, and late into fall
Collards: keep in garden
Corn: freeze whole kernel
Cucumber: pickles
Eggplant: freeze as part of prepared casserole
Onions: hang in braids or net bags, cold and dry
Parsley: green in pot on windowsill, or dry
Parsnip: store in ground in garden, harvest after ground has frozen and/or in spring
Peas: freeze
Peppers: freeze
Potatoes: root cellar
Pumpkin: store in dry, warmish spot (under kitchen table) freeze purée in late winter
Rhubarb: freeze
Rutabaga: root cellar in sand or sawdust
Spinach: freeze

Squash, summer: freeze, purée or grated
Squash, winter: dry storage, about 50°F. (under the bed), freeze purée in late winter
Tomatoes: can juice, purée and whole
Turnip: root cellar in sand or sawdust

Fruits

Apple: can applesauce, dry leather and slices, store apples in root cellar
Apricot: can
Blackberry: jelly
Blueberry: freeze
Cantaloupe: freeze
Cherry, sour: can
Cherry, sweet: can
Currant: jelly
Elderberry: shrub (drink)
Grapes: can juice, wine
Peach: can
Pear: can, and store in root cellar
Plum: can
Raspberry: freeze, or preserves
Strawberry: freeze, or preserves

six months. Over a longer storage time some losses occur even at 0°F. For example, beans, broccoli, cauliflower, and spinach may lose from one-third to three-quarters of their vitamin C when stored for a year at 0°F.

All this would indicate that the differences in food-preservation methods will be substantially counteracted and the losses kept to a minimum by:

- preserving only garden-fresh, ripe produce;
- using heat in processing for no more than the recommended time;
- storing canned foods in a cold, dark place; frozen foods at 0°F. or less;
- cooking foods for the table as briefly and with as little water as possible;
- making use of all cooking and blanching liquid either with the food cooked or in soup stock or gravy in order to save the nutrients dissolved in it.

CHAPTER 2

Freezing

W e simply can't imagine preserving without freezing — there are no two ways about it. Freezing is easy and fast, holds color, flavor, and nutrients, is suited to more foods than canning, is safe and convenient — and is expensive compared to other methods. Bear in mind, however, that the cost is variable, based on full or partial operation, cost of containers, electric rates, turnover rate, and whether or not you grow your own produce.

We started with an upright, manual-defrost freezer the first year that our garden was really big. We haven't stopped appreciating it yet. Not only does it allow time to enjoy summer, which is all too short in the northern states, but also it is a convenience all year long. It holds extra pies and baked goods, leftovers, meat specials, and holiday cooking. Casseroles can be frozen using oven-proof dishes lined with aluminum foil. (After it has frozen, remove the dish, and replace it when you are ready to heat the casserole.) Our freezer proves itself every time we have a cheesecake dotted with extra-large "fresh" strawberries straight from the freezer, or corn in mid-winter that tastes just picked.

Once, the freezer came unplugged by accident, ruining our early-summer frozen fruit. I cried, plugged in the freezer, cleaned up the mess, and bought a screw-in plug (a minor investment that can save you countless dollars in goods — it simply keeps a plug from being pulled out by accident). Even with that problem, plus the expense that perhaps makes a freezer a luxury, we would never forsake it. This is not to suggest that other methods aren't good, too. We make pickles, can fruit, make relishes, jams, and jellies, cold-store and dry food, but the freezer is the backbone of our home storage.

Maybe because of laziness the idea of washing fruit, packaging it, and putting it in the freezer appeals. Then there is time for a swim with the children. But, like everything else, not all of it is that simple. There are rules as with all the other methods.

Most of us have a freezer section in our refrigerator. If it is within the refrigerator itself, it is too warm for anything except short-term holding.

A separate door is one step better but still not adequate for long-term storage. To insure good quality, a freezer should maintain a minimum of 0°F. For each 10° above zero, the storage life of your food will be cut in half. Keep your freezer compartment for quick-rotation foods such as ice cream and popsicles. This will save on the constant "in and out" that makes running a freezer more expensive and defrosting a problem.

An upright freezer, which generally comes in models rated at 16 and 21 cubic feet, is easier than a chest type to find things in and takes up less floor space. On the other hand, cold spills out each time it is opened, making it slightly more costly to run. Use containers that stack well, since odd-shaped packages tend to fall out. With the chest freezer, the cold settles in when the lid is opened. Chest freezers do take up more floor space and are considerably harder to locate packages in, but the lid can provide counter space if the freezer is conveniently located. Chest freezers come in sizes ranging from 5 to 25 or more cubic feet.

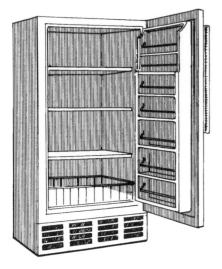

Upright freezer. In some models, each shelf contains freezing coils on which food is placed. The inside of the door is used for frozen juices and other smaller packages.

How Big a Freezer for Your Family?

Never, never underbuy. The cost of replacing a too-small freezer or adding a second one is excessive. Rent a freezer locker the first year to discover how much space you will need, or figure 3-4 cubic feet of vegetables per person.

- four-person family: 4 x 4 equals 16 cubic feet
- six-person family: 4 x 6 equals 24 cubic feet

If you raise your own meat or buy on special, allow at least 6 cubic feet per person. It seems wiser to buy a freezer slightly larger than you think you may need, as you are certain to find a use for the extra space.

Manual or Automatic Defrost

We can't say enough for a manual defrost. The expense of running one is significantly less than the automatic, frost-free models. A frost-free motor must turn on periodically to chill off the freezer each time the defrost mechanism finishes. With a manual, *you* are the defrost mechanism. We may be lazy, but not too lazy to defrost a freezer once a year, and the automatic-defrost freezers should be shut down once a year to be cleaned, anyway.

Defrosting is easy. Wait for a cold day late in the winter, when the freezer stock is low. Then turn down the freezer as far as possible overnight, so the food is as cold as possible. The next day turn off the freezer, unload the contents and place them out of doors, open the freezer door, and turn on a fan in the interior or put pans of hot water inside. I scrape with a blunt instrument, preferably the kind that comes

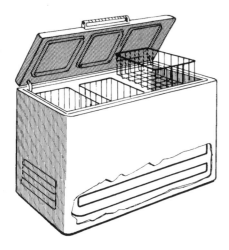

Chest freezer. This cut-away view shows the freezing coils in the walls. These coils are on all four sides of the freezer. Wire racks roll on tracks for easier access to lower level.

with a refrigerator or freezer. Wrapping frozen packages in newspaper and covering them with a blanket or sleeping bag will keep the food frozen even indoors during defrost. After defrosting, wash the interior with warm water and baking soda and wipe dry before reloading.

Frost need not build up to defrosting levels more than once a year if care is used. A half inch of frost indicates defrosting time. Do the defrosting before you start your summer freezing.

Features to Look For

Either type of freezer should have controls so that the temperature can be regulated. A minimum high temperature for quality is 0°F. For the best quality, freezers should be adjustable to -20°F. for a quick initial freeze that helps prevent large ice crystals. Some freezers have a special quick-freeze area. Otherwise, you can put packages to be frozen directly over the coils. A refrigerator-freezer thermometer is an asset, so you can quickly check your freezer's calibration.

Hints on Using Your Freezer Wisely

- Freeze realistically. Don't freeze more of anything than you can use in one year. If you know they will only be thrown away the following summer, resist the temptation to freeze several more cartons of zucchini just because it's there. Too many other things could take its place.
- Try moving a week's supply of food from your big freezer to your freezer-refrigerator. It will keep frost buildup to a minimum.
- If possible, you should have a full freezer at all times. The operating cost of a freezer is less at three-quarters full than at three-quarters empty. We heard of one woman who stuffed a sleeping bag in a half-full freezer so that it would operate at maximum efficiency. A more practical suggestion would be to keep large bags of ice cubes in the freezer during the summer when it is not full.
- Test-freeze any food that you have never frozen before to make certain that you are satisfied with the quality. This will not, however, indicate its keeping ability.

WHAT TO FREEZE

If you have all the preserving options available, freezing will be only part of your food storage plan. You should freeze only what freezes best. Potatoes will keep in a cold-cellar, tomatoes and relishes can be canned, apples will dry, but the bulk of your vegetables and fruits and all your meat will freeze. If your freezer is small, you will have to be more selective. Pick only foods that definitely have an edge on quality when frozen.

Applesauce is as good canned and quicker to use on short notice, but you would definitely freeze strawberries. Broccoli, Brussels sprouts, and cauliflower discolor and become stronger in flavor when canned, so freeze them. On the other hand, beets change texture when frozen, and radishes, lettuce, and green onions just don't freeze. Be selective and think out your priorities.

KEEPING TRACK

To get the most value and enjoyment out of your frozen foods you have to know what's left in store. Chest-type freezers especially defy a storage system that allows visual checking. Just as the new year's strawberries are ripening, you'll find a forgotten supply of the frozen berries you thought had long been used up.

The only answer is an *inventory checklist*, posted by the freezer or in the kitchen. Draft it up on a large cardboard from the totals you keep while freezing. Down the left-hand side list alphabetically all the fruits and vegetables you have frozen — meat cuts, too, if you wish. To the right of each food provide a square to mark off a package each time you use it. In the first square write the total you start with. You'll need as many squares as the largest number of packages of any of the foods you freeze. For instance, if you put up forty pints of kernel corn, the figure "40" goes in the first square and there are thirty-nine squares following to be filled as you use it up.

This way you can always tell what's left of any food. You won't end up with nothing but spinach — and you won't be forgetting those strawberries.

Once you have decided on your food choices, choose your varieties. Check seed packages and seed catalogues for the varieties that freeze better than others. For instance, Freezonia peas are especially adapted for freezing.

HOW TO FREEZE

1. Select only prime quality produce. Only the best is good enough; freezing won't improve the quality. Process vegetables as quickly as possible. Freeze fruit only when you would eat it fresh, when the flavor is completely matured.
2. Use the most sanitary conditions and equipment.
3. Organize your equipment and work area, as well as your time. Although freezing takes far less time and equipment than canning, you don't want to be interrupted by a last-minute trip to the store.
4. Sort for uniform size, as this makes for better appearance and consistent blanching and cooking.
5. Prepare as for fresh cooking. Wash or scrub thoroughly. Peel and slice as needed. Blanch vegetables and cool them quickly in ice water. (Blanching times are given in specific instructions, Chapter 9.)
6. Package promptly, expelling as much air as possible from the container. Allow headspace since foods expand, but leave as few air pockets as possible. A dry pack needs no headroom.
7. Label and place in your freezer's "cold zone" for as quick a freeze as possible. Don't put in more than one layer, and be sure that the packages are not touching each other. Put in no more than your freezer can freeze solid in 24 hours — 2 to 3 pounds per cubic foot of freezer capacity.
8. To use vegetables, don't defrost. The vegetables already are partially cooked, so they need be cooked only a short time until tender. Add ½ inch of water, cover, and boil.
9. Fruits don't need to be defrosted completely. A few ice crystals will prevent the fruit from becoming limp.

Packaging

There is more room for flexibility in packaging for a freezer than in canning, but for maximum quality, certain criteria must be met. Packages should be proof against air, moisture, and vapor. The seal should prevent odors from being absorbed from the freezer into the food. *Freezer burn*, a condition caused by exposure to the dry air of the freezer that causes a loss of moisture, can be prevented by a good seal. Gear your packaging sizes to family size. Pick the container size that will make one-meal servings.

Rigid containers. This means glass jars, plastic boxes, or wax-coated cardboard containers. The glass jars should be designated as appropriate for a freezer — with flared or straight sides to get out unthawed food. Always leave the recommended headspace when freezing in jars. Without it jars will break when the food expands during freezing. To speed the thawing of food in glass containers, put the cold jars in cold water — never hot water.

SALAD SPINNER AS FREEZING TOOL

Best quality in frozen foods depends on speedy chilling in ice water after blanching, then thorough drying of the food before freezing. Try using your salad spinner to remove excess moisture from beans, greens, and other vegetables. It's quick and thorough, will cut down on ice crystal formation, and will help keep the pieces separate.

For variety in preparation of beans, try french-style. Use the slotted end of a peeler, pressing beans through lengthwise.

Plastic containers stack better in the freezer and store compactly when empty. They are a substantial initial investment but are handy also for storing leftovers in the refrigerator and are reuseable. Headroom is marked on the plastic containers.

Freezer bags. These are not reuseable, as most rigid containers are, but the initial investment is much less. They are awkward to store compactly in the freezer but will retain a more rigid form when used with reuseable boxes. Put the food in the bag, using the box as a form. Force excess air out of the bag and close with a twistie. Freeze in the box until the package is solid. Then you can remove the box, allowing it to be used again — though if left on, the box protects the bag from tears.

Never put hot food into the bags, and be especially careful to get the heavy-duty bags. They come in pint, quart, two-quart, one-gallon, and two-gallon sizes. Special funnels and racks for easy filling are available.

Today's zipper-type freezer bags are also very convenient. They are thicker than traditional freezer bags, reducing the risk of tearing, and, providing there are no leaks, can be washed in hot soapy water, rinsed, and reused.

Boil-in bags. These are a relative newcomer to the frozen-food packaging field and a luxurious convenience. Special bags are filled and heat-sealed with a sealer mechanism and then frozen. The food is heated in the bags in boiling water. There is less nutrient loss from the food because it comes in contact with water only during blanching before freezing. Some people have experienced uneven cooking with these bags, but they are excellent for vegetables such as corn-on-the-cob or for vegetables frozen in a sauce or with butter.

Freeze wrap. To insure freshness, use the special papers and plastic wraps that have been developed especially for wrapping meats, pies, bread. Seal with freezer tape. Wax paper and aluminum foil will allow a deterioration in quality.

Improvised containers. Let your imagination loose and improvise. Just remember to get a good seal with pressure-sensitive tape. Scotch tape and masking tape won't do, as their stickiness releases in the cold. You can use plastic cottage cheese, ice cream, and margarine containers, reinforced with tape, but the quality may not be as good as with conventional freezer containers. You can use canning jars if the manufacturer so specifies. Use and reuse aluminum foil containers. Freeze cookies in coffee cans. Freeze fresh fish in ice in waxed milk cartons. Put homemade baby food or purée in ice cube trays until frozen, and then place the frozen cubes in freezer bags for easy access.

Labeling Containers

Using an indelible marking pen, label each container with the food variety, the date, and any other pertinent information. If you have ever stood in front of your open freezer trying to find that one special unlabeled package, you'll understand. Labeling becomes crucial if you've used opaque packaging, but see-through plastic box lids are no substitute for labeling — spinach looks just like broccoli!

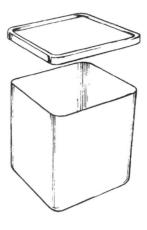
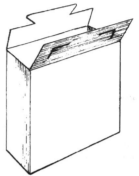
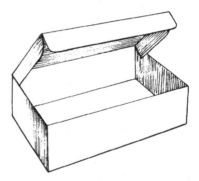

Freezer containers. The one at top is plastic with a snap-on lid and can be used for freezing anything. The center and bottom ones are made of plastic-coated cardboard and can be reused, but they wear out quickly. These should be used with plastic freezer bags as liners, and the lids should be closed firmly with freezer tape. All come in half-pint, pint, quart, and two-quart sizes.

The date is especially important, since shelf life in freezing is more complicated than in canning. Following is a chart for shelf life:

Fruits, citrus	3-4 months
Fruits, other	12 months
Vegetables (except onions)	12 months
Onions	3-6 months
Corn-on-the-cob	8-10 months
Mushrooms	8-10 months

Note that the keeping quality of fruits and vegetables varies greatly. Nothing should stay in your freezer for more than one year.

WHAT TO DO IF THE POWER FAILS

If the power fails, *don't* open the freezer door — resist the temptation to peek. A closed freezer will keep food frozen for two days if full, for one day if half full. In most cases the power will return before then. In more extreme cases, keep the freezer covered with blankets. If available, put in as much dry ice as you can (on cardboard and using gloves), or move your frozen food to a food locker or a friend's freezer.

If the food has started to thaw before the power returns, what can you refreeze? *Refreeze only those foods that still have ice crystals.* This will be food at a temperature of 40° or below. Look at and feel the food. Food with no ice crystals is said to be defrosted and should not be refrozen — with the exception of bread. If fruit is still cold, however, it can be refrozen with a marked decrease in quality. Label it again and use it first.

Bacteria that cause spoilage in food are not destroyed by freezing, only kept inactive as long as the food is stored at 0°F. Should the food thaw, the bacteria will start to grow, and food poisoning is possible. You should throw the food away.

If the freezer itself fails, check your warranty, as many will cover a certain portion of your food loss.

DRY ICE

For years home-freezer owners have been advised that if the power fails to pack chunks of dry ice into their freezers. Fifty pounds of it should hold an average freezer load of food at 0°F. for 36 hours.

The problem is where to find the dry ice — which is solid carbon dioxide that melts (turns to gas) at *minus* 110°F. In case of a prolonged power failure or non-functioning freezer, dry ice might be the best remedy, so locating a source ahead of time is a good idea. Most often it is used by ice cream manufacturers and medical laboratories.

Handle dry ice *very carefully* — with thick gloves; its extremely low temperature will damage bare skin instantly. And it should be kept separate from your food supply by putting it on top of cardboard.

Freezing Fruit

Few items are as easy or rewarding to preserve as fruit. And almost all fruits are suitable for freezing. The requirements and rules are simple. (For specific instructions on freezing each kind of fruit, refer to Chapter 10.)

- Pick or process small quantities. The first time we picked strawberries at a local farm we developed a temporary loathing for them after processing dozens of quarts at one time.
- All fruit should be ripe when preserved, as opposed to vegetables, which are at their best when slightly immature. (This is because the sugar in vegetables turns quickly to starch as they ripen, while the starch in fruit breaks down into sugar. The sugar is what pleases the palate.)

- A mellow flavor in peaches, plums, figs, and some berries is acquired by letting them sit at room temperature to mature overnight. Apples may require several days to develop maximum flavor. Pears usually are picked green and allowed to ripen in the dark for several days.
- All fruit should be sorted for uniformity to make an attractive product. Freeze only those fruits that you would want to eat fresh. Slightly bruised or overripe fruit makes excellent jelly.
- Prepare fruits much as you would for the table. Wash the fruit *gently* in cool water to minimize damage. Don't let fruits soak in water, or they will become waterlogged.
- Avoid iron utensils, which may darken fruits; use stainless steel or enamelware instead.
- Most fruits are best packed in rigid containers so that their shape is retained. Seal, label, and freeze.

SUGAR: TO USE OR NOT?

Fruits can be packed several ways, depending on their eventual use. Adding sugar sometimes helps to hold the color and bring out the flavor, but if you are trying to cut down your consumption of refined sugar it can be left out or other natural sweeteners such as honey can be tried. A *syrup pack* often is used for desserts or fresh use, while either a *dry pack* or an *unsweetened pack* is generally used for cooking, as in pies or jellies.

An unsweetened pack calls for cutting and washing the fruit, draining it, and putting it directly into containers or covering it first with an ascorbic-acid solution (see Anti-Oxidants, page 20) or the fruit's own juices. A dry or sugar pack refers to sprinkling sugar over the fruit and mixing *gently*, then leaving it for several hours to draw out a syrup.

Sugar syrups can be made of any density, but a 40 percent syrup generally is recommended. It is made up of 3 cups sugar to 4 cups water, yielding 5½ cups. Dissolve the sugar in hot or cold water and use the syrup cold. It can be made ahead of time and stored in the refrigerator. Sour fruits may take a heavier syrup, while mild-flavored fruits need a lighter syrup. See page 20.

OTHER SYRUPS

Sugar syrups also can be made by dissolving the sugar, using the same amounts as above, in fruit juice extracted from less perfect fruit. The flavor will be superior to a sugar-and-water syrup. Honey or corn syrup can be substituted for the sugar in either water or juice. If you replace only a quarter of the sugar with an alternative sweetener there will be little flavor change; above that the difference will be noticeable. Experiment!

Cover the fruit completely with syrup. Most fruits will float, so crumple wax paper and place it between the top of the syrup and the lid, to keep the fruit below the surface during freezing. Remove the wax paper when thawing the fruit for use.

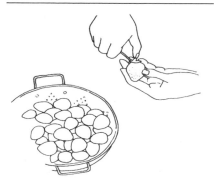

1. Sort and wash ripe, red strawberries. Remove hulls and green spots. Wash again.

2. For sugar pack, add ¾ cup sugar to 1 quart fruit. Mix thoroughly and let sit until juices start to flow.

3. Pack into containers, leaving appropriate headroom (see chart, page 170). Seal, label, and freeze.

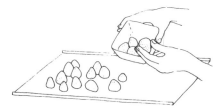

4. For whole, perfect strawberries, flash freeze on a metal sheet. Transfer when solid to freeze containers.

ANTI-OXIDANTS

Many fruits darken quickly when they are peeled, especially peaches and apples, so you may want to use an anti-oxidant to prevent this discoloration. Ascorbic acid (vitamin C), which comes as tablets or crystals, is an anti-oxidant and is available at drugstores. The crystalline form is easier to use. Dissolve the powder or tablets in cold water according to directions.

Syrup pack. Add the dissolved ascorbic acid to the syrup before adding it to the fruit.

Sugar pack. Sprinkle the ascorbic-acid solution over the fruit before adding sugar.

Unsweetened pack. Sprinkle the ascorbic-acid solution over the fruit and mix before packaging.

Fruit Fresh ascorbic-acid powders are made of ascorbic acid, sugar, and silica aerogel. Directions simply require sprinkling the granular powder over the fruit before packaging. These powders are very convenient but not quite as effective as ascorbic-acid solutions. Lemon juice is a simple substitute for either, but is not quite as effective and lends a lemony flavor to fruit.

Vitamin C tablets, which are economical and available year round, can be used as well. Buy 500 mg. tablets. Crush and dissolve 6 tablets per 1 gallon of water as a treatment solution.

FLASH FREEZING

Flash freezing is reserved for super-quality fruits. Wash extra large, perfect fruits, drain *well*, and place them on a metal sheet, separated from each other. Place the sheet in the coldest area of the freezer until the fruits are frozen solid. Then package in rigid containers. Used semi-thawed, they will retain their shape. The fruits will separate easily in case you need only a few at a time. They make excellent decorations for cakes and pies.

Don't overlook buying already-frozen fruits from local stores that sell in large-quantity containers. They can be canned in smaller quantities or broken apart (blueberries, for example) and frozen in more convenient portions. Individually frozen unsweetened berries can also be used later to make jams, jellies, and preserves. These stores often offer good buys, too, on citrus fruits sold fresh by the case.

Syrups for Freezing Fruits

TYPE OF SYRUP	SUGAR (in cups)	WATER (in cups)	YIELD OF SYRUP (in cups)
30% (thin)	2	4	5
40% (medium)	3	4	5½
50% (heavy)	4¾	4	6½
60% (extra heavy)	7	4	7¾

Approximate Yield of Frozen Fruits

FRUIT	FRESH	FROZEN
Apples	1 bu. (48 lb.) 1 box (44 lb.) 1¼ to 1½ lb.	32 to 40 pt. 29 to 35 pt. 1 pt.
Apricots	1 bu. (48 lb.) 1 crate (22 lb.) ⅔ to ⅘ lb.	60 to 72 pt. 28 to 33 pt. 1 pt.
Berries	1 crate (24 qt.) 1⅓ to 1½ pt.	32 to 36 pt. 1 pt.
Cantaloupes	1 dozen (28 lb.) 1 to 1¼ lb.	22 pt. 1 pt.
Cherries, sweet or sour	1 bu. (56 lb.) 1¼ to 1½ lb.	36 to 44 pt. 1 pt.
Cranberries	1 box (25 lb.) 1 peck (8 lb.) ½ lb.	50 pt. 16 pt. 1 pt.
Currants	2 qt. (3 lb.) ¾ lb.	4 pt. 1 pt.
Peaches	1 bu. (48 lb.) 1 lug box (20 lb.) 1 to 1½ lb.	32 to 48 pt. 13 to 20 pt. 1 pt.
Pears	1 bu. (50 lb.) 1 western box (46 lb.) 1 to 1¼ lb.	40 to 50 pt. 37 to 46 pt. 1 pt.
Pineapple	5 lb.	4 pt.
Plums and prunes	1 bu. (56 lb.) 1 crate (20 lb.) 1 to 1½ lb.	38 to 56 pt. 13 to 20 pt. 1 pt.
Raspberries	1 crate (24 pt.) 1 pt.	24 pt. 1 pt.
Rhubarb	15 lb. ⅔ to 1 lb.	15 to 22 pt. 1 pt.
Strawberries	1 crate (24 qt.) ⅔ qt.	38 pt. 1 pt.

Freezing Vegetables

If you have ever bought fresh green beans from the supermarket in mid-winter and compared them with your own frozen green beans, the merits of freezing should be obvious. There is no comparison in quality. Following are general directions for freezing vegetables. For specific information on each vegetable, refer to Chapter 9.

- Check the seed catalogues and seed packages to be sure you have chosen a variety that freezes well.
- Pick only tender, young vegetables ready for table use or even slightly younger. Nothing but the best is worth freezing. (If you must pick or buy before you are ready to freeze, put the vegetables in the refrigerator or spread them out in a well-ventilated area.)
- Wash the vegetables thoroughly by rinsing, repeatedly if necessary, and using a vegetable brush, an indispensable kitchen gadget. Lift the vegetables out of the water rather than draining the water, which allows the dirt to settle back on them. Don't let them soak so long that they become waterlogged. Sort according to size and keep only the best. Generally, prepare the vegetables as you would for table use.
- References to blanching often produce puzzled looks among novices, but it's really simple and essential. It means scalding the vegetables, usually by steaming or immersing them in boiling water, the easier method, although a microwave oven can also be used for blanching vegetables. (See page 24 for information on how to blanch vegetables for freezing.) Blanching sets color and stops the action of the enzymes that otherwise will continue to mature the vegetables in color and flavor beyond the optimum. It also helps to retain vitamins. Consult the specific instructions for blanching times in Chapter 9, as they vary from vegetable to vegetable. Only peppers and herbs do not require blanching.
- One secret to good, crisp vegetables is *prompt cooling* to stop the cooking process. Prepare plenty of ice in advance if you plan to do a lot of freezing. Fill the sink with ice water and put the hot, drained vegetables in, swishing them around. Don't let them soak. The cooling will take approximately as long as the blanching did.
- Drain the vegetables as completely as possible, even rolling them gently in towels if necessary. Proper drainage will prevent the formation of large ice crystals. A small portable fan can be helpful in further drying off cooled food.
- All of this requires the timing of a juggler, as there usually are vegetables being cut, blanched, cooled, and packed at approximately the same time. Allow space and time, and be organized. Have help if possible. Children can help by cutting beans or shelling peas. Make it an assembly-line process.
- Put vegetables in freezer containers, allowing appropriate headroom (see box on page 170). Vegetables expand very little after cooling, so pack firmly but not tightly. Seal and label. Put the containers in the quick-freeze area of your freezer in a single layer so that they are not touching each other until frozen solid in 24 hours.

BURNS

Never underestimate the hazard of burns when working around a stove, especially if you have small children. Canning and blanching both require large kettles of boiling water. Take precautions and always have first-aid remedies and know-how nearby in case of an accident.

BEAN MUSH

Have you been plagued some years with fine-looking frozen snap beans that turned out mushy when used? We've traced it back to two errors. Our basic mistake was trying to blanch too many beans at once, with the result that the re-boil was slow and the beans were over-blanched. Then, too, we found we weren't, in these large batches, chilling them fast enough or long enough. This year we tried smaller batches, and the results are crisp and delicious.

Approximate Yield of Frozen Vegetables

VEGETABLE	FRESH	FROZEN
Asparagus	1 crate (12 2-lb. bunches) 1 to 1½ lb.	15 to 22 pt. 1 pt.
Beans, lima (in pods)	1 bu. (32 lb.) 2 to 2½ lb.	12 to 16 pt. 1 pt.
Beans, snap, green, and wax	1 bu. (30 lb.) ⅔ to 1 lb.	30 to 45 pt. 1 pt.
Beet greens	15 lb. 1 to 1½ lb.	10 to 15 pt. 1 pt.
Beets (without tops)	1 bu. (52 lb.) 1¼ to 1½ lb.	35 to 42 pt. 1 pt.
Broccoli	1 crate (25 lb.) 1 lb.	24 pt. 1 pt.
Brussels sprouts	4 quart boxes 1 lb.	6 pt. 1 pt.
Carrots (without tops)	1 bu. (50 lb.) 1¼ to 1½ lb.	32 to 40 pt. 1 pt.
Cauliflower	2 medium heads 1⅓ lb.	3 pt. 1 pt.
Chard	1 bu. (12 lb.) 1 to 1½ lb.	8 to 12 pt. 1 pt.
Collards	1 bu. (12 lb.) 1 to 1½ lb.	8 to 12 pt. 1 pt.
Corn, sweet (in husks)	1 bu. (35 lb.) 2 to 2½ lb.	14 to 17 pt. 1 pt.
Kale	1 bu. (18 lb.) 1 to 1½ lb.	12 to 18 pt. 1 pt.
Mustard greens	1 bu. (12 lb.) 1 to 1½ lb.	8 to 12 pt. 1 pt.
Peas (in pods)	1 bu. (30 lb.) 2 to 2½ lb.	12 to 15 pt. 1 pt.
Peppers, sweet	⅔ lb. (3 peppers)	1 pt.
Pumpkin	3 lb.	2 pt.
Spinach	1 bu. (18 lb.) 1 to 1½ lb.	12 to 18 pt. 1 pt.
Squash, summer	1 bu. (40 lb.) 1 to 1¼ lb.	32 to 40 pt. 1 pt.
Squash, winter	3 lb.	2 pt.
Sweet potatoes	⅔ lb.	1 pt.

1. Wash by scrubbing with a vegetable brush to remove any sand. Cut off tough ends or snap at the brittle point. Cut into pieces or sort spears.

2. Blanch for 2-4 minutes in boiling water, depending on size.

3. Cool immediately in cold water. Drain.

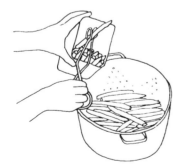

4. Pack into containers, leaving no headroom. For spears, alternate tips and ends. Seal, label, and freeze.

• To cook, remove the vegetables from the freezer. Place about ½ inch of water in a saucepan and bring to a rolling boil. Add the vegetables, cover, and count the cooking time from the return of the rolling boil. Don't overcook. Remember they have been partially precooked. Save the water for soups and stews. That's where many of the vitamins are.

Also try oven-cooking frozen vegetables. Place them frozen in a covered dish with a little water (about 1 tablespoon) and butter and seasonings if desired. Cook at 325°F. until tender (10 to 20 minutes, depending on the vegetable).

BLANCHING VEGETABLES

There are three methods of blanching vegetables for freezing: immersion in boiling water, steaming, and microwaving. The first two methods can be described quickly and easily, but — if you have a microwave — the third method may *be* the easiest. The microwave not only saves time in blanching, but vegetables done in this manner also taste fresher and lose fewer nutrients than in any other method of blanching. In addition, a Cornell University study has shown that when broccoli, green beans, peas, cauliflower, corn-on-the-cob, and kernel corn are microwave-blanched, 100 percent of the enzymes are killed.

Boiling water. Bring 1 gallon of water to a rolling boil in a large kettle. Prepare no more than 1 pound of vegetables at a time. Put the vegetables in a wire basket or other device that will allow all the vegetables to be removed from the water at the same time — to avoid overcooking — and place them in the kettle. Count your processing time from the *return* of the rolling boil.

Steam. Use a blancher or a steamer, a perforated insert that can hold the vegetables above the water. Put 2 to 3 inches of water in the bottom and bring to a boil. Put the vegetables in the steamer and lower it into place. Start timing when steam appears after you have replaced the lid. Don't steam large amounts at one time. When steaming, add 2 to 3 minutes to the recommended blanching times for boiling water.

Microwave. Research done by Dr. Gertrude Armbruster at the New York State College of Human Ecology at Cornell University has resulted in the following instructions for microwaving vegetables for freezing in resealable zip-type plastic bags intended for use in the freezer or the microwave. (Instructions for microwave blanching in other types of containers can be found on page 26.) No-mess-no-fuss freezing! These instructions are meant for use with a 600-700-watt oven. For optimum results, test temperatures with a temperature probe. Effective blanching occurs when the internal temperature reaches 190°F. If your microwave has a lower wattage, you can adjust the times accordingly by using a temperature probe. As with all other preserving directions, remember that the product you put by is only as good as the original. All rules for cleanliness apply here as well.

1. Choose the freshest produce only. Wash and trim according to the chart on page 28.
2. Fold back the bag neck to form a 1-inch cuff.
3. Fill bags to the bottom of the neck with water and vegetables as recommended. Uncuff, wipe zipper-closure clean, and seal, leaving a 1-inch center opening for steam to escape. Microwave one bag at a time, according to the chart. Cook to 190°F. or use the recommended time on the chart.
4. Carefully remove the bag from the oven (it will be hot!). Plunge it into ice water, submerging all of the food in the bag, but not allowing water to enter.
5. When thoroughly cooled, remove the bag from the ice water, press out excess air, wipe zipper clean, and seal. Label and freeze.

FREEZING CORN

1. Husk corn and remove silk for strictly fresh ears. Process quickly.

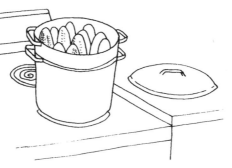

2. For whole-kernel corn, blanch for 4 minutes in boiling water. For corn-on-the-cob, blanch small ears 7 minutes, medium ears 9 minutes, and large ears 11 minutes.

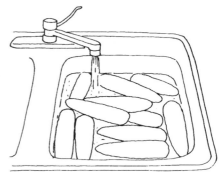

3. Cool immediately in cold water. Drain well.

4. For whole-kernel corn, cut kernels from the cob at about ⅔ their depth.

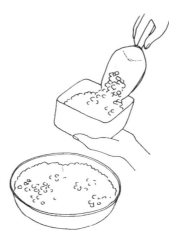

5. Pack into containers, leaving appropriate headroom (see page 170). Seal, label, and freeze.

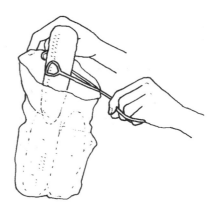

6. For corn-on-the-cob, pack into freezer bags after blanching and cooling, expelling as much air as possible. Seal, label, and freeze.

If you prefer to use your own freezer bags, boxes, or containers, the following directions for microwave blanching should be followed:

1. Prepare vegetables as indicated in the amounts specified on the chart on page 28. Add water as indicated, but no salt. Cook in a covered 2-quart microwaveable casserole, stirring or rearranging the vegetable halfway through the cooking time.
2. Cook for the minimum time, then check for doneness. The vegetable should be evenly heated — again, a temperature probe is the safest method, cooking to 190°F. — and have a bright color throughout. Continue cooking if needed, using the maximum time on the chart.
3. Plunge immediately into ice water and chill for an amount of time equal to the cooking time. Drain well and pat dry with paper toweling.
4. Package in moisture-vapor-proof half-pint or one-pint freezer containers or freezer-weight plastic bags. Seal, label, and freeze.
5. Please note that times are given for both the 600-700-watt and 500-watt units and that all times are meant for cooking on high.

Timetable for Blanching Vegetables in Boiling Water or Steam

VEGETABLE		BLANCHING TIME (minutes)	
		BOILING WATER (1 gal./1#veg.)	STEAM (1#veg.)
Asparagus	small stalks	2	4
	medium stalks	3	5
	thick stalks	4	6
Beans, green & wax	whole (tender small)	3	4
	cut	2	3
	french-sliced	1	2
Beans, lima	baby	2	4
	medium	3	5
	large	4	6
Beets		see page 126	
Broccoli		3	5
Brussels sprouts	small	3	
	medium	4	
	large	5	
Cabbage	wedges	3	
	shredded	1½	
Carrots	small whole	5	6
	diced or sliced	2	3
Cauliflower		3 (add 4 tsp. salt or lemon juice)	5
Celery		3	

VEGETABLE		BLANCHING TIME (minutes)		
		BOILING WATER (1 gal./1#veg.)		STEAM (1#veg.)
Corn, whole kernel & cream style		4	(cut off kernels after blanching)	
Corn-on-the-cob	small (up to 1¼" dia.)	7		
	medium (1¼-1½")	9		
	large (over 1½")	11		
Eggplant		4	(add ½ cup lemon juice)	5
Greens	dandelion	1½		
	all others	2		
	except collards	3		
Kohlrabi	whole (small)	3		5
Mushrooms	whole button	5		5
	sliced	3		4
Okra	small	3		
	large	4		
Onions	chopped			
	whole (small)	3-7	(blanching unnecessary)	
Parsley		½-1	(blanching optional)	
Parsnips	whole (small)	4		6
	diced or sliced	2		3
Peas, field		2		3
Peas, green		1½		2
Peas, sugar		1½		2
Peppers, green sweet	whole or half	3	(blanching optional)	4
Peppers, hot	diced or sliced	2	(blanching unnecessary)	3
Pimientos		see page 148		
Potatoes, new	whole (small)	4-10		
Potatoes, sweet		see page 149		
Pumpkin		boil or bake until soft		
Rutabagas	cubed	2		
	mashed	see page 152		
Soybeans		5	(blanch in pod, squeeze out beans)	
Squash, winter		boil or bake until soft		
Turnip	cubed or sliced	2½-3		3½
	mashed	see page 162		
Zucchini and summer squash	cubed or sliced	3		

Microwave Blanching in Zip-Type Bags

VEGETABLE	BAG SIZE	VEGETABLE AMOUNT	WATER AMOUNT	600-700-WATT MINUTES
Asparagus (2-inch pieces)	pint	2 cups	2 tbsp.	2:30
	quart	4 cups	4 tbsp.	3:00-4:30
Broccoli (2-inch pieces)	pint	2 cups	3 tbsp.	3:00
	quart	4 cups	4 tbsp.	5:00
Carrots (¼-inch slices)	pint	2 cups	3 tbsp.	2:30-3:00
	quart	4 cups	5 tbsp.	4:30-5:30
Cauliflower (1½-inch)	pint	2 cups	3 tbsp.	4:00
	quart	4 cups	4 tbsp.	6:00
Corn kernels	pint	2 cups	2 tbsp.	4:00
Corn-on-the-cob (5-inch length)	quart	2 ears	2 tbsp.	4:00
		(omit water if corn is very fresh)		
Green beans (1½-inch pieces)	pint	2 cups	3 tbsp.	3:00
	quart	4 cups	5 tbsp.	6:00
Okra (whole)	pint	2 cups	2 tbsp.	1:30-2:00
	quart	4 cups	4 tbsp.	3:00-3:30
Parsnips (¼-inch slices)	pint	2 cups	3 tbsp.	1:30-2:00
	quart	4 cups	5 tbsp.	3:30-4:00
Peas	pint	2 cups	2 tbsp.	3:00
	quart	4 cups	4 tbsp.	5:00
Spinach (leaves)	pint	4 cups	none	1:00
	quart	8 cups	none	1:00-1:30
Summer squash (¼-inch slices)	pint	2 cups	2 tbsp.	2:00-2:30
	quart	4 cups	4 tbsp.	2:30-3:00
Turnips (¾-inch slices)	pint	2 cups	3 tbsp.	2:00-2:30
	quart	4 cups	5 tbsp.	3:30-4:00
Zucchini (¼-inch slices)	pint	2 cups	2 tbsp.	2:00-2:30
	quart	4 cups	4 tbsp.	3:00-4:00

Microwave Blanching in Other Containers

VEGETABLE	VEGETABLE AMOUNT	WATER AMOUNT	600-700-WATT MINUTES	500-WATT MINUTES
Asparagus (cut into 1-2- inch lengths)	2 cups	¼ cup	2½-3½	4-5½
Beans, green or wax (cut in 1-2- inch pieces)	3 cups	½ cup	3½-5½	5-8½
Broccoli (cut in 1- inch pieces)	2 cups	½ cup	4-6	6-9
Carrots (½- inch slices)	2 cups	¼ cup	4½-5½	7-8½
Cauliflower (florets)	2 cups	½ cup	4-5	6-7½
Corn kernels	2 cups	¼ cup	4-5	6-7½
Corn-on-the-cob (cook in a single layer)	4 ears	¼ cup	5-7	7½-10½
Peas	2 cups	¼ cup	3½-4½	4½-7
Spinach (Note: do not cover casserole)	12 cups	none	3½-4½	5-6½
Summer squash (zucchini or yellow, ½-inch slices)	4 cups	¼ cup	3-4½	4½-6½
Turnips (cubed uniformly)	3 cups	¼ cup	2½-4	4-6

CHAPTER 3

Canning

ome-canned vegetables are at least as good as store-bought ones, and perhaps better when you have grown them yourself and know exactly how they have been handled and what types of pesticides and fertilizers have (or have not) been used on them. Canned foods have an advantage over frozen in that they require no expensive equipment to keep them — just a shelf in a cool, dark, dry place.

The first time that we made yeast bread it was with much hesitation and faltering, stopping constantly to read and reread what seemed endlessly complicated directions. Now we breeze through, yet without skimping on accuracy. The same is true with canning. The first time it was time-consuming, frustrating, and a little frightening, but now we do it with confidence and skill. So read through the following instructions and cautions carefully, then proceed. You will find few more gratifying sights than the rows of sparkling jars of tomatoes, pickles, relishes, vegetables, and fruits you have produced.

Good planning is the secret to rewarding and satisfying canning. Be prepared with all the necessary utensils, ingredients, and information. Set aside more than enough time, so that you don't have to cut corners on processing times. Clear a large surface, since canning takes space. Then organize before starting.

CANNING EQUIPMENT

Jars are the canner's stock in trade. They are an investment that will repay you in the years ahead. But jars seem to come in a multitude of confusing sizes and shapes. First, let's settle the word *Mason*. John L. Mason invented the first practical canning jar in 1858. Mason jars, as such, are no longer manufactured, but all similar canning jars now are called Mason, denoting a type rather than a manufacturer.

Most processing times specify using pint or quart jars. They are easiest to find and seem to fit most families' needs. They come with either a wide or a regular mouth. Wide mouths are easier to fill but cost slightly more than regular-mouth jars. Definitely use wide mouths if you freeze in jars, so that the contents will come out before thawing.

Jars also are available in half pints and half gallons. The processing times for half pints are the same as those for pints. The half pint is ideal for jellies and relishes that are used only in small quantities. Many come with decorative lids and molded designs on the sides. They make attractive gifts of a practical size.

Half gallons are for large families, but they have several drawbacks. Processing times are difficult to find, and dense, low-acid foods don't process adequately due to the bulk. In addition, few water-bath canners are tall enough to handle half gallons. If you use them for high-acid foods in a boiling-water bath, a rule of thumb is to add 10 minutes to the time required for quarts.

Canadian canning jars are available in many northern states. They come in conventional American-size pints and quarts, and their lids are interchangeable with American regular-mouth jars. The jars are squarish, which makes storage and stacking easy.

Many of the foods we buy come in jars that can be used as home-canning jars. Most commercially bottled mayonnaise or salad dressing comes in pint and quart jars that can be used with two-piece lids for canning acid foods in a boiling-water bath. Be careful to thoroughly check these jars for any cracks, scratches, or nicks around the rim.

You should expect more seal failures and breakage using these jars. As a general rule, they have a narrower sealing edge than the standard Mason jar and may have become weakened with the repeated use of metal utensils to get at the contents. Although a scratch appears harmless, it may have weakened the glass just enough to cause breakage in the canning process. *Never* use these jars in any process requiring pressure.

The USDA no longer recommends the old-fashioned bail-wire-clamp or Lightning jars for use as canning jars, as they too often fail to seal properly. Sometimes, a seemingly safe seal can be weakened with the passage of only a short period of time and the resulting possibility of botulism can be deadly. It is not a chance worth taking. These jars can, however, be used to store dry foods and for a variety of decorative purposes. The USDA also no longer recommends the use of the one-piece porcelain-lined caps or the two-piece glass lid with rubber seal. These, too, often fail to seal properly.

If you're lucky enough to have found old canning jars in a family attic or at a flea market, you may own either valuable collector's items or some practical canning jars. Make sure which they are before canning. The blue glass jars are especially valuable, selling for prices that would have made your grandmother blush.

Test the jars by running your finger around the lip. If there are any cracks or flaws, the jars are *not* up to canning standards and will not seal. Many old jars are still around for which lids are no longer being made. Don't improvise for canning. They make lovely canisters.

We have not mentioned metal cans, since this method of canning has become increasingly rare. During the Depression, extension agents traveled from community to community with tin-can canning equipment. Equipment and cans are costly, cumbersome, and hard to find, although the cans themselves are much cheaper than jars. They can't be recycled, whereas jars can be used year after year. For a thorough treatment of tin-can canning, the U.S. Department of Agriculture has published bulletins available by writing to the USDA in Washington, D.C. The processing times and instructions in this book are for glass jars only.

Lids

The lids for standard, modern canning jars are two-part: a *screwband* and a *one-use lid*. The soft compound on the inside of the lid completes the seal. When a jar of food is heated, the contents expand and steam forms, forcing air out of the jar. As the contents contract and steam condenses during cooling, a vacuum is formed, which will hold the lid in place aided by the rubber compound on the dome lid. The screwband holds the lid in place until it is sealed — after which it is unnecessary. For this reason screwbands can be removed after cooling. Leaving them on is optional but is similar to leaving a pattern pinned to a dress after it is completed. To prove the point, you can actually lift a jar by the dome lid after the screwband is removed, provided you have a good seal. Once removed, screwbands should be stored in a dry place where they won't rust and used again next year. *Don't* reuse the dome lids, however, as the rubber is good for only one sealing.

The methods of using these lids, which are made by different manufacturers, may differ slightly. To be sure, always read the directions that come with them. First, wash the lids and screwbands in hot, soapy water, rinse, place in a pan, and cover with boiling water. Do not actually place them on the stove to boil, as this would damage the sealing compound. When a jar has been filled with food, remove air bubbles by running a rubber spatula carefully around inside the jar. Wipe off the top of the jar to be sure no specks of food will catch between the sealing compound and the glass, then put the lid in place and screw the band on tight. The jar is now ready to be processed.

You can open a jar of home-canned food with a bottle opener or a punch can-opener, which puts a hole in the dome lid and further reminds you that it can't be used again.

People often ask if all Mason-jar screwbands and dome lids are interchangeable among modern canning jars of the same size mouth. Yes. If you bought jars from one company and lids from another, you will have no problem.

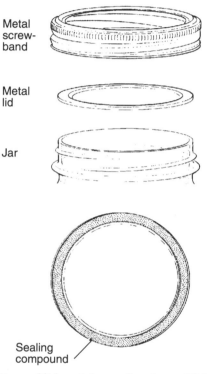

Metal screw-band

Metal lid

Jar

Sealing compound

Jar and lid: metal screwband, metal lid.

How to Test for a Perfect Seal

There are four tests for Mason-jar seals recommended by the major canning companies.

• First, you can hear it seal. As a jar completes the seal, it will make a *kerplunking* sound. This test is only reliable, however, if you are doing

one jar at a time. If you have a dozen jars cooling on your counter, it is difficult to keep track of which jar is *kerplunking*.
• Second, you can see the seal. The lid should curve down in the middle.
• Third, after the jar has cooled, feel that the lid is down and stays down.
• Finally, tap the center of the lid with a spoon. It should make a clear, ringing sound if the seal is perfect.

After the jars have cooled, in approximately 12 hours, test the seals. If the jars didn't seal properly, you can re-process them *within 24 hours* of the original processing, *using new dome lids* — or you can eat the food. Re-processing will result in a less satisfactory product, because the full canning time must be repeated.

If your jars come unsealed later during storage, discard the contents, being sure that neither children nor animals can find and eat them, and *sterilize* the containers.

Canning Equipment Checklist

Having everything out, clean and ready, before starting will help things go smoothly. You'll need:

• Jars. Check for cracks or nicks in the rims, wash thoroughly in hot soapy water, rinse, and keep hot until ready to fill.
• Lids and bands. Prepare as manufacturer instructs.
• Jar lifter.
• Hot pads.
• Canning funnel.
• Food preparation tools: knives, cutting boards, kettle, colander, etc.
• *For boiling-water bath.* Deep kettle with lid and rack; also, a teakettle for adding hot water if necessary.
• *For pressure canning.* Pressure canner and rack.

New Terms You'll Run Into

Nothing is more frustrating when starting something new than to encounter unfamiliar terminology that an author takes for granted you already know. To avoid this we have defined below some of the terms used in canning.

Raw or cold pack. These phrases are used interchangeably. They refer to prepared but uncooked fruits or vegetables, packed in jars to which a hot liquid is added, and then processed.

Hot pack. Hot pack refers to foods that are precooked to some degree, then put into jars for processing. This makes for more compact packing, particularly with greens. A hot pack sometimes requires less cooking time, since the food is already partially cooked. Sometimes it takes as long or longer because of the denser pack.

The specific instructions for each vegetable and fruit will indicate whether hot or raw pack is better. Raw pack has the advantage of holding the shape of lower-density foods. If you want tomatoes, for instance, to retain their shape, cold-pack them. Take the precaution of packing tightly, since raw pack tends to shrink in processing.

CHECKING THE LIDS

Taking a lead from the baby-food manufacturers, Owens-Illinois is marketing Mason-jar lids with a "Magic Button." This button in the center of the lid pulls down under vacuum and pops up clearly if the seal isn't perfect.

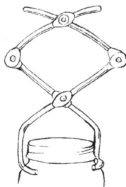

Jar lifters for removing jars from the canner.

Headroom or headspace. These terms refer to the space between the top of the food and the top of the jar. Generally ½ inch is allowed, with the exception of starchy foods such as corn and peas, which expand more; they require 1 inch or more. As bad as leaving too little headroom (which causes jars to overflow during processing and thereby ruins the seal) is leaving too much. Allowing too much headroom means too much air and the possibility of an improper seal. If you have only enough of a fruit or vegetable to fill half a jar, use it fresh or find a smaller jar.

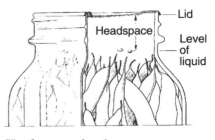

Headroom or headspace.

Boiling-Water-Bath Canning

A boiling-water bath is the cheapest and easiest method of canning for preserving *high-acid foods*. These include all fruits, all pickles, and those vegetables to which sufficient vinegar has been added to raise the acidity level high enough. It is this acidity that makes a boiling-water bath possible for these foods. The heat achieved in a boiling-water bath is simply that of boiling water (212°F.). This is not sufficient to kill the heat-resistant bacteria that cause spoilage, but they are inhibited from growing by the presence of high acidity.

See the table on page 40 for pH values of common foods. A low number means *high* acidity, and a high number means *low* acidity. A food with a pH value of 4.5 or higher is considered low acid for canning purposes and *must* be processed in a pressure canner rather than a boiling-water bath. Only a pressure canner can produce temperatures that are high enough to kill the bacteria that cause botulism. Although tomatoes are generally considered an acid food, some varieties actually have a pH value slightly above 4.6. Check your variety to see if it is labeled as a low-acid tomato. If it is, it can be acidified to a pH of 4.6 or lower with lemon juice or citric acid.

Vegetables are low in acid and, therefore, *unsuitable for a boiling-water bath* unless pickled, such as dilled beans or pickled beets. Our grandmothers may have processed vegetables in a boiling-water bath, but dozens of jars were thrown away due to spoilage — not to mention the occasional case of food poisoning.

Boiling-water-bath canning requires a kettle deep enough to cover your jars with 1-2 inches of water plus room for a *rolling* boil, which is necessary for canning and must never be turned down to a gentle boil or simmer. So you need a canner deep enough to avoid splashing over.

A rack on the bottom is necessary, too, to provide complete circulation of the boiling water under the jars. A lid on the kettle will help to maintain the rolling boil. Since most quart jars are 7 to 7½ inches tall, you will need a canner 11 to 12 inches deep.

Most people use a conventional black enamel canner with white spots, which is resistant to acids and salt solutions and so can double for processing pickles or brining vegetables. An aluminum kettle won't serve for this. A lobster pot or large camping kettle or a large pressure canner may make a perfectly adequate water-bath canner provided the lid is left unlocked and the vent open. You can use old screwbands or bent coat hangers to improvise a bottom rack. It is important for maximum heat circulation that the jars don't touch each other.

If you purchase a boiling-water-bath canner, invest the extra money and buy the large model. It will accommodate quarts, which are the most practical size for the bulk of home canning. Don't do as one woman we heard about who processed her tomatoes in a too-small canner with the jar tops out of water. Then she turned them over to process the other halves!

STERILIZATION OF EMPTY JARS

All jams, jellies, and pickled products to be processed in a boiling-water bath for less than 10 minutes should be put into *sterile* jars. To sterilize empty jars, put them right side up on the rack in a boiling-water canner. Fill the canner and jars with hot (not boiling) water to 1 inch above the tops of the jars. Boil 10 minutes at altitudes of less than 1,000 feet. (At higher elevations, boil 1 additional minute for each additional 1,000 feet of elevation.) Remove and drain the hot sterilized jars one at a time. Save the hot water for processing filled jars. Fill the jars with food, add lids, and tighten screwbands.

Jars used for vegetables, meats, and fruits to be processed in a pressure canner need not be pre-sterilized. It is also unnecessary to pre-sterilize jars for fruits, tomatoes, and pickled or fermented foods that will be processed 10 minutes or longer in a boiling-water canner.

STEP BY STEP

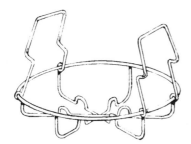

Rack for boiling-water-bath canning. Use in a pot with a lid.

Check the jar rims to be sure there are no nicks or cracks. Discard old screwbands that are rusty or warped. Use only new Mason-jar lids. Wash your jars and screwbands in hot soapy water and rinse. A scale or hardwater film on jars can be removed by soaking jars for several hours in a solution of 1 cup vinegar to 1 gallon water. Put the kettle on the stove half full of water and begin simmering.

Wash dome lids in hot soapy water and rinse. Place them in a pan, cover with boiling water, and leave them until needed.

Place your raw- or hot-packed food in the clean, hot jars, leaving the recommended headroom. You can add 1 teaspoon of salt to a quart of vegetables, although this isn't necessary for preservation — only for flavor.

Run a rubber spatula around the inside edge of each jar to release any air bubbles. Slice through densely packed greens to aid heat penetration to the center of the jar. Wipe the top of each jar with a damp cloth if your syrup contains sugar, or with a dry towel if not. Do this thoroughly and carefully to prevent any small particles from interfering with the seal. Place the lids and screwbands on and tighten them as firmly as possible.

Boiling-water bath. Cutaway shows jars in position.

Lower the jars into the simmering water with a jar lifter, another indispensable gadget. (*Note:* Cold jars should be put into water that is warm, not simmering; they will crack from a sudden change in temperature.) Make sure that the jars are not touching, so you will get good heat

CANNING TOMATOES
(raw pack, with a boiling-water bath)

1. *Wash and sort tomatoes. Dip into boiling water for ½ minute. Remove to cold water to cool for 1 minute.*

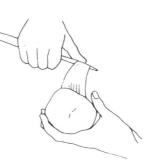

2. *Pull off skins. Cut off the stem as well as blemishes and green spots. Cut into sections.*

3. *Pack tightly into jars, pushing down so that the tomatoes are covered by their own juice, leaving ½ inch headspace.*

4. *Run a rubber spatula around the inside of the jar to release trapped air bubbles.*

5. *Wipe the jar rims with a clean cloth. Place lid in position and tighten screwband.*

6. *Place jars in a boiling-water-bath canner. Cover with 1-2 inches of water. Cover. Start timing when you have a rolling boil — 40 minutes for pints, 45 minutes for quarts.*

circulation. Add water to cover the jars by 2 or 3 inches. Put on the kettle lid, bring the water to a rolling boil, and then (*not before*) start keeping track of the processing time.

When the recommended time is up, remove the kettle from the heat and take out the jars with a lifter. Leaving them in longer will result in overcooking. (But old jars should be treated with extra care, so leave them in the water until the boil has stopped.) Put the jars on a cake rack or towel in a draft-free area. Be careful not to knock them together, since they will shatter easily when hot. Don't cover the cooling jars unless there is a draft.

Leave jars until thoroughly cooled, then test the seal. If it isn't good, you can reprocess within 24 hours of the original processing. Try to find out *why* your jars didn't seal. The most frequent reasons are a bit of food caught between lid and jar rim, and cracks on the jar rim. Both of these can be avoided with care.

If the seal is good, remove the screwbands from the jars. Wipe the jars dry and label them with the product name, its origin, and the date. This information will be helpful in deciding how and what to can next year.

Store the jars in a cool, dry, dark place. Dampness rusts the dome lids and causes the seals to deteriorate. Light tends to destroy vitamins and fade colors. Freezing and thawing will deteriorate the food's quality and possibly break the seals.

Store for no more than one year, since quality will have deteriorated by that time. The food may be safe to eat after a year, but why settle for old canned goods when next year's harvest will supply good fresh produce?

Now enjoy your garden's bounty, when the snow is four feet deep and summer is long past!

Approximate Yield of Canned Food

The number of quarts of canned food you can get from a given amount of fresh vegetables or fruit depends on quality, condition, maturity, and variety, size of pieces, and the way it is packed — raw- or hot-pack.

Generally, the following amounts of fresh vegetables and fruits (as purchased or picked) make 1 quart of canned food:

VEGETABLE	POUNDS
Asparagus	2½ to 4½
Beans, lima, in pods	3 to 5
Beans, snap	1½ to 2½
Beets, without tops	2 to 3½
Carrots, without tops	2 to 3
Corn, sweet, in husks	3 to 6
Okra	1½
Peas, green, in pods	3 to 6
Pumpkin or winter squash	1½ to 3
Spinach and other greens	2 to 6
Squash, summer	2 to 4
Sweet potatoes	2 to 3

FRUIT	POUNDS
Apples	2½ to 3
Berries, except strawberries	1½ to 3
	(1 to 2 qt. boxes)
Cherries (canned unpitted)	2 to 2½
Peaches	2 to 3
Pears	2 to 3
Plums	1½ to 2½
Tomatoes	2½ to 3½

In 1 pound there are about 3 medium apples and pears, 4 medium peaches or tomatoes, or 8 medium plums.

Altitude Chart
for Boiling-Water-Bath Canning

If you live at an altitude of 1,000 feet or more, you have to increase the processing time in the canning directions for a boiling-water bath, as follows:

	INCREASE IN PROCESSING TIME IF THE TIME CALLED FOR IS —	
ALTITUDE	20 MINUTES OR LESS	MORE THAN 20 MINUTES
1,000 feet	1 minute	2 minutes
2,000 feet	2 minutes	4 minutes
3,000 feet	3 minutes	6 minutes
4,000 feet	4 minutes	8 minutes
5,000 feet	5 minutes	10 minutes

HOT-WATER-BATH CANNING

A hot-water bath is used *only* for sweet or acid fruit juices in jars. It involves a pasteurizing process (in which the jars are simmered at 175° to 190°F. in a water-bath canner) and is *not* to be confused with a *boiling-water bath*. In this method there is less loss of vitamins and flavor. There is also an increased risk of poor seals.

STEAM CANNING

Although the steam canner may appear to offer an interesting and energy-efficient alternative for preserving high-acid foods, this type of canner does not maintain an even temperature, so it is impossible to know if the heat has penetrated properly. The USDA does not recommend steam canning due to inadequate research on the process.

Pressure-Canning Vegetables

All vegetables are *low-acid* (except tomatoes, sauerkraut, and pickles) and must be processed in a *pressure* canner (not to be confused with the steam canner).

There are old cookbooks still on our shelves that say processing low-acid foods for three hours in a boiling-water bath is a substitute for using a pressure canner. However, no matter how long you boil water the temperature will not go above 212°F., and you cannot be *sure* that the botulinum bacteria have been destroyed. We shudder when we talk with a homemaker who says she has "always canned vegetables without a pressure canner and hasn't had a problem yet."

It takes only one spoonful from one jar of poisoned food to cause serious illness or death. So *please*, for your family's sake, *always* use a

ACID STRENGTH OF VEGETABLES AND FRUITS

	1 -	
	2 -	cranberry, pickle gooseberry, plum apple
High Acid	3 -	blackberry, sour cherry rhubarb, prune apricot, grapefruit orange, strawberry sauerkraut
	4 -	peach, blueberry sweet cherry pear pineapple tomato
	5 -	fig, pimiento
		okra, pumpkin carrot, cucumber turnip, cabbage pepper, squash parsnip, beet snap bean, sweet potato greens, asparagus cauliflower
Low Acid	6 -	broccoli, Brussels sprouts mushroom
		lima bean, white potato pea, corn olive (ripe)
	7 -	

Process at 212°F. in boiling-water bath

Process at 240°F. in pressure canner

Adapted from *Ball Blue Book*, Ball Corp., 1974.

pressure canner with low-acid foods. If you cannot buy one, look into sharing the cost with a relative or friend, or borrow one. It may be the most important investment you ever make.

There are several types of pressure canners, but they all work according to the same principle. The pan has a tight-sealing lid with some type of regulator. When a small amount of water is heated in the canner (usually 1 to 2 inches of water), it is converted to steam, which, as it builds up pressure, reaches temperatures substantially higher than boiling. At 10-15 pounds pressure the temperature is 240°-250°F. The pressure used for canning is 10 or 11 pounds, depending on the type of canner used (unless otherwise noted). (At altitudes more than 1,000 feet above sea level higher pressure must be reached to achieve the right temperatures. See the table on page 39.)

The canner is fitted with safety features that are designed to maintain pressure at reasonable levels, and to "let go" if the pressure should become too high. It is essential that you become familiar with the directions for your type of canner, and follow those directions exactly. The booklet that accompanies each new canner should be read thoroughly; if you have no booklet, read the following information carefully.

Please note: Use only Mason jars. Other glass jars, in which you have bought mayonnaise or peanut butter, for example, are not suitable for home pressure canning. The shock of heat and pressure changes can cause them to shatter, with great danger to the people working with them. Controlled conditions in a commercial cannery make it possible for them to be used there.

There are two types of pressure canners: those with a *dial gauge* that shows the pressure, and those with a *weight control* that makes a noise when it reaches the required pressure. Before using any pressure canner, check all of its parts to be sure all are in good working order, and give all a thorough cleaning. Use only canners that have the Underwriter's Laboratory (UL) approval to ensure their safety.

DIAL-GAUGE CANNERS

The dial gauge registers the pounds of steam pressure being produced in the canner. *The gauge should be checked for accuracy each year before any canning is done.* Ask your local Extension Service or a store where canners are sold where you can have it checked. Gauges can be checked at most county Cooperative Extension Agencies. Replace gauges if they read high by more than 1 pound at 5, 10, or 15 pounds of pressure. Low readings cause overprocessing and may indicate that the accuracy of the gauge is unpredictable. Replace the gauge whenever there is a question.

The dial gauge is a delicate mechanism and should be handled with care. It must not be immersed in water, so the lid should never be washed in water. Use a wet cloth to wash the inside and outside of the lid, and wipe the gauge carefully. To protect the gauge, always store the cover upside down on the pan. This will also prevent the inside of the canner from becoming musty.

Dial-gauge canners come with either a *rubber gasket* in the cover that seals it to the pan, or a *metal-to-metal* closure with screw clamps.

Rubber-Gasket Canners

Automatic air vent. The air vent is both an air regulator and a safety feature. It automatically vents air from the canner during the initial heating, and allows air to flow back in when pressure is reduced after processing, thus preventing the formation of a vacuum in the canner. It serves as an emergency pressure release designed to "blow out" if the vent pipe is clogged and pressure cannot be released normally. Check to see if the rubber part of the air vent is soft and pliable. If not, it should be replaced.

To clean the air vent, remove it by pushing down on it from the top. After cleaning, insert it by pushing it up through the opening from the underside of the cover. When in place, the slightly rounded face of the automatic air vent will be exposed on the outside of the cover.

Pressure regulator and vent pipe. The pressure regulator is placed on the vent pipe, and controls the amount of pressure that can be built up in the canner. The maximum pressure is 15 pounds, above which the regulator will rock to release excess pressure.

The regulator will not hold the pressure at 11 pounds, which is the pressure used for canning in a dial-gauge canner. It is up to the operator to watch the indicator closely and reduce the heat to maintain 11 pounds. (Fruits and tomatoes can be processed in a boiling-water bath in your pressure canner with the pressure regulator removed and water filled up over the tops of the jars.)

To clean, wipe out the interior of the regulator. The vent pipe should be cleaned regularly by drawing a pipe cleaner or tiny brush through it.

Sealing ring. The sealing ring fits into the canner cover and forms a pressure-tight seal during cooking or processing. After the canner has been in use for a considerable period, the sealing ring may shrink. If there is an escape of steam around the edges of the cover, replace the sealing ring.

The sealing ring should be washed after each use, and the groove in the lid into which it sets should be washed with a brush. Be sure it is thoroughly dry before replacing the ring.

Metal-to-Metal Canners

Control valve. Metal-to-metal canners have a control valve rather than a pressure regulator and vent pipe. In the *open* (upright) position, air and steam can escape from the canner during initial heating. It is closed (pushed down) to build up pressure for processing. When processing is over and the canner has cooled to zero pressure, the control valve is opened to allow air to flow back into the canner, preventing a vacuum from forming.

Water in Pressure Canners

SIZE OF CANNER	AMOUNT OF WATER FOR PROCESSING
4-quart	1 quart
6-quart	1½ quarts
8-quart	1½ quarts
16-quart	2 quarts
21-quart	2 quarts

Increase the recommended amount of water by 1 pint if the canner is not filled to capacity with jars.

When cooking food for meals or canning in tin cans (but *not* when canning with glass jars), the control valve is opened soon after processing to release the steam; liquid cannot escape from cans.

Clean the control valve by using a toothpick to keep the holes clear, so air and steam can escape through them.

Closure. Canners with a metal-to-metal seal have knobs that screw down to lock the cover. Put a drop of oil on the threads of each of these before using. To close this type of canner, place the cover on the pan, evenly lined up with the knobs. Tighten all knobs slightly, doing two opposite ones at the same time to keep the cover level. Then tighten all knobs firmly, using hand pressure only, and again always doing two opposite ones at a time.

When these pressure canners are used for canning *only*, the metal-to-metal seal must be lubricated with oil, paraffin, or wax to prevent scratching and sticking of the seal.

To maintain a good sealing edge, be careful not to knock utensils against the rim of the pan or the sealing edge of the cover (such as knocking a metal spoon on the rim of the cooker to clean it of food after stirring). Also do not clean with metal scouring pads.

How to Operate a Dial-Gauge Canner

1. Have basket or rack in place. *For foods canned by the hot-pack method*: Put boiling water about 2 inches deep into the canner. See table on page 42 for exact amount to use. Set canner on low heat. *For foods canned by the raw-pack method (with cold food)*: Pour the same amount of hot, but not boiling, water into the canner. Set on low heat and do not allow to reach simmering temperature until you put the cover on.
2. Place each prepared jar upright in the canner. Jars must not be touching each other or the bottom of canner, so be sure the rack or basket is in place.
3. Place cover on canner and lock securely. Do not build up pressure in any canner until the cover is securely locked into closed position.

   Rubber-gasket canners. The lid may have arrows pointing to a closed position, or the handles may need to be centered over each other. Turn the lid until it reaches the locked position. Do *not* put pressure regulator on vent pipe yet.

   Metal-to-metal canners. Screw down the thumb-screws, always tightening two opposite knobs at the same time. Be sure control valve is in open (upright) position.

4. Set burner to highest heat. When steam flows freely from the vent pipe or control valve, reduce heat slightly to maintain a strong steam flow. Steam should flow freely from all four holes in the control valve on metal-to-metal canners. Allow steam to vent for 10 minutes to eliminate all air from canner and jars. If air is not vented in this way, it will throw off the accuracy of your canning process.
5. Now place the pressure regulator on the vent pipe, or close the control valve by turning down valve stem to horizontal position.
6. Steam will build up in the canner.

Rubber-gasket canners: Soon the automatic air vent will rise and seal the canner. If it does not, gently touch the metal plunger in it with something other than your hand (it is hot!) — perhaps something is stuck in the opening that is preventing the plunger from sealing.

7. Keep the heat on high, and the pressure will gradually rise to 11 pounds. Watch the gauge closely and when the dial is almost at 11 pounds, turn the heat down to low on electric and gas ranges. If you are using a coal or wood stove, wait until the pressure reaches 11 pounds, then move the canner to a cooler spot on the stove. *Start counting the processing time as soon as the required pressure is reached.*

8. Make minor adjustments in the heat if necessary to keep the pressure at 11 pounds. It is important to keep the pressure steady; fluctuations in pressure can cause liquid to be lost from the jars. Do not touch or remove the pressure regulator during the processing period; steam would be released, causing a sudden drop in pressure. If the pressure drops below 11 pounds, you must start over again, so watch the canner closely.

9. As soon as the processing time is up, turn off gas burner, or remove canner from electric burner or constant-heat unit such as a wood stove.

10. Allow the pressure to return to zero naturally. Do *not* try to speed the cooling process by running cold water over the canner or removing the pressure regulator or opening the control valve. This could cause the jars to break or lose liquid, spoiling the seal. Worse, forced cooling may result in food spoilage.

Rubber-gasket canners. When the dial reaches zero and the automatic air vent has dropped, remove the pressure regulator from the vent pipe. Let the canner cool another 1 or 2 minutes.

Metal-to-metal canners. When the dial reaches zero, open the control valve very slowly so that any pressure left is released gradually.

11. Release the cover from locked position and remove *carefully*. To avoid getting a faceful of steam, lift up the far edge of the cover first and remove, shielding yourself with the cover.

12. Remove jars from canner and set on a rack or towel to cool.

13. If you're processing another batch of jars, be sure there is enough water in the canner before starting.

WEIGHT-CONTROL CANNERS

Automatic pressure control. This type of canner has a one-piece, unbreakable metal-weight-type control. It has three different settings, for 5, 10, and 15 pounds of pressure. The control is placed on the vent pipe and automatically releases pressure greater than the amount for which it is set. For example, to set the control for 10 pounds pressure, the required amount for a weight-control canner, place the control with the hole marked "10" on the vent pipe. When the pressure builds up to 10 pounds, the control will begin to jiggle, releasing steam and preventing the pressure from rising further.

Rather than having to watch a dial, the operator listens for the jiggling sound that indicates the canner has reached the required pressure. The heat is then adjusted so that the control will jiggle only two or three times a minute. Low to medium-low temperature on a gas or electric range will usually be right; experiment until you find the right temperature. If the control doesn't jiggle enough, too little pressure is being maintained, meaning the temperature is too low for proper processing; if it jiggles too much, a substantial amount of steam may escape, which over a long period of time could cause the canner to run dry, overheating the cooker and possibly wrecking both it and your canned goods.

"Jiggling" is not the same as the slight shaking and sizzling the control makes as pressure is building up — there is a distinct change in sound when it reaches the jiggling point, which you will recognize as soon as you hear it.

Because this control is unbreakable, it does not have to be checked for accuracy each year as does the dial gauge. It is also self-cleaning by the action of the steam on it, but it can be washed in hot clean suds and rinsed thoroughly to insure that it is free of any obstructive particles that might hamper its operation.

The vent pipe that it fits onto should be cleaned regularly by running a pipe cleaner or small brush back and forth through it. The whole cover can be washed along with the rest of the cooker.

Self-sealing gasket. This is similar to the sealing ring on dial-gauge canners, and should be cared for in the same way. See page 42.

Safety fuse. In the lid of these canners is a small round plug. It will release and drop into the cooker if the cooker becomes overheated due to lack of water, or it will "blow out" if the vent tube becomes clogged. If the proper amount of water and heat is used and the vent tube is kept clear, the fuse should never blow. If it does, replacements can be purchased. Do not pick or scratch at fuses while cleaning the lid.

How to Operate a Weight-Control Canner

1. Set rack in canner and add enough water to be about 2 inches deep in canner. (See the table on page 42.) *For hot-pack canning*: Add boiling water and set on burner over low heat. *For raw-pack canning:* Use warm water and set on low heat; do not allow to simmer until canner is covered.
2. Set prepared jars on rack in canner.
3. Close canner, making sure the cover is locked in position with handles aligned over each other. Turn heat on high. Allow air to vent from the canner and jars for 10 minutes (see manufacturer's directions). Then put pressure control on vent pipe. Set at 10 pounds pressure (5 pounds for tomatoes and fruits).
4. It may take up to 45 minutes to bring a canner up to 10 pounds pressure when filled to capacity with raw-packed quarts of vegetables. When the control begins to jiggle vigorously, start to count the processing time. Reduce heat, but keep it high enough that the control

1. Wash spinach, lifting it to let dirt settle out. Remove tough stems and wilted leaves. Steam ½-1 pound of spinach at a time until it is well wilted (8-10 minutes).

2. Pack loosely into hot jars. Add boiling water or cooking liquid, leaving ½ inch headroom.

3. Run a spatula around the inside of the jar to release air bubbles.

4. Wipe rim carefully with a damp cloth to remove pieces of food.

5. Put on Mason lids with sealing compound down against the glass. Put on the screwband and tighten firmly.

6. Set jars in hot water (1-2 inches deep) on rack in pressure canner.

7. Tighten lid of pressure canner securely. Follow manufacturer's directions for operating canner, or refer to pages 43-47. Time spinach 70 minutes for pints, 90 minutes for quarts. When time is up, remove canner from the heat and allow to cool slowly.

8. When pressure returns to zero, slowly remove weighted gauge or open petcock. Remove cover, tilting far side up so steam escapes away from you. Lift jars out and set upright on a cloth away from drafts.

9. Allow jars to cool several hours. Test for a good seal (see page 33), remove screwbands, wash jars, label, and store in a cool dark place.

jiggles at least two or three times a minute. Avoid rapid temperature changes or drafts blowing on the canner, as this will cause uneven pressure, which forces liquid from the jars.

5. When processing time is up, turn off the heat. Remove canner from electric burners or constant-heat units such as wood stoves. Move it carefully, as it is hot and heavy. Do not dislodge the control.

6. Allow to cool naturally. Do not rush cooling by running cold water over the canner or by lifting the control. It will take at least 20 minutes (up to 45 minutes in larger canners) for the pressure to drop in a canner filled with jars.

7. When a reasonable length of time has passed, check to see if the pressure has returned to zero by lifting the control *slightly* with a fork. If you see steam spurt out, pressure is still up, so replace the control and wait a while longer. If you do not *see* steam, pressure is down and the control can be removed all the way. You may hear a hissing sound in either case, indicating either steam coming out or air rushing in — so trust your sight rather than your ears!

8. After removing the pressure control, unlock the cover and lift it off. Protect yourself from the steam by lifting the far edge off first and shielding your body with the cover as you remove it.

9. Remove jars from canner and carefully place them upright on a towel or rack, not touching, in a draft-free spot. Do not let them bump into each other as this may cause them to crack.

HINTS FOR ALL TYPES OF PRESSURE CANNING

Aluminum Canners

The inside of a used aluminum canner may be discolored because of the action of acids, iron, or various minerals in water and foods. These stains are harmless, but some may be removed if desired by using a solution of water and cream of tartar. (A strong vinegar solution also can be used.) Pour enough of the solution into the canner to cover the discoloration (do not fill over two-thirds full), then close cover securely. Place pressure regulator on vent pipe and heat until pressure regulator rocks gently. Remove canner from heat; allow to stand 3 to 4 hours. Remove pressure regulator, open canner, and empty contents. Wash and rinse thoroughly and dry.

To prevent water stains in a canner or on jars, add 1 tablespoon vinegar or 1 teaspoon cream of tartar to the water when processing.

Stacking Jars

In large canners half-pint and pint jars can be stacked in more than one layer. It is not essential to put a rack between the layers, but it is recommended because it helps the steam to circulate more evenly.

Pressure Saucepans

Small jars can sometimes be canned in small pressure cookers if: (1) the pressure can be regulated at 10 pounds (most saucepans can only be

---

PRESSURE CANNING WITH A WOOD STOVE

The old kitchen range is ideal, because of its extended and variable heat, for cooking down tomatoes for ketchup, sauce, and paste, and for jellies and jams, too. When it comes to drying herbs and some fruits and vegetables, its warming shelves and oven are hard to beat.

It is another matter, though, if you're doing pressure canning, when it is critical that a *constant* steam pressure be held — sometimes for as long as 65 minutes. It can be done on a wood-fired range, but it takes constant attention and some quick shifting of the cooker to hotter or cooler parts of the stove top. Most people who cook with wood stoves, however, find they make the kitchen unbearably hot at the height of the freezing and canning season, and they resort to the less economical but more even and directed heat of a gas, electric, or kerosene burner for canning.

regulated at 15 pounds, so check this closely), and (2) there is adequate room for the jars to fit inside the cover when locked in place. It is generally recommended to add 5 percent to the processing time when a pressure saucepan is used, because of the quicker heating and cooling times. Be sure to let it cool down naturally, without putting it under running water or otherwise trying to speed up the cooling process.

What Causes Liquid to Boil Out of Jars?

- Jars packed too solidly with food.
- Filling jars too full. Allow ½ inch of headroom for most fruits and vegetables except shelled beans, corn, peas, and sweet potatoes, which require 1 inch or more.
- Temperature or pressure too high.
- Sudden fluctuations in temperature or pressure. When processing food in a pressure canner, the pressure regulator or control should not be removed or bumped, and pressure should be allowed to return to zero naturally.
- Failure to adjust lids properly before processing.

What Causes Jars to Break?

- Cracked or weakened jars, or using jars other than standard canning (Mason) jars.
- Jars packed too tightly or too full.
- Jars touching the bottom of the canner.
- Improper tightening of lids before processing.
- Sudden heat or pressure change, especially cooling the canner too rapidly after processing.
- Putting cold jars into boiling water; bumping together hot jars after removing them from the canner; or putting hot jars in a cold, drafty place to cool.

Why Don't Jars Seal?

- The jar or lid may be defective.
- Food may have been caught under sealing compound on rim, or may have been forced out of jar with liquid.

Capacities of Canners

SIZE OF CANNER	CAPACITY					
	HALF PINTS		PINTS		QUARTS	
4 quart	4	or	4		-	
6 quart	7	or	7		-	
8 quart	14*	or	7	or	4	
16 quart	20*	or	9	or	7	
21 quart	-	or	18*	or	7	

*If jars are stacked.

If a jar does not seal, either refrigerate and eat contents soon or reprocess it within 24 hours. Remember it must be processed as long as the first time, and both flavor and food value will suffer. Another possibility is to adjust the headspace in the jar to 1½ inches and freeze if you have the room.

To reprocess, open the jar, inspect it for defects, and clean the rim carefully. Put on a *new* dome lid (the same screwband can be washed and reused), and process for the full length of time specified in the directions.

Insure Safe, Quality Canned Foods

Scrupulously wash all produce. Soil-borne spores are the hardest to kill later, but will wash off before processing. Wash your produce several times, lifting the food out of the water rather than swishing it around. Change the water often and rinse the sink or pan repeatedly. This is especially important with leafy vegetables such as chard and spinach, which are frequently sand covered.

DETECTING SPOILAGE

To detect spoilage, check a container of food before opening it. Does the can end or the jar lid bulge? If it does, the food may be spoiled. *Don't taste it.*

Open the container. Is there any mold or cloudiness? Any peculiar smell? Did the liquid spurt when you opened the container? All these indicate spoilage. *Don't taste it.*

You can't be certain that low-acid foods are safe even if they pass these two tests. Botulism can't be seen or smelled. Always boil the food for 15 minutes (20 minutes for corn and greens) in a covered pan. This will make an off-odor more evident. If the food has that odor, or if it foams or simply doesn't look right, *discard it* — and that means burning it or disposing of it so that no person or animal will accidentally eat it.

Containers that have contained food suspected of being botulism-poisoned must also be destroyed. First, cover jars and lids with boiling water in a kettle and boil for 30 minutes. When they have cooled, break jars and bend or break lids, so someone else won't come along and pick them up. Then discard. Wash hands and pots thoroughly, adding a tablespoon of bleach to each gallon of wash water. Thoroughly clean all surfaces that jars, lids, or foods may have touched, and discard sponges and cloths used in the cleanup process.

Types of Food Spoilage

Flat sour is easy to recognize by its sour acid taste and offensive odor. It is caused by a heat-resistant organism. Flat sour can be avoided by not canning over-mature food, by not letting cooked foods sit in jars too long before processing, and by cooling jars quickly after processing.

Bacteria, molds, and yeasts are everywhere — in the air, soil, and water — and they must be destroyed by proper heat to prevent spoilage.

Molds are found on canned fruits, tomatoes, and jellies and on non-canned foods.

"DON'T" METHODS

Over the years, certain questionable preserving methods have been developed and have been passed on by word of mouth. These include *aspirin canning* and *oven canning*. Rather than risk confusion, we have avoided any references to these methods. *None of them is safe or acceptable.* And there can be no compromise on this point. Similarly, we do not believe microwave ovens should be used for canning.

Also, remember that getting a good seal won't prevent spoilage if the food should become contaminated between kettle and jar.

Timetable for Pressure-Canning Vegetables*

VEGETABLE	METHOD	HEADROOM (inches)	MINUTES TO PRECOOK	MINUTES TO PROCESS PINTS	QUARTS
Asparagus	Raw Pack	½	-	30	40
	Hot Pack	½	2-3	30	40
Beans, dry with sauce		(see page 123)		65	75
Beans, fresh lima	Raw Pack	(see page 125)		40	50
	Hot Pack	1	bring to boil	40	50
Beans, snap	Raw Pack	½	-	20	25
	Hot Pack	½	5	20	25
Beets	Hot Pack Only	½	15	30	35
Broccoli	Hot Pack Only	1	3	30	35
Brussels sprouts	Hot Pack Only	1	3	30	35
Cabbage	Hot Pack Only	1	3	45	55
Carrots	Raw Pack	1		25	30
Cauliflower	Hot Pack Only	1	3	30	35
Celery	Hot Pack Only	1	3	30	35
Corn, cream style	Hot Pack Only	1	bring to boil	85	pints only
Corn, whole kernel	Raw Pack	1	-	55	85**
	Hot Pack	1	bring to boil	55	85**
Eggplant	Hot Pack Only	1	5	30	40
Mushrooms	Hot Pack Only	½	(see page 140)	45 (half-pints-30)	-
Okra	Hot Pack Only	½	1	25	40
Parsnips	Hot Pack Only	1	3	30	35
Peas, field	Raw Pack	1½-pints	-	35	40
	Hot Pack	2-quarts	bring to boil	35	40
Peas, fresh green	Raw Pack	1	-	40	40
	Hot Pack	1	bring to boil	40	40
Peppers	Hot Pack Only	1	3	35	half-pints or pints only
Potatoes, white-whole	Hot Pack Only	½	10	35	40
Potatoes, cubed	Hot Pack Only	½	2	35	40
Pumpkin, cubed	Hot Pack Only	½	bring to boil	55	90
Pumpkin, strained	Hot Pack Only	½	bring to boil	65	80
Soybeans	Hot Pack Only	1	bring to boil	55	65
Spinach & other greens	Hot Pack Only	½	steam 10 min.	70	90
Squash, summer	Hot Pack Only	½	bring to boil	30	40
Squash, winter (see pumpkin)					
Sweet Potatoes	Dry Pack	1	20-30	65	90
	Hot Pack	1	20	65	90

Tomatoes (see page 155)

*Process in a dial-gauge pressure canner at 11 pounds pressure or a weighted-control pressure canner at 10 pounds pressure.
**Corn darkens when processed this long, so we recommend that corn be canned only in pint jars.

Yeasts cause foods to ferment, and thrive on fruits, tomatoes, jams, jellies, and pickles. Both yeasts and molds usually can be destroyed by being heated to the temperature of boiling water (212°F.) for several minutes. Heat of the required degree and duration, proper sealing methods, plus cleanliness are the strongest weapons against yeasts and molds.

Fermentation in foods is caused primarily by yeasts. Bubbles are formed from a sour-smelling gas, which generally breaks the seal. This is usually the result of under-processing the food.

Putrefaction spoilage is caused by bacteria and appears in meat and vegetables. Pickles, where it is often found, become soft and slimy with a bad odor. Again, under-processing may be the reason.

Enzymes are present in all foods and are beneficial; enzymatic action is responsible for the maturing of color, flavor, and texture. But unless this action is stopped the fruit or vegetable will continue to mature. When the optimum point is past, color, flavor, and texture will begin to deteriorate. The simple application of heat, as in blanching, will retard enzyme growth.

Clostridium botulinum are frightening words and for good reason. While rare, an attack of botulism is usually fatal. The bacteria botulinum are found throughout the environment in water and soil and are harmless there. However, in an anaerobic (airless) environment, such as a sealed canning jar, the spores divide and produce poisonous toxins and gas. The spores are extremely heat-resistant, but can be destroyed in vegetables by processing in a pressure canner at 240°F. for the times called for in the instructions. Fruits and pickles can be processed safely in a boiling-water bath (212°F.), because their high acidity inhibits the formation of these toxins.

Signs of botulism poisoning begin within 12 to 36 hours after a person eats contaminated foods. Symptoms include double vision, inability to swallow, speech difficulty, and progressive paralysis of the respiratory system. Obtain medical help immediately, as there are antitoxins available that are effective if symptoms are identified soon enough.

Risks of Canning

If the potential risks and dangers of home canning are honestly and simply weighed, people can make their own evaluations. Do try to keep the topic in perspective, however. In recent years there have been few deaths in the United States from botulism.

Remember that the keys to successful canning are careful handling and perfect seal *along with* proper processing times and temperatures. If you use the proper methods and equipment, you will have satisfactory results.

A CHECKLIST OF PRECAUTIONS

1. Prime, quality produce is good insurance. Bruises encourage the growth of bacteria.
2. Wash all produce carefully and completely.
3. Be sure all equipment and work surfaces are scrupulously clean and in good working order.
4. Make sure of a good seal.
5. Most important, process for the *correct time* and at the *correct temperature*. This is the final key and the crucial factor which, along with the seal, cannot be over-stressed.
6. *Don't, don't* take short cuts. Follow directions carefully so that the result will justify all your time and effort.

CHAPTER 4

Jams and Jellies

ams and jellies are a special treat for children and grownups alike. They can be made from any fruit or berry, and also from such things as tomatoes, wine, and herbs, particularly mint. This is an area of preserving in which your imagination and taste can take full rein to suit your family's tastes and to create gifts with a homemade, personal touch.

Our family joins in the fun of picking berries and fruits from early summer to fall, and after we have sated ourselves on fresh fruit, the rest is frozen or made into preserves. In our own garden we pick rhubarb in May, strawberries in June, and raspberries in July. Later in the summer and fall there are wild black caps in the woods nearby, tart grapes growing along the fence, and bright red crab apples down the road. Many area orchards provide an abundance of apples in the fall. The mint that grows around our house can be made into jelly either with apples as the base or with store-bought fruit pectin.

Jams and jellies can be made in season when the fruit is freshly picked, or you can use canned or frozen fruits and fruit juices (your own or bought) during other times of the year. (Do not use commercially canned fruit juice, however, as it does not contain enough acid or pectin.)

In addition to jams and jellies, there are preserves, conserves, marmalades, fruit butters, and chutneys. The methods for making these are similar. Traditionally all were preserved by the open-kettle method of canning. However, unless your storage facilities are cold (below 50°F.), it is now recommended that all these products be sealed in sterilized canning jars and processed in a boiling-water bath for at least 5 minutes.

Jellies are made from fruit juices or other flavored juices, jelled enough to be shimmeringly firm. *Jams* are made from ground or crushed fruit and have enough jell to hold their shape. *Preserves* contain whole or large pieces of fruit in a slightly jelled syrup. (The word *preserves* is often used to mean all of these different types.) *Conserves* usually consist of mixed fruits and citrus, with raisins and nuts. *Marmalades* are clear jellies in which pieces of citrus or other fruit are mixed. Fruit pulp cooked with sugar until thick is called a *butter*; and *chutneys* (see Chapter 5) are a spicier mixture of fruits and spices cooked with sugar and vinegar. Recipes for all of these products are included throughout this chapter (and the next), but the instructions here will focus on jellies and jams.

All of these preserves contain fruit and sugar, with pectin and some form of acid either naturally present or added. The fruit provides the distinctive flavor and nutrient base for the jelly. In some cases it also provides the pectin that makes it jell. Apples and quinces are especially high in pectin, while most other fruits require the addition of pectin. Apples can be used as the pectin source for other types of fruit, or you can buy commercially prepared fruit pectin in a powder or liquid form. Most fruits have some natural pectin, more when underripe than ripe. If you make preserves without adding pectin, use all slightly underripe or ¼ underripe with ¾ ripe fruit to provide enough natural pectin.

The correct level of acidity also is critical to the jelling process. Many fruits have plenty of natural acid, especially when they are underripe. If there is not enough acid present, the jelly or jam will not set. If too much acid is present, the product will "weep" (liquid will separate from the finished product). For less acidic fruits, such as peaches, pears, and apricots, recipes may call for the addition of acid in the form of lemon juice to aid in the jelling process. Commercially marketed pectin products contain acids as well. You can also substitute ⅛ teaspoon crystalline citric acid (available at a drugstore) for 1 tablespoon lemon juice.

Sugar is most important as a preservative in these products. It also helps the jelling process and of course adds to the flavor. It is possible to make diet jellies and other preserves with a sugar substitute recommended by your doctor. However, these must be refrigerated or frozen unless they are cooked the long way and processed in a boiling-water bath, since they lack the preserving qualities of sugar. You can also replace part of the sugar with honey or corn syrup. For jelly, one-fourth of the sugar can be replaced with honey or corn syrup; and for jams and other preserves, half of the sugar can be replaced. Corn syrup and honey will mask the fruit flavor as well as alter the jell structure. Use only tested recipes for replacing sugar with honey or corn syrup. Do not try to reduce the amount of sugar in traditional recipes. Too little sugar prevents jelling and may allow molds and yeasts to grow.

According to the USDA, even though sugar helps preserve jellies and jams, molds can grow on the surface of these products. Research now indicates that the mold that people usually scrape off the surface of jellies may not be as harmless as it seems. Mycotoxins are known to cause cancer in animals; their effects on humans are still being researched. Because of possible mold contamination, paraffin or wax seals are no longer recommended for any sweet spread, including jellies. To prevent growth of molds and loss of good flavor and color, fill products hot into *sterile* Mason jars (see page 36), leaving ¼ inch headroom, seal with self-sealing lids, and process 5 minutes in a boiling-water canner.

🍂 MAPLE SYRUP

Sugaring starts around Town Meeting Day in New England, the first Tuesday in March, and it's a sure sign of spring. Whether you buy or boil your own, you want to store some for later use. The syrup that comes packed in tins is vacuum-sealed, but once it is opened, mold, unattractive but not dangerous, can start to grow. The syrup is so high in sugar that it is not a good medium for the growth of bacteria, but if some water separates and comes to the top, that creates a better medium.

To get rid of the mold, skim off as much as you can and heat the syrup to just below the boiling point (boiling will crystallize the sugar). Then pour the syrup into hot, sterilized Mason jars for storage. Adjust lids. Process for 5 minutes in a boiling-water bath to insure a good seal.

Always work with small batches when making preserves. Cook only 4 to 8 cups of juice or fruit at a time. When you have a large quantity to do, divide it up. It will not take much longer to boil several small batches than to boil one large one, and the results will be superior. Large batches require a longer time to cook, are harder to handle, may refuse to jell, or may have a poor flavor.

Use a kettle that seems three times too big (8 quarts or larger) and that preferably is stainless steel, with a wide, flat bottom. It is amazing how high the juice and foam will rise when boiling, especially if you are using honey, and boiled-over jelly is no fun to clean off the top of your stove. To reduce the amount of foam and help prevent the juice from boiling over, add ½-1 teaspoon of butter before boiling.

Use a candy, jelly, or deep-fry thermometer when making jellies and jams; it takes the guesswork out of deciding when you have reached the jellying stage. The jellying point for jelly is 220°F. (8°F. over the boiling point of water), and for jams it is 221°F. (9°F. over the boiling point of water). If you live at an altitude 1,000 or more feet above sea level, measure the temperature of boiling water with your thermometer, and add 8°F. to that for jelly and 9°F. for jams to reach the jellying point. Since changes in atmospheric pressure can affect this temperature from day to day, test your thermometer on the day you are planning to make jelly or jam.

If you are using commercial pectin, follow the directions provided by the manufacturer, or use only recipes that specifically refer to the kind of pectin you have. Never substitute the liquid type for the powdered or vice versa, since the fruits are cooked differently, and the pectins are added at different points in the cooking process. More sugar is usually required with the liquid than the powder type. In other respects — cost, cooking times, and quality of the final product — they are similar.

Also do *not* use a commercial pectin recipe if you are not adding any pectin. It just won't work! Jellies and jams made without added pectin must be boiled much longer for them to jell. Besides, less sugar is used than with store-bought pectin. You will end up with smaller quantities and the jelly will have a darker color because it has cooked longer.

Storage

All preserved foods should be stored in a cold, dark, dry place. Temperatures should be between 32° and 50°F. to preserve flavor, color, and the nutrients that light will destroy, and to prevent the growth of molds and bacteria. Use only standard canning jars that can be processed in a boiling-water bath for 5 minutes. Jars must be sterilized before filling.

Jelly Glasses and Jars

Manufacturers of canning jars produce attractive jelly glasses with colorful, decorated lids and decorations embossed in the glass. These serve as a mold for the jelly and can easily be turned over onto a serving

HOMEMADE FRUIT PECTIN

You can make and can your own "pectin" to use with strawberries, peaches, and other low-pectin fruits. Choose hard, tart, ripe apples. Weigh, wash, and cut up fine, leaving on stems and cores. Add 1 pint water and 1 tablespoon lemon juice for each pound of apples. Cover and boil rapidly for 30 minutes, stirring occasionally to prevent scorching. Press through a jelly bag or damp cheesecloth, then strain through several layers of damp cheesecloth without squeezing. Heat back to the boiling point, seal in canning jars, and process in a boiling-water bath for 5 minutes. To use, mix equal parts with juice of a low-pectin fruit. Use the pectin test (see above) on the mixed juices to determine whether enough pectin is present. Proceed as for other jellies, using ¾ to 1 cup sugar per cup of mixed juice.

dish, leaving a pretty pattern in the jelly. There are also less expensive, plain glasses, which make for an attractive, smoother-surfaced, molded jelly.

Canning jars with decorated lids made especially for preserves and relishes make lovely gifts. Don't forget, however, that unless they have straight or flared sides, they cannot be used as a mold for the jelly.

Other Equipment Needed

In addition to glasses or jars, lids, a large kettle, and a thermometer, you will need:

- jelly bag or cheesecloth for jellies
- a stand or colander to set it on
- measuring cups
- dishes for holding fruit
- vegetable brush for washing hard fruits such as apples
- potato or other masher
- paring knife
- wooden spoons for stirring
- a timer to measure exactly 1 minute when adding pectin
- a damp cloth for wiping jar rims
- a slotted spoon to skim off foam
- a rack or towel to cool hot jars on

A pad to separate the pot from the burner will help prevent scorching your fruits, and, if you can find one, a "jelmeter" is a help in measuring the pectin content of a fruit juice.

Jelly bags can be bought, or you can make your own from a piece of unbleached muslin or flannel (napped side in) or several layers of cheesecloth. Sew the material together around a hoop made from a coat hanger, or tie the corners together and suspend it over a bowl from a handy hook or cupboard door. You may want to try the old trick of turning a chair upside down on a table, and suspending the bag by tying the corners with string to the chair legs. Place a bowl underneath on the upturned chair seat. (This is a great conversation piece if the neighbors drop by!)

Or if you have a food press (the cone-shaped type that fits into a frame), you can use the frame to hold the bag, attaching it with clothespins. The simplest method is to put 4 layers of damp cheesecloth inside a colander and set it in a bowl.

Preparation of Equipment — Sterilizing

Unless you are going to process your preserves in a boiling-water bath for more than 10 minutes (and only 5 minutes is recommended), you *must* sterilize your jars. To do this, wash them in hot soapy water, and rinse thoroughly. Put them in a kettle, cover with hot water, and boil rapidly for 10 minutes at altitudes less than 1,000 feet; boil 1 additional minute for each additional 1,000 feet in altitude. Leave the jars in the hot water, until you are almost ready to use them. Remove the jars, drain, and invert them on a cloth while the jelly is in its last minutes of cooking. Some dishwashers have a sterilizing cycle, which may be used to sterilize your jars. Leave them hot in the dishwasher until needed.

If you are using canning jars, follow the manufacturer's directions on how to prepare the self-sealing Mason lids. These should be washed with hot soapy water, rinsed, put in a bowl or pan, and covered with boiling water. Do not actually boil the lids on the stove, as this can spoil the sealing compound. Leave the lids in the hot water until ready to use.

Fruits to Use

Fruits that usually contain enough pectin to jell by themselves include sour apples, crab apples, currants, underripe Concord grapes, quinces, lemons, blueberries, raspberries, blackberries, cranberries, wild cherries, and green gooseberries.

Fruits usually too low in pectin and acid include apricots, peaches, pears, strawberries, elderberries, cherries, and oranges. They can be cooked with cut-up apples or with fruit pectin, and often lemon juice or citric acid is added. Since the pectin content decreases as the fruit ripens, even the high-pectin fruits may need to be treated in this way if fully ripe when used. If you intend to add commercial fruit pectin, fully ripe fruit generally is specified.

Testing Fruit for Pectin and Acid

It is possible to make a simple test to see if your fruit juice has enough pectin and acid for it to jell properly.

Pectin test. After extracting your fruit juice (see page 58), put 1 teaspoon of the juice into a glass and add 1 tablespoon of rubbing alcohol (70 percent alcohol). *Do not taste!* Stir in gently. If there is enough pectin in the juice, a gelatinous mass will form that you can pick up with a fork. If there is not enough pectin, a few pieces of jelly-like material will form. You can add 1 tablespoon liquid pectin for each cup of juice to increase the pectin content, testing again to see if this is enough. When the pectin content is high enough, you can proceed to cook the juice for jelly by the long-cook method.

Acid test. This is a taste test. Compare the acid flavor of the fruit juice with that of a mixture containing 1 teaspoon lemon juice, 3 tablespoons water, and ½ teaspoon sugar. If the fruit juice is not as tart, add 1 tablespoon of lemon juice for each cup of fruit juice.

Amount of Sugar to Use

If the fruit juice contains an adequate amount of pectin, use ¾-1 cup sugar per cup of juice; if slightly less pectin, use ⅔-¾ cup sugar. Too much sugar will make a syrupy jelly. These directions apply only if you are going to cook the jelly by the long method rather than following directions for a commercial pectin.

🌿
JAMS AND JELLIES WITH REDUCED SUGAR

Noncaloric sweeteners can be used to make jams and jellies if they are made with modified pectin, gelatin, or gums. Currently, there are two types of modified pectin available for home use. One makes a fine product using one-third less sugar. The other is low-methoxyl pectin, which works with calcium salts to form a jell. Jars of these jams and jellies must be processed longer in a boiling-water canner to prevent spoiling. It is important to follow recipes and directions for processing when using any of these methods to produce the freshest-tasting and safest product possible.

Making Jelly

Jellies can be made from any clear juice if you use a commercial pectin such as Sure-Gel (powder) or Certo (liquid), and they can be made from the clear juice of a fruit naturally high in pectin without a jell additive. (Since commercial pectins are made from apples or citrus fruits, their use is not really "unnatural.")

Be sure to wash the fruit thoroughly in cold water before using. Never let it soak in the water, however, as you will lose much of the flavor and juice.

Hard fruits such as apples and grapes can be cut up or crushed, covered with water, and boiled to extract their juice. Soft berries can be crushed and put through a food mill to draw the juice, or else simmered with little or no water.

When the juicy pulp is ready, it is put into a damp jelly bag, and the juice allowed to drip into a bowl.

For a sparkling clear jelly, resist the temptation to squeeze the jelly bag. Just let it drip for several hours. The resulting juice should be perfectly clear and will make the most attractive jelly. The pulp can be turned back into the pan, some water added, and cooked briefly. Then repeat the dripping process. This second extraction will not be as clear as the first, but will make satisfactory jelly.

If you are not fussy or if the jelly is to be used in cakes or jelly rolls, you can squeeze to get more juice. This juice can be strained through several layers of damp cheesecloth to remove most of the impurities, or allowed to settle overnight in the refrigerator to get a clearer juice. Since crystals form in grape juice, it always should be allowed to settle overnight. Then carefully pour off the clear juice without disturbing the sediment at the bottom.

The juice can be used immediately, or can be frozen or canned to be used later. (See Chapter 10 for directions on preserving juices.)

COOKING JELLY THE LONG WAY

Follow these directions if you are *not* adding commercial pectin.

Measure the juice, using only 4 to 6 cups for each batch. Bring the juice to a boil and let boil for a couple of minutes. Then add ¾ to 1 cup of sugar for each cup of juice. Boil rapidly, stirring frequently. Stay right with it to be sure it does not boil over. If you are using a candy thermometer, place it in the kettle, completely covered with jelly but not touching the bottom.

Testing for the Jelly Stage

The jelling point for jelly is 220°F. (or 8° above the boiling temperature of water for the elevation where you live). When your thermometer reaches this temperature, remove the kettle immediately from the heat.

If you are not using a candy thermometer, you can tell when the jelly is done by one of two methods.

The sheet test. With a cold metal spoon, dip out some boiling jelly, hold it well above the kettle and tip it so the juice runs out. Before the jelly is done, it will usually drip off the spoon in two separate drops. When the jelly comes off the spoon in a sheet or when two drops come together before dripping off, the jelly is done.

The refrigerator test. Put some jelly on a plate and place it in the freezing compartment of your refrigerator for 5 minutes. If it is jelled by then, it is done. During this test, remove the rest of the jelly from the heat so it will not overcook.

When the jelly is done, remove from heat, let it settle down, and skim off every bit of foam on the surface. A slotted spoon works well for this. Sometimes there is a lot of foam, which seems wasteful. We put it aside and use it on toast; the children call it a special treat. If it is left on the jelly it will spoil the appearance and texture.

Sealing Jelly

Immediately ladle or pour the boiling hot jelly into hot, sterilized containers, being careful not to spill any on the rim of the jars or on the inside edge of the glasses. Leave ¼ inch headroom. Wipe the rim of each jar with a clean, damp cloth to be sure no jelly is left on the rim to spoil the seal. Seal each jar as soon as it is filled. Take Mason lids from hot water and place on jar, then screw the band on tightly (as tightly as an average person can without using a jar tightener).

Processing Jelly

Place the jars on a rack in a kettle full of simmering water, adding more water if necessary to bring the level to 1 or 2 inches above the tops of the jars.

Put on cover, bring to a full rolling boil, and time for just 5 minutes or the time recommended by a specific recipe. When the time is up, remove jars immediately from the kettle and place them on a rack or towel out of drafts to cool. When completely cool, check for a good seal. If any are not sealed, either refrigerate and use soon, or reprocess after cleaning rim of jar and checking for defects, using a new lid. When the jars have cooled, remove the screwbands from the sealed jars, wash the jars, and label them.

Attractive labels come with some types of jars or can be bought separately; they can add a personal touch to your jellies. Store in a cool, dark place.

NO-COOK JAMS AND JELLIES

For a change you might want to try freezer jams and jellies that require absolutely no cooking. These are made with commercial pectin, the powder or the liquid type, and many recipes are included in the directions that come with the pectin. The color is bright and the flavor delicious—more like the fresh fruit because it has not been cooked. Some drawbacks to this type of jam or jelly are that they must be stored in the refrigerator and used within three weeks, or else stored in the freezer for longer periods. They also require *twice* the amount of pectin needed for ordinary jams and jellies.

MAKING JELLY WITH ADDED PECTIN

Use fully ripe fruit, and prepare the fruit juice as above. (See also the paragraph on the use of a commercial pectin under Hints, page 55.)

Powdered pectin: Add the pectin to the unheated fruit juice, bring to a boil, and then add the sugar.

1. Crush 2½ quarts of washed, hulled, ripe strawberries.

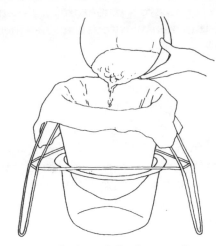

2. Put pulp into jelly bag or damp cheesecloth and allow juice to drip through. For clearer jelly, drip, don't squeeze, through cheesecloth a second time.

3. Measure 3¾ cups juice into large saucepan. Add ¼ cup lemon juice and 7½ cups sugar. Place over high heat and bring to a boil, stirring constantly. Stir in Certo (liquid pectin), bring to a full rolling boil, and boil hard for 1 minute, stirring constantly.

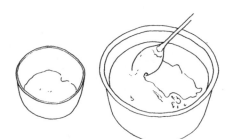

4. Remove from heat and skim off all foam with a metal spoon.

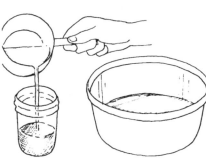

5. Pour quickly into hot, sterilized glasses, leaving ¼ inch headroom. Wipe rims clean.

6. Adjust lids and process in a boiling-water bath for 5 minutes to insure a good seal. Set upright to cool.

Liquid pectin. Add sugar to the fruit juice, bring to a boil, and then add liquid pectin.

With both kinds of pectin, follow specific recipe directions for quantities to use. Bring the jelly to a full rolling boil after all ingredients have been added and boil hard for exactly 1 minute, then remove immediately from the heat.

Skim off all the foam and ladle or pour the boiling hot jelly into hot, sterilized containers. Seal with appropriate canning lids as you would for the long-cook method, page 61.

Please note: Directions and many recipes are included in the booklets that come with commercial pectin, and we recommend you follow them closely. When using these recipes, it is important to make no more than double the recipe amount at a time, and not to change the amount of sugar or pectin called for. With the liquid pectin (Certo), the recipe book is wrapped around the bottle under the label. A folder comes in the box with the powder Sure-Gel. For some jams and jellies, one bottle of Certo will make a doubled recipe; two boxes of Sure-Gel are needed for the same quantity. The amount of juice (or fruit with jams) can be adjusted slightly if you prefer a softer (or firmer) jelly or jam. For a softer jelly, use ¼ to ½ cup more juice or fruit than the recipe calls for; for a firmer jelly or jam, use ¼ or ½ cup less juice or fruit.

Making Jams

Jams are made from crushed fruit with or without added pectin. They are simpler to make than jellies because there is no first cooking and juice extraction. Otherwise, making jam is similar to making jelly.

COOKING JAM THE LONG WAY

Wash the fruit quickly in cold water, taking care not to let it stay in the water long. Peel, cut up, and hull or pit the fruit, depending on variety. Crush soft fruits; cut hard fruits into small pieces. Add sugar or honey (usually ¾ to 1 cup per cup of fruit), and bring the mixture slowly to a boil.

Sometimes hard fruits are cooked in a water-and-sugar syrup to soften, or the sugar and fruit are allowed to stand several hours to draw the juices before cooking. Fruits with small seeds that are difficult to remove, such as grapes and raspberries, can be put through a food press or food mill for a seedless jam with a purée consistency.

When jam is cooking, the pieces of fruit tend to stick to the pan and scorch unless you stir constantly. Boil the jam rapidly until it reaches the jellying point, which for a firm jam is 221°F. (or 9°F. above the boiling point of water). This may take anywhere from 15 to 45 minutes, depending on the pectin quantity in the fruit. Rather than cooking the low-pectin fruits too long, you can stop the cooking when they begin to thicken and be satisfied with a soft jam, or else use a commercial pectin. If you have no candy or jelly thermometer, the refrigerator test can be used (see page 59), or cook until the jam thickens. The sheet test does not work for jams.

When the proper temperature is reached, remove the jam from the heat and skim off all foam on the surface. Then stir and skim constantly for about 5 minutes, allowing the jam to cool slightly. This will prevent the fruit from floating to the top of the jam. Or shake the filled jars gently several times after sealing.

Pour or ladle the hot jam into hot, sterilized jelly glasses or canning jars, leaving ¼ inch headroom. Adjust lids and process in a boiling-water bath for 10-15 minutes. Let the jam cool undisturbed. Check for good seals, remove screwbands from canning jars, label, and store in a cool, dark place.

MAKING JAM WITH ADDED PECTIN

As with jellies, be sure you do not substitute the liquid for the powdered pectin or vice versa, since the methods of adding them to the fruit are different. The results are similar, however. Both are different from the long way of cooking in that they require more sugar, have a shorter cooking time, and take less guesswork in knowing when they are ready. The colors also are brighter because they are not cooked as much.

Use fully ripe fruit and prepare it as you would for the long-cook method, page 61.

Powdered pectin. Add pectin and lemon juice, if called for, to the fruit, and stir to dissolve the pectin completely. Bring the combined ingredients quickly to a boil over high heat, stirring constantly. When the mixture comes to a full boil (bubbles over entire surface), add the sugar. Stir and again bring rapidly to a full rolling boil. Boil hard for 1 minute, then remove immediately from the heat.

Skim off all foam and stir the jam for 5 minutes to help prevent the fruit from floating, or shake the filled jars gently several times after sealing.

Liquid pectin. Add sugar to measured fruit and lemon juice, if called for, and mix thoroughly. Place over high heat and bring to a full rolling boil, stirring constantly. Boil hard for exactly 1 minute, then remove from heat and immediately add the liquid pectin. Skim off the foam and stir the jam for 5 minutes to cool slightly and prevent the fruit from floating, or shake the filled jars gently several times after sealing.

Pour or ladle the hot jam into hot, sterilized jelly glasses or canning jars, leaving ¼ inch headroom. Adjust lids and process in a boiling-water bath for 10-15 minutes. Let the jam cool undisturbed. Check for good seals, remove screwbands from canning jars, label, and store in a cool, dark place.

WHAT WENT WRONG?

Most of us who have made jelly have experienced the frustration of ending up with either syrup or what might pass for rubber, and yet we don't know what went wrong. Sometimes the weather or even the strawberry grower gets blamed!

Syrupy jelly or jam is still good (and messy) on toast, makes a delicious topping for ice cream, and can be enjoyed with milk as an interesting milkshake. To avoid it the next time, however, follow directions to the letter, making small batches, using a candy thermometer, and for the long-cook method, using fruit that is ¼ underripe and ¾ ripe.

The weather really *can* be the culprit, since the boiling point will vary according to the weather. So, on the day you plan to use it, test your candy thermometer for the boiling point of water, and add 8°F. to that for jelly and 9°F. for jams and preserves.

The following are some of the most common problems people have with jams and jellies, and ways to avoid them:

1. **Jelly that is too soft.** This may be caused by too much juice, too little sugar, too little acid, or trying to make too large a batch at one time. If too soft to use, you can try to remake the jelly, doing only 4-8 cups at a time.

   Without added pectin. Re-boil the jelly until the jelly point is reached according to your thermometer or the sheet or refrigerator test. Remove the jelly from the heat, skim off the foam, pour into hot, sterilized containers, and seal.

   With powdered pectin. Measure the jelly. For each quart of jelly, measure ¼ cup sugar, ¼ cup water, and 4 teaspoons powdered pectin. Mix the pectin and water, and bring to a boil, stirring constantly to prevent scorching. Add the jelly and sugar. Stir thoroughly. Bring to a full rolling boil over high heat, stirring constantly. Boil mixture hard for ½ minute. Remove jelly from the heat, skim off foam, pour into hot, sterilized containers, and seal.

   With liquid pectin. Measure the jelly to be re-cooked. For each quart of jelly measure ¾ cup sugar, 2 tablespoons lemon juice, and 2 tablespoons liquid pectin. Bring jelly to a boil over high heat. Quickly add the sugar, lemon juice, and pectin, and bring to a full, rolling boil, stirring constantly. Boil mixture hard for 1 minute. Remove jelly from the heat, skim off foam, pour into hot, sterilized containers, and seal.

2. **Jam that is too soft.** Jam may be too soft for the same reasons as jelly, but because of its consistency it is usually still satisfactory to use without trying to re-cook. Next time, cook until thicker, or if using a candy thermometer, be sure to stir the jam before reading the thermometer, measure the temperature in the middle of the kettle, and make sure the jam completely covers the bulb of the thermometer and that the bulb is not touching the bottom of the kettle.

3. **Syrupy jelly.** Using much too much sugar can cause syrupy jelly, and no amount of cooking will make it jell. This can also be caused by too little pectin, acid, or sugar.

4. **Jelly or jam that is too stiff.** Overcooking or too much pectin, either added or natural, may cause stiff jelly or jam. Too much of the fruit may have been underripe. For the long-cook method, use ¼ underripe and ¾ ripe fruit. Use fully ripe fruit when adding pectin. To make a softer jelly or jam, next time add ¼ to ½ cup more juice or fruit than called for in the commercial pectin recipes.

5. **Tough jelly.** The jelly may have been cooked too long before reaching the jelly stage because too little sugar was used.

6. **Gummy jelly.** This can be caused by overcooking.

7. **Fermentation of jelly.** The jar was sealed improperly, or too little sugar may have been used. *Throw away!*

8. **Cloudy jelly.** Speed is important when transferring the cooked jelly from kettle to glasses. It may become cloudy if poured too slowly or allowed to sit too long in the kettle. Cloudiness also can be caused by improper straining that leaves pulp in the juice, or if it sets too fast as a result of too green fruit.

9. **Mold on jelly or jam.** If the seal is imperfect to begin with or is broken by weeping jelly or mishandling, air and mold will get into the container. *Throw away!*

10. **Jelly or jam that darkens at the top of the container.** This can be caused by warm storage or an improper seal that lets in air. Throw away if the seal was improper.
11. **Faded jelly or jam.** Storage that is too warm or long, or exposure to light can cause fading, particularly in red fruits such as strawberries and raspberries.
12. **Floating fruit in jam.** To prevent this, allow jam to cool slightly and stir for 5 minutes before putting it in glasses; or after sealed in jars, shake it gently. Other causes of floating may be underripe fruit, fruit that was not sufficiently crushed or ground, or fruit that was not cooked long enough.

Recipes

GRAPE JELLY

6 pounds grapes, ¼ underripe and
 ¾ ripe
6 cups sugar

Wash, stem, and crush grapes. Add a small amount of water (about 1½ cups), cover, and bring to a boil over high heat. Reduce heat and simmer 15 minutes. Turn into jelly bag and drip, or squeeze and re-strain through several layers of damp cheesecloth. Let sit overnight in refrigerator, and pour off clear juice or re-strain the next day to remove crystals. Measure 8 cups juice into kettle and bring to a boil. Add sugar (¾ cup for each cup of juice) and stir. Boil until the jelly stage is reached according to thermometer (8°F. over the boiling point of water) or sheet test or refrigerator test (see page 59). Remove from heat and skim off foam with a slotted spoon. Pour immediately into hot, sterilized containers, leaving ¼ inch headroom. Adjust lids and process in a boiling-water bath for 5 minutes.

Yields seven or eight 8-ounce glasses.

MINT JELLY

3 cups apple juice (prepared as for
 Apple Jelly, page 66)
2 cups sugar
½-1 cup fresh mint leaves (washed
 and chopped, or cut up fine if
 you plan to leave them in the
 jelly)
green food coloring (optional)
2 tablespoons lemon juice (if
 apples are sweet)

Measure juice into kettle and bring to a boil. Add sugar and stir until dissolved. Boil 2 minutes, then add mint leaves. Boil rapidly until the jelly stage is reached according to thermometer (8°F. over the boiling point of water) or sheet or refrigerator test (see page 59). Add a little green food coloring and lemon juice, if desired.

Remove from heat and skim off foam with a slotted spoon. Pour through strainer (unless you want the pieces of mint in the jelly) into hot, sterilized containers, leaving ¼ inch headroom. Adjust lids and process in a boiling-water bath for 5 minutes.

Yields three or four 8-ounce glasses.

This recipe and the two that follow can be used to make jelly with blackberries, boysenberries, dewberries, loganberries, red raspberries, strawberries, or youngberries.

Berry Jelly with Powdered Pectin

4 cups loganberries or red raspberries — about 2½ quarts fully ripe berries
1 box packaged powdered pectin
5 cups sugar (5½ cups for loganberries and red raspberries)

If necessary, wash berries quickly in cold water and drain on paper towels. Do not let them stand in the water. Remove stems and caps, and cut out bad spots. Crush thoroughly, place in jelly bag, and squeeze out juice. (For clearer jelly, let drip only — you will need 1½ to 2 times as much fruit.) Measure 3½ cups juice into kettle. Mix powdered pectin with the juice to dissolve. Bring to a boil on high heat, stirring occasionally. Add sugar all at once, stir, and bring to a full rolling boil (a boil that cannot be stirred down); boil hard for exactly 1 minute, stirring constantly. Remove from heat and skim off foam with a metal spoon. Pour immediately into hot, sterilized jelly glasses, leaving ¼ inch headroom. Adjust lids and process in a boiling-water bath for 5 minutes. Remove jars and cool on a towel or rack. Check seals and store properly.

Yields five or six 8-ounce glasses.

Berry Jelly with Liquid Pectin

4 cups berry juice — about 2½ quarts fully ripe berries (for strawberries and blackberries, 3 ¾ cups juice plus ¼ cup lemon juice, strained)
7½ cups (3¼ pounds) sugar
1 bottle liquid pectin

Measure prepared juice into kettle. Add the sugar and mix well. Bring to a boil over high heat, stirring constantly. At once stir in liquid pectin and bring to a full rolling boil. Boil hard for exactly 1 minute, stirring constantly. Remove from heat, skim off foam with a metal spoon. Pour immediately into hot, sterilized containers, leaving ¼ inch headroom. Adjust lids and process in a boiling-water bath for 5 minutes. Remove jars and cool on a towel or rack. Check seals and store properly.

Yields seven or eight 8-ounce glasses.

Berry Jelly: The Long-Cook Method

8 cups berry juice — blackberries or raspberries only (about 5 quart boxes with ¼ underripe and ¾ ripe, plus 1½ cups water)
6 cups sugar

Measure prepared juice into kettle, add sugar, and stir well. (For less than 8 cups juice, add ¾ cup sugar for each cup of juice.) Bring to a boil over high heat, and boil until the jelly stage is reached according to thermometer (8°F. over the boiling point of water) or the sheet or refrigerator test (page 59). Remove from heat and skim off foam with a metal spoon. Pour immediately into hot, sterilized containers, leaving ¼ inch headroom. Adjust lids and process in a boiling-water bath for 5 minutes. Remove jars and cool on a towel or rack. Check seals and store properly.

Yields seven or eight 8-ounce glasses.

ORANGE-PEACH MARMALADE

4 pounds of fully ripe peaches
2 medium oranges
peel of 1 orange, shredded very
    fine
2 tablespoons lemon juice
3 cups sugar

Wash peaches, and remove stems, skins, pits, and bad spots. Chop or grind them up fine. Remove peel and seeds from oranges. Leave some of the white rind on the oranges, as it contains much of the pectin of the fruit. Chop or grind the oranges up fine. Measure 5 cups peaches and 1 cup oranges into kettle and add the remaining ingredients. Stir to mix thoroughly. Bring to a boil rapidly over high heat, stirring constantly. Boil until the mixture thickens, or until it reaches 9°F. above the boiling point of water. Remove from heat and skim off the foam. Ladle into hot, sterilized canning jars, leaving ¼ inch headroom, and seal. Process in a boiling-water bath for 15 minutes.

Yields six or seven half-pint jars.

AUNT SARAH'S TOMATO MARMALADE

The donor of this recipe says it will please adults and children, and recommends placing homemade-bread toast underneath it.

8 pounds plum tomatoes
3 oranges, chopped fine, skin and
    all, removing only the seeds
3 lemons, treated the same
1 tablespoon whole cloves
8 cinnamon sticks
sugar (see recipe instructions)

Skin and chop up tomatoes to provide 4 quarts. Let stand in bowl until most of the liquid can be poured off and used elsewhere. Place chopped oranges and lemons in kettle. Add cloves and cinnamon sticks.

Add tomatoes, adding 1 cup of sugar for each cup of tomatoes. Bring to a boil, stirring as sugar dissolves. Then boil, stirring constantly to prevent burning, until the marmalade sheets off the spoon. (If you are using a candy thermometer, the marmalade is cooked when thermometer registers 8° above the boiling point of water.) Fish out cinnamon sticks and as many of the cloves as can be found. Spoon into hot, sterilized jars, leaving ¼ inch headroom. Adjust lids and process in a boiling-water bath for 10 minutes.

APPLE JELLY

3 pounds apples and 3 cups water
2 tablespoons strained lemon juice
    (if apples are very sweet)
3 cups sugar

Use tart apples, about ¼ of them underripe and ¾ ripe. Wash thoroughly, cut off blossom and stem ends and bad spots. Leave on skins but remove core. Cut the apples into small pieces, add water, cover, and bring to a boil. Lower heat and simmer until soft (about 25 minutes). Turn into jelly bag and let drip for clearest jelly; for more, less-clear jelly, squeeze bag and re-strain through 4 layers of damp cheesecloth. Measure 4 cups juice into kettle. Add lemon juice and sugar and stir well. Rapidly bring mixture to a full boil over high heat, and continue to boil until it reaches the jelly point (8°F. over the boiling point of water on candy thermometer, or use the sheet or refrigerator test, page 59).

Remove from heat and quickly skim off all the foam. Pour boiling hot into hot, sterilized containers, leaving ¼ inch headroom. Adjust seals and process in a boiling-water canner for 5 minutes.

Yields four or five 8-ounce glasses.

APPLE JELLY WITH HONEY

7 pounds apples
juice of lemon
4 cloves
1 stick cinnamon
¼ teaspoon allspice
2½ cups honey

Wash and quarter apples. Cover with water, adding lemon juice, and simmer until soft. Drain through a jelly bag. Measure 4 cups juice into kettle and boil 5 minutes. Add spices tied in a cheesecloth bag and honey. Boil for 8 more minutes. Pour into hot, sterilized jelly glasses, leaving ¼ inch headroom. Adjust lids and process in a boiling-water bath for 5 minutes. Makes four 8-ounce glasses.

JAMS MADE WITH BERRIES

This recipe and the two that follow can be used to make jam with blackberries, boysenberries, dewberries, strawberries, youngberries, loganberries, red raspberries, or gooseberries.

Berry Jam with Powdered Pectin

6 cups crushed berries — about 3 quart boxes of fully ripe berries (grind gooseberries instead of crushing)
1 package powdered pectin
8½ cups sugar

Measure crushed berries into a large saucepan. Add powdered pectin and stir well to dissolve. Bring to a hard boil over high heat, stirring constantly. Add sugar all at once, and, stirring, bring to a full rolling boil (a boil that cannot be stirred down) and boil hard for exactly 1 minute. Remove from heat and skim off foam with metal spoon. Stir and skim for 5 minutes to cool slightly and prevent fruit from floating. Ladle into hot, sterilized containers, leaving ¼ inch headroom in jars, and seal. Process canning jars in a boiling-water bath for 10 minutes.

Yields eleven or twelve half-pint jars.

Berry Jam with Liquid Pectin

4 cups crushed fruit — about 2 quarts fully ripe berries (or
3¾ cups fruit and ¼ cup lemon juice for strawberries or other berries that lack tartness)
7 cups sugar (6½ cups for loganberries and red raspberries; 6 cups for gooseberries)
½ bottle liquid pectin

Measure 4 cups fruit (or fruit and lemon juice) into large saucepan and add sugar. Mix well. Bring to a full, rolling boil over high heat and boil exactly 1 minute, stirring constantly. Remove from heat and stir in liquid pectin at once. Skim off foam with metal spoon, then stir and skim for 5 minutes to cool slightly and prevent fruit from floating. Ladle into hot, sterilized containers, leaving ¼ inch headroom, and seal. Process in a boiling-water bath for 10 minutes.

Yields eight or nine half-pint jars.

Berry Jam: The Long-Cook Method

4 cups crushed berries (about 2 quarts berries, ¼ underripe and ¾ ripe)
3 cups sugar
2-4 tablespoons lemon juice (optional with strawberries and other berries that are not very tart)

Measure berries into kettle. Bring slowly to a boil over low heat, stirring frequently. Add sugar (¾ cup for each cup fruit), stir constantly, and boil rapidly until thick (or for a firm jam, until mixture reaches 9°F. over the boiling point of water). Remove from the heat, skim off foam, and ladle into hot, sterilized canning jars, leaving ¼ inch headroom. Seal. Process in a boiling-water bath for 15 minutes.

Yields three or four half-pint jars.

CHRISTMAS MARMALADE

3 oranges
1 lemon
1 large can (1 pound 14 ounces)
    crushed pineapple
3 pounds sugar
1 small jar maraschino cherries,
    chopped

Put oranges and lemon through food chopper. Add pineapple and sugar. Cook ½ hour, then add cherries. Pour into hot, sterilized jars, leaving ¼ inch headroom, and adjust lids. Process in a boiling-water bath for 10 minutes.

STRAWBERRY PRESERVES

6 cups prepared strawberries
    (about 2 quart boxes of large,
    firm, tart strawberries)
4½ cups sugar

Combine the berries and sugar in alternate layers and let stand for 8 hours or overnight in the refrigerator or other cool place. Heat the fruit and sugar mixture to boiling, stirring gently. Boil rapidly, stirring often to prevent sticking or scorching. Cook to 9°F. above the boiling point of water, or until the syrup thickens (about 15 to 20 minutes). Remove from heat and skim off the foam. Ladle into hot, sterilized canning jars, leaving ¼ inch headroom, and seal. Process in a boiling-water bath for 20 minutes.

Yields about four half-pint jars.

GRAPE CONSERVE

4½ cups Concord grapes (about 4
    pounds) with skins
    removed and set aside
1 orange
4 cups sugar
1 cup seedless raisins
½ teaspoon salt
skins from grapes
1 cup nuts, chopped fine

Measure skinned grapes into a kettle and boil, stirring constantly, for about 10 minutes, or until seeds show. Press through a sieve to remove seeds. Wash and chop the orange up fine without peeling. Add orange, sugar, raisins, and salt to sieved grapes. Boil rapidly, stirring constantly, until the mixture begins to thicken (about 10 minutes). Add grape skins and boil, stirring constantly, to 9°F. above the boiling point of water (about 10 minutes). Do not overcook; the mixture will thicken more on cooling. Add nuts and stir well. Remove from heat and skim off foam. Ladle into hot, sterilized canning jars, leaving ¼ inch head-room, and seal. Process in a boiling-water bath for 15 minutes.

Yields eight or nine half-pint jars.

APPLE BUTTER

6 pounds apples (24-26 medium apples)
2 quarts water
1 quart sweet cider
3 cups sugar
cinnamon, ground
cloves, ground

Wash the apples and cut into small pieces, leaving the skins and cores. Add the water and boil the apples until they are soft (about 30 minutes). Put through a food mill or rub through a sieve.

In the meantime, boil down the cider to half its volume, add the hot apple pulp, sugar, and ground spices to taste, and cook until thick enough to spread. Stir occasionally to prevent sticking or scorching. Ladle into hot, sterilized canning jars, leaving ¼ inch headroom, and seal. Process in a boiling-water bath for 10 minutes.

Yields five or six pints.

GREEN PEPPER JELLY

This unusual jelly is excellent with cream cheese on crackers or melba toast as an appetizer. It also can be used as an accompaniment for meat or game.

½ cup chopped or ground hot red or green peppers (6-8 whole)
1½ cups chopped or ground sweet green or red peppers (12 whole)
6½ cups sugar
1½ cups vinegar
1 bottle liquid pectin

Mix peppers, sugar, and vinegar in a stainless or enameled pan and bring to a brisk boil. Boil for 3 minutes. Add pectin and boil for 1 minute longer. Remove from heat and let stand 5 minutes. Pour into hot, sterile jars, leaving ¼ inch headroom, and adjust seals. Process in a boiling-water canner for 15 minutes. Remove jars from canner and let them cool.

Yields six to eight half-pints.

CHAPTER 5

Pickles and Relishes

M ost beginners start with pickling because it is the "fun" part of preserving. It's easy, and the results are satisfying. Pickling refers to adding vinegar and salt, with a variety of spices and sometimes sugar, to fruit and vegetables. There is variety and room for creativity, but there still are hard and fast rules for safe and successful results.

The pickles most often encountered are made with cucumbers. There are many varieties of cucumbers; some are "picklers" while others are "slicers" or table types. Choose the pickler varieties to grow or buy for use as pickles. Their texture (especially their spiny skin), shape, and flavor are superior to table varieties for canning, and they are good for table use, too. The slicers often have a tough, smooth skin developed for its durability in shipping and keeping, but definitely not tender in a pickle.

Picklers can be harvested at any size. They are picked when tiny for use as little dill or sweet gherkins. As they become more mature (4 to 6 inches long), they can be cross-cut for bread-and-butter pickles or dill chips, or sliced lengthwise for spicy or dill spears. (This is the stage, before the seeds have had a chance to get very big, when they also are excellent served fresh like a slicer.) Make sure you discard a $1/16$-$1/4$-inch slice from the blossom end of the cucumbers. The blossoms sometimes contain an enzyme that can cause excessive softening of the preserved pickles. Crisp pickles are far better than soft, limp ones. When you have put up all you need of these types of pickles and have had your fill of fresh cucumbers, allow the rest to mature to the ripe yellow or white (depending on the type) stage. These big, ripe cukes can be peeled and seeded, and the crisp, thick flesh cut into bite-size chunks and made into sweet "tongue" pickles, "turmerics," "golden glows," or other autumn specialties.

If you don't pressure-can or freeze or if you just want variety, you can look to pickling as a way of preserving your vegetables safely in jars. The addition of the acid vinegar brings the pH level low enough to stop the growth of heat-resistant bacteria. Beans or corn that are pickled are as safe as any cucumber pickle. Try pickled beets, corn relish, dilled beans, pickled carrots, or green tomato relish for colorful and tasty side dishes.

Fruits pickle, too, and the process adds a whole new dimension to apples, pears, and peaches. Watermelon rind, spiced apple slices, mincemeat, and chutneys are just samplings of the variety of pickled fruits available.

PROCESSING

First and most important is the question of processing. Pickled vegetables and fruits should receive a boiling-water bath for safety, to stop bacteria that cause spoilage, to stop enzyme action, and to insure a good seal and high quality. Processing kills the heat-sensitive bacteria that still can grow in high-acid foods. (You can process cucumber pickles — and *only* cucumber pickles — for 30 minutes in water that is 180°F. to prevent spoilage, but it is *imperative* that you use an accurate candy or jelly thermometer to make sure the 180° is maintained throughout processing.) Do use new recipes. You may have a favored old family recipe, but undoubtedly it will not have a processing time. There are many older recipes that have been adapted to newer methods.

For any pickle that is to be processed less than 10 minutes in a boiling-water bath, the canning jars must be sterilized in order to be safe (see page 36).

INGREDIENTS

Use a canning salt, which is sold in 5-pound bags at most groceries. It is additive-free and is also one of the best buys around. Table salt should not be used for pickling, as the additives that prevent caking can cause clouding. Do not use rock salt, since it is impure.

Vinegar is the key ingredient in pickling, providing flavor and storing qualities. The prime consideration with vinegar is acidity. Check the label, as 5-6 percent acidity is necessary. Homemade vinegars may vary in strength, so save them for salads. Use either the cider type or distilled white vinegar. Don't use commercial wine vinegars. And again, *don't* use old recipes. They may have been geared to a less- or more-acid vinegar that would throw off your proportions. White vinegar makes a clearer pickle juice and has a sharp, tart taste, while cider vinegar has a mellower, fruity flavor. Buy vinegar in bulk (gallons) if you're doing many pickles, as you will use large quantities. Don't be tempted to water down your vinegar if you should run short, for this will lower the acidity and possibly compromise the quality.

🌱

CHECKLIST FOR SUCCESSFUL PICKLING

1. Fresh cucumbers are best picked in the early morning, before the sun has had a chance to warm them. Results will be poorer with cucumbers that have been picked and then refrigerated.
2. Remove and discard $\frac{1}{16}$-$\frac{1}{4}$ inch of the blossom end of the cucumber.
3. Use only canning or pickling salt, distilled white or cider vinegar of 5-6 percent acidity, and soft or distilled water.
4. Make sure any fresh herbs you are adding are indeed fresh. The same goes for dried herbs and spices. A food cooperative or natural foods store is a great source for bulk herbs and spices, or vinegar.
5. Wash cucumbers thoroughly.
6. Follow specific recipes and directions for processing times exactly, checking to make sure your jars are sealed properly.

Crispness is a part of good pickles. Simply adding grape or cherry leaves will help maintain crispness, or follow the tip on this page for a lime-water solution soak. Do not use alum, as it is unnecessary and does not improve the firmness of pickles.

Spices are the flavor-makers, and their use allows for creativity in pickling. Quantities and varieties can be varied with no danger except to taste. Always use fresh spices, since they lose quality when stored from one year to the next. The use of a cheesecloth pickling bag for mixed spices will distribute the flavor evenly without causing bland or hot spots. Some pickling spices come ready-mixed.

Recipes often call for peppercorns, cinnamon sticks, cloves, ginger, turmeric (which produces a yellow color), hot pepper, or large quantities of mustard seed. Don't forget to grow your own garlic, which is far superior fresh and is called for in many pickle recipes. The same is true of dill flower and onions. Small onions grown from sets are ideal and go far in saving on expense.

You can use either brown or white sugar, although brown makes a darker pickle. Or you can substitute honey for half of the sugar called for.

Soft water is a luxury in some areas, but it is a necessity for pickling, since hard water interferes with fermentation. Boil hard water, skim off the scum, and let it sit for 24 hours before using it. Then carefully ladle water from the container, so as not to disturb the sediment on the bottom. Distilled water can also be used.

Dill, the key ingredient for dill pickles, is sometimes difficult to find fresh, but it is as easy to grow as a weed and will frequently re-seed. Usually it matures before the cucumbers, unless it is planted late. Dill is easy to air-dry or freeze. To freeze, just put the unwashed dill heads in a container and freeze until pickling time. Fresh dill seems to have more of a wallop than commercial, dried dill seed, so you may want to adjust for that.

POSSIBLE PROBLEMS

Soft pickles. Vinegar too weak.

Hollow pickles. Too mature or poorly developed cucumbers, or too long between harvesting and pickling.

Dark pickles. Iodized salt, too much spice, or the use of iron, copper, or brass utensils.

Shriveling. Sweet pickles in a too-heavy syrup or too-strong vinegar, overcooking, or over-processing.

Soft and slippery pickles. Growth of bacteria from a poor seal. *Throw away.*

EQUIPMENT

Don't use brass, copper, or iron utensils, which react with the salt and vinegar and can affect the color in your pickles. Use enameled, glass, or stainless steel pots instead.

Wide-mouth jars are a great convenience in pickling. Dill spears go in and come out far easier than with a regular jar. However, don't pack your cucumbers so tight that they won't be completely surrounded by the juice.

There are several slicers on the market that adapt to the uniform slicing of cucumbers, but a good chopping knife is perfectly adequate.

According to the USDA, food-grade lime can be used in a lime-water solution for soaking fresh cucumbers for 12-24 hours before pickling. The cucumbers must then be drained and rinsed and soaked in clean, cold water for an hour, *three separate times* before pickling. This improves the crispness of the final product.

Recipes

Recipes are the heart of good pickling. There is only one way to freeze or can properly, but there are hundreds of options in pickling, so it's impossible to come up with one classic example. Whole books have been written on the subject.

Remember that pickles improve with age — the flavor mellows (but try to use them up within a year). The shriveling often encountered in dilly beans will disappear after several weeks on the shelf, so be patient and wait for a month to six weeks.

Do try more than one recipe the first year. You may find that you made a great pickle but not a family favorite. Also, mark your recipes so that you remember which ones to try again. Keeping a small notebook of successes and failures is a good idea.

QUICK DILL PICKLES

3 cups white vinegar
3 cups water
⅓ cup canning salt
4 pounds cucumbers, washed and cut into spears
6 heads dill or 6 tablespoons dill seed
3 peeled garlic cloves (optional)
9 peppercorns

Combine liquids and salt and heat to boiling. Pack cucumbers into hot, clean quart jars. Add to each jar 2 heads dill or 2 tablespoons dill seed, 1 clove garlic, and 3 peppercorns. Fill the jars with the hot pickling syrup, leaving ½ inch headroom. Adjust lids. Process in a boiling-water bath for 20 minutes. Yields three quarts.

TWO-DAY MUSTARD PICKLES

This recipe is a gardener's delight, since when it's served, he or she can exclaim with pride, "That's from my garden — and that and that and that." It demands vegetables from six different rows, all of which can be found in most gardens in August.

1 head cauliflower (about 1½ quarts), broken into florets
1 quart small white onions, peeled
1 quart small cucumbers
1 quart small green tomatoes
2 large green peppers, chopped and with seeds removed
2 large sweet red peppers, treated in like manner
3 quarts cold water
½ cup canning salt
2 quarts cider vinegar
6 tablespoons prepared mustard
1½ cups light brown sugar
⅔ cup flour
2 tablespoons turmeric

First day: Tidy up vegetables, place them in a large bowl, and cover them with a brine made of 3 quarts of cold water and ½ cup of salt. (Use a total of 4 cups of chopped peppers; the ratio of green to red is not important.) Cover and let sit for 24 hours.

Second day: Using a colander and a large pan, drain salt solution from vegetables, catching them in colander and liquid in saucepan. Heat solution to boiling and pour over vegetables in colander, this time discarding it. Let vegetables drain.

Combine vinegar, mustard, brown sugar, flour, and turmeric. Stir, then heat gradually, stirring constantly, until mixture is thick and smooth. Add drained vegetables and cook gently until they are tender but have not lost their individuality. Stir (with heavy wooden spoon) to prevent scorching.

Pack into hot, sterilized pint jars, leaving ½ inch headroom. Process in a boiling-water bath for 10 minutes. This will produce more than 5 quarts of pickles — excellent gifts for fellow gardeners.

SUNSHINE PICKLES

4 quarts chunked ripe yellow
    cucumbers (about 1½ x ½-inch
    pieces)
4 large onions, sliced
1 tablespoon canning salt
1 tablespoon celery seed
1 tablespoon turmeric powder
4 cups white sugar
2 ¾ cups cider vinegar
¼ cup water

Mix all but cucumbers and onions in a kettle. Bring to a boil. Put in cucumbers and onions, stirring occasionally until cukes turn transparent. Don't overcook. Pack in hot, sterilized jars. Cover to within ½ inch of rim. Adjust lids. Process pints 10 minutes in a boiling-water bath. These pickles can be used immediately if desired.

DILLY BEANS

2 pounds green beans, trimmed
1 teaspoon cayenne pepper
4 cloves garlic
4 heads dill
2½ cups water
2½ cups vinegar
¼ cup canning salt

Pack beans lengthwise into hot, sterilized pint jars, leaving ½ inch headroom. To each pint add ¼ teaspoon cayenne pepper, 1 clove garlic, and 1 head dill. Combine remaining ingredients in a kettle and bring to a boil. Pour boiling hot over beans, leaving ½ inch headroom. Adjust caps. Process pints (or quarts) 5 minutes in a boiling-water bath. Yields four pints.

For best flavor, let the canned beans stand for at least two weeks before serving. This allows the flavor to develop. And don't worry if they look shriveled right after processing — they'll plump up in a few weeks.

MIXED PICKLES

4 quarts cucumbers
1 quart onions
1 green pepper
3 cups cauliflower florets
3 cloves garlic
⅓ cup canning salt
ice cubes
5 cups sugar
2 tablespoons mustard seed
½ tablespoon celery seed
1 quart cider vinegar

Slice cucumbers and onions and pepper thin. Combine all vegetables with garlic and add salt. Cover with ice cubes, mix, and let stand for 3 hours. Drain well.

Combine remaining ingredients and pour over vegetables. Bring to a boil. Put in clean, hot pint jars, allowing ½ inch headroom. Seal and process in a boiling-water bath for 15 minutes. Yields eight pints.

BREAD-AND-BUTTER PICKLES

6 pounds cucumbers
1 pound onions
2 large, peeled garlic cloves
⅓ cup canning salt
2 trays ice cubes
4½ cups sugar
1½ teaspoons turmeric
1½ teaspoons celery seed
2 tablespoons mustard seed
3 cups cider vinegar

Wash and slice cucumbers. Peel and slice 1½ cups onions. Combine. Add garlic cloves, canning salt, and mix. Cover with 2 trays of ice cubes and let stand 3 hours. Rinse and drain. Remove garlic. Combine sugar, turmeric, celery seed, mustard seed, and vinegar in large pot. Stir, then add drained cucumbers and onions. Heat for 5 minutes. Pack hot pickles into hot, sterilized jars, leaving ½ inch headroom. Adjust jar lids. Process in a boiling-water bath for 10 minutes for pints or quarts. Yields seven pints.

SHORT-CUT BREAD-AND-BUTTER PICKLES

½ gallon of your own or store-
   bought dill pickles
1 clove garlic, cut into pieces
4 cups sugar
2 cups cider vinegar
2 sticks cinnamon
2 tablespoons celery seed
1 tablespoon dry mustard

Drain pickles and cut them into ½-inch slices. Put them back into jar with garlic. Combine sugar and vinegar and boil. Add cinnamon, celery seed, and mustard and pour over pickles. Keep in refrigerator for 1 week before serving. These are not to be resealed.

ZUCCHINI BREAD-AND-BUTTER PICKLES

2 pounds fresh firm zucchini
2 small (or medium) onions
¼ cup salt (canning salt is best)
ice, cubes or cracked
2 cups white sugar
1 teaspoon celery seed
1 teaspoon turmeric
2 teaspoons mustard seed
3 cups cider vinegar

Wash zucchini and cut into thin slices. Peel onions, then slice very thin. Add to zucchini. Cover zucchini and onions with water and add salt. Cover with ice, and let stand 2 hours. Rinse and drain thoroughly. Bring remaining ingredients to boiling. Pour over zucchini and onions. Let stand 2 hours. Bring all ingredients to boiling point and heat 5 minutes. Pack into hot, sterilized jars. Leave ½ inch headroom. Adjust caps and process in a boiling-water bath for 10 minutes. Yields about three pints.

ZUCCHINI RELISH

4 cups chopped zucchini
3 cups chopped carrots
3 cups chopped onions
1½ cups chopped green or red
    sweet peppers
¼ cup sugar
2 tablespoons table salt
2¼ cups white vinegar
1 tablespoon celery seed
¾ teaspoon dry mustard

Mix all ingredients in a large skillet. Cook for 15 minutes or until all vegetables are tender but still crisp. Pack in hot, clean jars, leaving ¼ inch headroom. Adjust lids and process in a boiling-water bath for 20 minutes. Makes four to five pints.

PICCALILLI

3 sweet red peppers
3 green peppers
2 quarts green tomatoes
10 small onions
3 cups cider vinegar
1¾ cups sugar
⅛ cup table salt
¼ cup mustard seed
⅓ tablespoon celery seed
½ teaspoon cinnamon
½ teaspoon allspice

Wash, seed, and quarter peppers. Wash and quarter tomatoes. Peel and quarter onions. Put all through a food mill. Drain off extra liquid. In a large kettle add vegetables and half of vinegar. Boil for ½ hour, stirring often. Drain and discard liquid. Add remaining vinegar, sugar, and spices, and simmer for 3 minutes. Pour into hot, sterilized pint jars, allowing ½ inch headroom, and process in a boiling-water bath for 5 minutes. Yields six pints. Ideal with hamburgers or mixed with ketchup for relish, or in potato salad.

CORN RELISH

8 cups raw corn cut from cob
3 cups chopped onions
½ cup chopped green pepper
½ cup chopped sweet red pepper
¾ cup packed brown sugar
½ cup white corn syrup
7 teaspoons canning salt
1 tablespoon dry mustard
3 cups cider vinegar

Mix all ingredients thoroughly. Cover and boil for 15 minutes, stirring often. Pour into clean, hot pint jars, leaving ½ inch headroom, and process in a boiling water bath for 15 minutes. Yields four or five pints.

CABBAGE & BEET RELISH

3 pints shredded cabbage
3 pints cooked, sliced beets
1 cup chopped onions
¾ cup grated horseradish
2 tablespoons canning salt
2½ cups vinegar
1 cup sugar

Mix vegetables and salt. Heat vinegar and sugar until dissolved. Add to vegetables and boil 12 minutes. Pack into hot, clean pint jars, leaving ½ inch headroom. Adjust lids and process in a boiling-water bath 15 minutes.

GREEN TOMATO MINCEMEAT WITHOUT MEAT

2 quarts green tomatoes
1 orange
2½ quarts apples
1 tablespoon table salt
1 pound seeded raisins
3½ cups brown sugar
2 teaspoons cinnamon
1 teaspoon cloves
½ teaspoon ginger
1 teaspoon nutmeg
½ cup vinegar

Wash and drain tomatoes, orange, and apples. Grind up tomatoes in a meat grinder, sprinkle with salt, and let stand for 1 hour. Drain and cover with boiling water for 5 minutes. Drain again. Grate rind and chop pulp of orange. Core, pare, and chop apples. Mix all ingredients and boil slowly until tender. Pour into hot, clean pint jars and seal, allowing ½ inch headroom. Process in a boiling-water bath for 25 minutes. Yields six pints. Ideal in pies or cookies.

GREEN TOMATO RELISH WITH HONEY

12 green tomatoes
4 large onions
1 red and 1 green sweet pepper
1 tablespoon table salt
1 cup dark honey
1 cup vinegar
1 tablespoon mustard seed
1 tablespoon celery seed

Chop tomatoes, onions, and peppers into chunks. Drain. Add remaining ingredients and mix. Cook slowly until tender, about 20 minutes. Put into hot, sterilized jars, leaving ½ inch headroom. Adjust lids. Process in a boiling-water bath — 10 minutes for pints, 15 minutes for quarts.

LINDA'S PICKLED PEARS

12 pears, pared, cored, and cut into
    quarters (d'anjou work well)
1½ cups honey
4 cups cranberry juice
1 cup red or white wine vinegar
6 cinnamon sticks
1 tablespoon ground ginger
1 tablespoon ground cloves

Combine all ingredients except pears and bring to a boil. Boil for 5 minutes. Add the pears and simmer until barely tender. Lift pears out of liquid and pack into hot, sterile pint jars. Bring liquid quickly back to a boil and pour into jars, distributing 1 cinnamon stick to each jar, leaving ½ inch headspace. Adjust lids. Process in a boiling-water bath for 10 minutes. Remove jars and let them cool. Yields six pints.

CONNIE'S PEAR CHUTNEY

10 cups (5 pounds) sliced, firm,
    ripe pears
½ cup finely chopped green
    peppers
1½ cups seedless raisins
4 cups sugar
1 cup chopped, crystallized ginger
3 cups cider vinegar
½ teaspoon table salt
½ teaspoon whole allspice
½ teaspoon whole cloves
3 cinnamon sticks, 2 inches long

Place pears and the next six ingredients in a saucepan. Tie allspice and cloves in a cheesecloth bag and add along with cinnamon. Cook slowly until pears are tender and mixture is thick, about 1 hour. Remove spices. Ladle into hot, sterilized jars, leaving ½ inch headroom. Adjust caps. Process 10 minutes in a boiling-water bath. Yields about ten half-pints.

WATERMELON RIND PICKLES

1 large watermelon
½ cup canning salt
2 quarts water
2 cups vinegar
3 cups white or brown sugar
1 lemon, sliced thin
2 sticks cinnamon
1 teaspoon allspice
1 teaspoon whole cloves

Remove skin and pink from rind. Cut rind into 1-inch cubes or chunks. You should have about 8 cups. Soak chunks overnight in brine mixture of ½ cup salt and 2 quarts water. Drain and rinse in fresh water. Drain again. Add more fresh water to cover, and simmer until tender. Drain. Make syrup of vinegar, sugar, lemon, and spices tied in a cheesecloth bag. Simmer 5 minutes. Add rind and cook until clear. Pack rind into hot, sterilized jars and fill with syrup, leaving ½ inch headroom. Adjust lids and process in a boiling-water bath for 10 minutes. Yields three pints.

SPICED APPLE SLICES

6 cups sugar
2 cups vinegar
4 sticks cinnamon in small pieces
2 teaspoons whole cloves
5 pounds firm apples, peeled,
    cored, and sliced thick

Boil sugar, vinegar, and spices; add apples and simmer uncovered until they are tender but not broken. Pack into hot, sterilized pint jars, leaving ½ inch headroom, and process in a boiling-water bath for 10 minutes. Yields three or four pints.

JAN RAYMOND'S TONGUE PICKLES

5 pounds ripe cucumbers
1 teaspoon cinnamon
1 teaspoon cloves
1 teaspoon ginger
½ teaspoon pepper
1 teaspoon canning salt
1½ pounds brown sugar
2 cups vinegar

Peel cukes, remove seeds, and cut into pieces about 2 inches long. Place in an enamel kettle or pot. Put spices in a mesh bag or cheesecloth tied at the top. Add sugar and vinegar and spice bag to pot. Cook until cukes are transparent. Let sit overnight. Reheat, put pickles in hot, sterilized jars and add liquid, leaving ¼ inch headroom. Adjust lids and process in a boiling-water bath for 10 minutes.

CHAPTER 6

Curing with Brine

S alting, an ancient method of preserving, was based on the discovery that large amounts of salt will inhibit spoilage. However, using a great deal of salt means that the food is not fit to eat until it has been desalted and freshened by soaking in several changes of water, resulting in the loss of many nutrients.

When small amounts of salt are used, however, fermentation occurs. The bacteria change the sugars of the vegetables to lactic acid, and the acid (with the salt) prevents other spoilage organisms from growing. This lactic-acid fermentation is the method used in making sauerkraut and other "sour" vegetables. Since the salting is so mild, the consumption of both vegetable and juice can be enjoyed, and nearly all the nutrients are preserved.

The Chinese may have been the first to preserve food by the fermentation process. The present-day *yen tsai* — meaning vegetables preserved in brine — is prepared with mixtures of various vegetables that have been available since ancient times. Turnips, radishes, cabbage, and other vegetables are used in these preparations, and salt is added if available.

Some of the vegetables that can be fermented in the home with success are cabbage, Chinese cabbage, turnips, rutabagas, lettuce, green tomatoes, and snap beans. Cucumbers also are fermented when brined the long way for pickles.

When properly prepared, all of these foods will be crisp but tender. They are pleasantly acid and salty in flavor, and they are good in salads (except for sauerkraut) or served whole on the relish tray, without freshening. They also are good cooked with meat.

GENERAL DIRECTIONS

1. As with all kinds of storage, choose only fresh, healthy, tender young produce for the best results.
2. Use pure "pickling" salt, which also is called "canning" salt. Ordinary table salt usually has iodine and starch added to it. Neither of these additives is harmful if used in salting, but the iodine may cause an off-color and the starch may interfere with the fermenting process and settle to the bottom of the jar, giving a cloudy appearance. Canning salt also is much cheaper than table salt. "Flakey" and medium salts, such as dairy, cheese, and kosher salts, also may be used, but be careful when measuring (see salt chart, page 85). Pound for pound these are the same as the granulated pickling salt, but by *measure* almost 1½ times as much is called for. Coarse salt is *not* recommended for use, because it dissolves too slowly and is harder to distribute evenly.
3. Weigh or measure the vegetables and salt accurately and follow directions exactly.
4. Keep the vegetables completely immersed in the brine at all times, during both fermentation and storage.
5. Never add fresh vegetables to a batch that has already started curing.
6. Clean the cloth and cover regularly and remove scum from surface of brine. A piece of cloth tied over the curing container will help keep insects and dust off the cover and out of the brine.
7. Discard *without tasting* any material that is slimy, soft, or has an off-odor or off-color. It is not fit to eat.

EQUIPMENT NEEDED

- Household scales to weigh vegetables and salt.
- Kraut-cutting board, or a large, very sharp knife and cutting board (for sauerkraut).
- Large pans for making brine and mixing vegetables and salt. These should be of stainless steel, glass, unchipped enamel, or plastic. Never use copper, brass, galvanized, or iron utensils for mixing or heating acid or salty solutions. They may react with the metal, causing undesirable compounds and color changes.
- Curing containers. For small quantities, use glass, quart to gallon wide-mouth containers with lids. Do not use zinc lids. For large quantities, use stone jars, crocks, paraffined wooden barrels, or large casseroles or kettles of unchipped enamelware.
- Cover for large containers: a round, flat board or china plate that will fit snugly *inside* the top of the container; or a large, waterproof plastic bag suitable for use with food.
- Weight to hold cover and vegetables below the level of the brine: something that can be washed thoroughly, such as a glass jar filled with sand or water.
- Sterile white cheesecloth or muslin to put on top of the vegetables.
- Wooden tamper, potato masher, or a clean, heavy bottle to tamp down cabbage and turnips.
- Canning jars and lids for processing fermented vegetables.

All equipment should be scrupulously clean. Containers that have been used before should be aired thoroughly and scalded. Do not use wooden containers or covers made of yellow or pitch pine, or the vegetables will develop a piney flavor. To paraffin wooden containers or covers, warm them and be sure they are thoroughly dry. Melt paraffin and apply with a brush, thin but thoroughly. Dry well before using.

SAUERKRAUT

The health-giving properties of sauerkraut have been well-recognized for two hundred years or more, and before vitamin C was discovered it was a preventative or cure for scurvy. This was, of course, because cabbage ranks high among foods for vitamin C value. Even though two-thirds of the vitamin C is lost in fermenting and processing, there are still 16 mg. in a 4-ounce serving, and only about twenty calories. Sauerkraut also happens to be inexpensive to make. You can use Chinese cabbage in this recipe as well as regular cabbage.

For 40 to 50 pounds of cabbage, 1 pound of salt is needed. Approximately 45 pounds of cabbage will fill a 5-gallon crock; about 8 pounds of cabbage will fill a 1-gallon jar. For each 5 pounds of cabbage, you will need 3 tablespoons of pickling salt.

1. Choose heavy, firm heads of cabbage of the long-growing, late variety. Let them stand at room temperature for several hours to wilt, and the leaves will become less brittle and less likely to break in cutting. Trim off the outer leaves and wash the heads. With a sharp knife cut the heads into quarters. The core may be cut out or left on and sliced thin with the rest of the cabbage. It contains as many nutrients as the rest of the cabbage, but is tough and somewhat bitter. Chinese cabbage has more flavor than regular cabbage does, due to more and sweeter natural juice.
2. Cut 5 pounds of cabbage at a time into thin shreds. If using a kraut-cutting board, set the blade to cut shreds about the thickness of a dime. Mix 5 pounds of cabbage with 3 tablespoons of salt in a large pan, and let it settle for 15 to 20 minutes or more while shredding the next batch. The salt will start working on the cabbage during this time, reducing the bulk (which makes it easier to pack), drawing juices (so less tamping is required), and softening it somewhat (helping to prevent breakage of the shreds when packed).
3. Pack the cabbage into clean containers, pressing firmly with hands or a tamper to remove air pockets and to draw the juice. Fill large containers to within 3 or 4 inches of the top with salted cabbage, pressing and tamping down after each layer. (Leave about 6 inches space above the cabbage if you're using a filled plastic bag for the cover; see #4.) Do not tamp so hard that you bruise or tear the shreds, for this can result in undesirable softening of the kraut. Juice should cover the surface of the kraut within 24 hours.
4. Wipe stray pieces of cabbage from around the edge of the container. Cover the cabbage with several layers of sterile white cheesecloth and tuck it down the sides. Then put on your cover. The size of the cover

---

KRAUT PROBLEMS

Here are some of the common causes of spoilage in sauerkraut, and the reasons the U.S. Department of Agriculture gives for them:

Softness. Insufficient salt, too-high temperature during fermentation, uneven distribution of salt, or air pockets caused by improper packing.

Pink kraut. Certain types of yeast grow on the surface of the kraut because of too much salt or an uneven distribution of salt, or when the kraut is improperly covered or weighted during fermentation.

Rotted. Usually found at the surface where the cabbage has not been covered sufficiently to exclude air during fermentation.

Dark kraut. Unwashed and improperly trimmed cabbage; insufficient juice to cover fermenting cabbage; uneven distribution of salt; exposure to air; high temperatures during fermentation, processing, or storage; or too long a storage period.

is important: it should fit snugly within the container to seal out air, preventing the growth of undesirable yeast and aerobic bacteria that can spoil the kraut. Keep flat, so that no air will be caught under it. On top of the cover place a weight of such heft that the juice will rise just above the cover. It may take several hours for this to happen. If the juice has not risen over the cover within 24 hours, add enough 2½ percent brine (see chart, below) to bring it to this level.

Instead of using cloth, cover, and weight, a large plastic bag of a type suitable for freezing food can be placed directly on the kraut and filled with enough water to keep the juice over the top of the kraut. A second or third bag can be put inside the first before filling to prevent leakage. The bag should be big enough to cover the kraut completely and fit tightly against the inside edge of the container. This will seal out air effectively. After putting cold tap water into the bag to the level of the top of the container, close it with metal twisties or rubber bands.

5. Room temperature of 68°-72°F. is recommended for fermenting cabbage, which will usually be ready in 5 to 6 weeks. Fermentation will be faster at 75°-80°F., and at 85°F. the cabbage will be ready in about 2 weeks. However, the chances of spoilage are much greater at these high temperatures, and the kraut may become soft.

Unless air is completely sealed out, a white scum will appear on the brine surface within a few days. If so, promptly remove the cover and carefully lift off the cloth, then skim off any scum that does not adhere to the cloth. Replace the cloth with a clean one, scald the cover, and replace it and the weight. Check the kraut daily, removing the scum and cleaning the cloth and cover as often as the scum forms. Adjust the weight to keep the brine level up above the kraut. Add more 2½ percent brine if the level becomes too low.

After a couple of weeks there may be a dramatic drop in the level of the juice, meaning fermentation is ceasing. Then add enough 2½ percent brine to cover the kraut. Bubbles will be visible on the surface of the kraut as long as fermentation continues. When no bubbles can be seen, fermentation is complete. After fermentation has ceased, put the kraut into a kettle and heat to simmering. Pack the hot sauerkraut into clean, hot jars. Cover with hot juice, leaving ½ inch headroom. Adjust lids. Process in a boiling-water bath — pints for 15 minutes, quarts for 20 minutes.

Salt Needed for Brines

STRENGTH OF BRINE (percent)	(oz./qt.)	BY WEIGHT ALL TYPES OF SALT (oz./gal.)	(lb./gal.)	BY VOLUME GRANULATED (cups/gal.)	FLAKE OR MEDIUM (cups/gal.)
2½	1 oz.	3½ oz.	¼ lb.	⅓ cup	½ cup
5	1¾	7½	½	¾	1
10	4	16	1	1½	2¼
15	6¼	25	1½	2½	3¾
20	9	36	2¼	3½	5¼

Equivalent Weights and Volumes of Salts

AMOUNT OF SALT (weight)	EQUIVALENT MEASURE	
	GRANULATED PICKLING	FLAKE OR MEDIUM
1 oz.	1 tbs. + 1 tsp.	3 tbs. +1½ tsp.
½ lb.	¾ cup	1 cup + 2 tbs.
1 lb.	1½ cups	2¼ cups

MEASURE	EQUIVALENT WEIGHT	
½ cup	5 oz.	3½ oz.
1 cup	10 oz.	7 oz.

Conversions: 1 tablespoon = 3 teaspoons
1 cup = 16 tablespoons

From USDA Farm Bulletin #1932.

Small-Batch Krauting

If you have just a few heads of cabbage, you may want to ferment them in individual containers. To ferment your kraut in quart or pint jars, proceed according to the directions, cutting and mixing 5 pounds of cabbage with 3 tablespoons of salt. Let it settle for 15 or 20 minutes, then pack tightly into jars. Insert two or three wooden sticks, cut slightly longer than the width of the jar mouth, into the jar, catching the ends up under the shoulders of the jars. This should hold the kraut down under the juice.

Add more 2½ percent brine to cover if enough does not form in 24 hours. The tops should be placed on the jars loosely so that gas formed during fermentation can escape. Place the jars on trays or newspapers to catch the juice that oozes out with the gas. The level of the kraut may sink enough in a week or two to make it necessary to combine the kraut from several jars — about 1 quart of kraut will be needed to supplement the contents of 4 other quarts. Do *not* add fresh vegetables to a batch of already-started sauerkraut or other salted vegetables.

If scum forms in these small containers, remove it with a spoon. If the level of the brine is so low that it is difficult to reach the scum, add more 2½ percent brine. The scum will rise to the surface of the brine, where it can be reached more easily.

After about 2 to 6 weeks the fermentation process will cease. The kraut should have a pleasantly acid taste and have changed color to a slightly translucent pale gold-white. At this point, kraut packed in large containers can be transferred to smaller canning jars to be processed for storage (see page 86), or it can be stored for several months in the original container in a cold (38°F.) place. For storage, put on a fresh cloth, be sure the brine covers the surface of the kraut, and cover with a tight-fitting lid.

For a change of pace, sauerkraut can be made more interesting by adding herbs (caraway or dill) or garlic cloves to small batches of the

🌿

LETTUCE KRAUT

Head lettuce of the Los Angeles or iceberg type can be made into kraut in the same manner as cabbage. It is milder in flavor than cabbage kraut, and is an excellent product if properly made.

cabbage before fermenting. Remove the garlic before cooking or before serving the finished kraut. A few sliced carrots, whole green tomatoes, or pieces of cauliflower or broccoli can be scattered in the cabbage to ferment with it. Or try a whole cabbage, for use as stuffed cabbage leaves, pickled in the kraut. Put salt into the cavity left by cutting out the core — about 2 teaspoons salt per pound of cabbage — and bury the whole cabbage, cavity side up, in the center of the shredded cabbage.

Canning Kraut

For longer or warmer storage, can the kraut as follows:

Hot-pack canning. Place the kraut in a kettle and heat to simmering (185°-210°F.) in its own juice. Stir gently so the kraut will heat evenly, but do not boil. Add more 2½ percent brine if there is not enough juice to cover the kraut. Pack into sterile, hot canning jars, press down to release air bubbles, and cover with hot juice, leaving ½ inch headroom. Adjust lids and process in a boiling-water bath:

> pints . . . . . . 10 minutes
> quarts. . . . . . 15 minutes

Remove jars and place on a towel or rack several inches apart to cool. If allowed to remain hot for too long a time, the kraut will darken and soften. When canned and cooled properly, the kraut will have much the flavor and texture of the fresh product.

Raw-pack canning. Fill hot, clean jars firmly with kraut and cover with juices, adding more 2½ percent brine if necessary. Leave ½ inch headroom. Adjust lids and process in a boiling-water bath:

> pints . . . . . . 20 minutes
> quarts. . . . . . 25 minutes

Remove jars and cool on a towel or rack.

WEAK BRINING WITH SALT AND VINEGAR

This is a method of preserving some vegetables if you have no other means. It also offers interesting flavor changes that you might like to try. Several vegetables can be stored by this method. They don't need to be soaked to remove the salt before serving, but if the flavor is too tart they can be rinsed well or soaked a short time before cooking. Vegetables that can be used are snap beans, beets, beet tops, carrots, cauliflower, mustard and turnip greens, kale, rutabagas, turnips, and small, whole green tomatoes.

1. Prepare the vegetables as for table use by trimming and washing. Cut the cauliflower or break it into florets, and slice or dice turnips and rutabagas. Wash greens thoroughly in several waters to remove all traces of grit. Wash small carrots, beets, and green tomatoes and remove stems (leave ½ inch of stem on the beets), but do not cut into pieces. Wash very tender snap green or wax beans and blanch for 5

When the snap beans come faster than your family can pick them — much less eat them — and the freezer has had its quota, try a small crock of them brined (see page 87), or better yet put up pint or larger jars of them as dilled beans, using your favorite dill pickle recipe (or see page 75). The dill comes into flower usually when your first bean crop is just running out and everybody's had enough fresh beans for a while.

TOO MANY?

When the snap beans come faster than your family can pick them — much less eat them — and the freezer has had its quota, try a small crock of them brined (see page 87), or better yet put up pint or larger jars of them as dilled beans, using your favorite dill pickle recipe (or see page 75). The dill comes into flower usually when your first bean crop is just running out and everybody's had enough fresh beans for a while.

minutes in boiling water or steam, and cool promptly. They can be cut into pieces crosswise or left whole.

2. Prepare a 5 percent brine. The amount needed will be about half the volume of the vegetables to be packed. To each gallon of water, add and dissolve ½ pound of salt. Add 1 cup of vinegar that has a 4 to 6 percent strength of acetic acid.

3. Pack the vegetables firmly into clean containers to within 3 or 4 inches of the top. Cover with several layers of sterile white cheesecloth or muslin and tuck in around the edge. On top of this place a weighted cover. Pour the brine over the vegetables until it comes up over the cover.

4. Store the containers in a cool place. Follow directions given for sauerkraut (page 84) about removing scum and washing the cloth and cover frequently. After fermentation for 10 days to 2 weeks, hot-pack the vegetables into canning jars and process in a boiling-water bath the same way as sauerkraut. If necessary, make more 5 percent brine to cover the vegetables in the jars, leaving ½ inch headroom.

SAUERRUBEN (SOUR TURNIPS)

Select sweet, young, juicy, purple-topped turnips for this specialty. Rutabagas also can be used.

Peel, shred, and mix 3 tablespoons of granulated pickling salt with each 5 pounds of turnips. Pack into clean containers and press down gently after all of it has been packed, to remove air pockets. Tamping layer-by-layer should be unnecessary if the turnips are juicy. Cover and weigh down as you would sauerkraut. Enough juice should form to cover the turnips within 24 hours. If not, add more 2½ percent brine to cover. (See chart, page 84.)

Kept at room temperature (68°-72°F.), it may take from a month to 6 weeks for the turnips to ferment. Be sure they remain covered with brine, and remove scum as it forms. Replace the cloth with a clean one and scald the cover daily.

When fermentation is complete, heat the sauerruben to simmering, and hot-pack it into clean, hot canning jars. Cover with its own juice, leaving ½ inch headroom. Adjust lids and process in a boiling-water bath:

> pints . . . . . . 15 minutes
> quarts. . . . . . 20 minutes

BRINE-CURED PICKLES

Curing cucumbers and other vegetables in a brine "strong enough to float an egg" is as much a part of our food heritage as salt pork or apple pie. A 10 percent brine will float a fresh egg, and in it we cure many vegetables that are then used for sour, spiced, and sweet pickles: cucumbers, green tomatoes, green beans, onions, and cauliflower.

SAUER BEANS OR SLICED GREEN TOMATOES

Wash young, tender, snap beans, snip off the ends, and cut into short lengths. Blanch them for 5 minutes in boiling water or steam. Cool promptly in ice cold water and drain. Wash green tomatoes, remove stem and core, and slice thick.

Mix, as evenly as possible, 4 ounces salt and 4 ounces (½ cup) vinegar with each 5 pounds of vegetables. If not enough brine forms to cover the vegetables completely within 24 hours, add more 5 percent brine. Pack firmly and proceed with each step as for making and processing sauerkraut.

Vegetables prepared this way will be attractive in appearance, crisp in texture, and slightly salty and acid in flavor. Since they do not need to be soaked in fresh water, they retain a fair share of their nutrients.

Beans should be boiled 10 minutes before tasting or serving. Discard *without tasting* any material that is soft or has an objectionable odor.

1. Prepare vegetables by washing, trimming, and removing stems and blossom ends. Use whole, immature cucumbers — from tiny gherkins up to 7 inches. Wipe rather than wash, unless very dirty. Beans should be blanched in boiling water or steamed for 5 minutes. Small green tomatoes and onions can be left whole. Cut cauliflower into florets.
2. Weigh vegetables and pack into a clean container. Cover with a cold brine of 1 pound pickling salt to 1 gallon of water. A gallon of brine will be needed for each 2 gallons of vegetables.
3. Cover the vegetables with a wooden cover or plate weighed down to keep the vegetables under the brine.
4. The following day add additional salt at the rate of ½ pound for each 5 pounds of vegetables. This is necessary to keep the brine strong enough despite the liquid drawn from the vegetables by the salt. Place the salt in a mound on top of the cover rather than directly into the brine, so it will not sink to the bottom.
5. At the end of the first week, and for 4 or 5 succeeding weeks, add ⅛ pound salt for each 5 pounds of vegetables. To help remember when and how much salt to add, tape a timetable to the crock, marking off each time the salt is added.
6. Remove any scum that forms, and be sure to keep every pickle completely submerged in the brine. Add more 10 percent brine if necessary.
7. Fermentation will continue 4 to 8 weeks, indicated by a few bubbles rising to the surface. The speed will depend on the storage temperature — 68°-72°F. is safest to avoid spoilage.

More vegetables *may* be added in this recipe for the first couple of weeks of the brining process, provided the brine is kept strong enough — at 10 percent. Go ahead and test it with an egg!

The cucumbers are ready when they are a consistent olive-green color, translucent throughout and without white spots. Before using for pickles, they should be desalted by soaking for 12 to 24 hours in large quantities of fresh water that is changed several times, or in equal parts water and vinegar.

FREEZING IN BRINE

Try packing your vegetables in brine, then freezing them. This is the advice in *Preparing Food for Your Freezer*, Circular 534, published by the Pennsylvania State University College of Agriculture. The advantage of doing this, the authors say, is that the brine helps to keep the color and texture of the vegetables. Mix ½ teaspoon salt in ½ cup water for each pint of vegetables. Follow all other instructions for freezing vegetables.

QUICK-BRINED PICKLES

20 pounds cucumbers
¾ cup whole mixed pickling spices
3 bunches fresh dill
2½ cups vinegar
2½ gallons water
1¾ cups canning salt

Never use overripe cucumbers. Be especially careful to wash completely, removing the blossom end. Put half the pickling spices and a layer of dill in a 5-gallon crock or glass jar. Fill with cucumbers, leaving 3 to 4 inches headspace. Put remaining dill and spices on top. Mix vinegar, water, and salt and pour on. Cover with a plate, using a canning jar filled with sand or water to keep the pickles below the brine surface. Cover crock with a sterile cloth. Leave at room temperature.

Remove scum every day, being sure cucumbers are completely covered. First scum forms in about 3 days. In about 3 weeks pickles will be ready to process. The brine may be cloudy; if you wish a clear brine, replace it with ½ cup salt and 4 cups vinegar to 1 gallon water. Pack in clean, hot, quart jars, adding some of the dill. Cover with boiling brine, leaving ½ inch headroom. Process in a boiling-water bath for 15 minutes.

1. Remove outer leaves from firm, mature heads of cabbage. Wash and drain. Remove core and shred with a knife or shredder.

2. Weigh 5 pounds carefully to insure correct cabbage-salt proportions.

3. Measure 3 tablespoons canning salt and sprinkle over 5 pounds prepared cabbage. Mix well with spoon or hands. Allow 15-20 minutes for cabbage to wilt slightly.

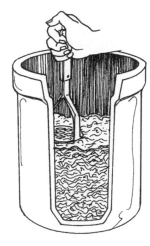

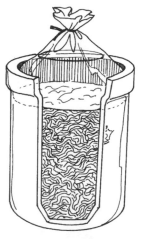

4. Pack cabbage into a 1-gallon jar. Press firmly with wooden spoon or hands until juice is drawn out to cover shredded cabbage.

5. Put a heavy-duty plastic bag on cabbage and fill with water until it sits firmly, allowing no air to reach the cabbage. Ferment for approximately 5 to 6 weeks. Gas bubbles indicate that fermentation is occurring. Temperatures between 68° and 72° are ideal for fermentation.

4. After fermentation has ceased, put kraut into a kettle and heat to simmering. Pack hot sauerkraut into clean, hot jars. Cover with hot juice, leaving ½ inch headroom. Adjust lids. Process in a boiling-water bath — pints for 15 minutes, quarts for 20 minutes.

OTHER METHODS

There are methods of heavily salting or brining vegetables using a 20 percent brine, but in order to prepare them for table use it is necessary to soak them for a long time in fresh water. Since this does a pretty good job of pouring nutrition down the drain, we do not recommend these methods unless you have absolutely no alternative. Any of the other storage or preserving methods in this book are nutritionally superior.

CHAPTER 7

Drying

D rying, one of the oldest forms of food preservation, has been generally neglected in the last few generations. It wasn't until the publication of *The Foxfire Book*'s chapter on drying that many of us gave it much thought. Then we heard of some of the old-time techniques of air-drying: leather britches, for instance, in which you string tender green beans on a thread, hang them in the shade to dry, and then store them in a paper bag. Leather britches demonstrate how little equipment you can get by with. Freezing and canning are certainly more expensive and time-consuming.

Other than that, why dry foods? If you are a hiker and have purchased freeze-dried foods done in a drying chamber (in which food is frozen and then vacuum heat applied to evaporate the ice into water vapor—a complicated and expensive undertaking), you will know their expense, lack of variety, and tastelessness. Your own dried foods will be cheaper and more flavorful, and you can be assured of no chemical preservatives. We reconstitute ours in soups and stews, and nibble the dried fruits. And don't forget fruit leathers, which are so expensive in the delicatessen departments. They are made of dried fruit purées and provide a healthful snack at any time.

But you don't need to be a hiker to appreciate dried foods. They are convenient to use, have a long shelf life (up to a year), and require little space, since they are reduced to a third or less of their original bulk. Since drying extracts the water, spoilage organisms can't grow and there is not as much danger of bacterial growth as there is in canning.

But don't expect dried foods to have true flavors or an enticing appearance. Until reconstituted, their looks leave much to be desired. The flavor is different, but once they have tasted dried apples, for instance, children and everyone else will demand more.

WHY DRY FOODS?

"Of all the methods of preserving food, drying is the simplest and most natural. It is also the least expensive, in energy expended, equipment and in storage space. Compared to canning, which requires special lids and processing equipment and a great deal of shelf space, or freezing, which requires special containers and a constant source of electricity, drying foods is the least complicated method of storing food for the winter months. You simply cut the food into small pieces and spread it out in the sun. When the drying is completed, you put it into a small container — almost any container — and store it in a cool, dark place."

Phyllis Hobson
Drying Vegetables, Fruits and Herbs

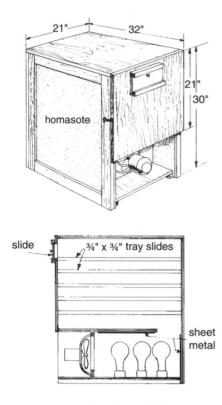

Construction details and dimensions for an electrical homemade dryer. Detail shows heating unit.

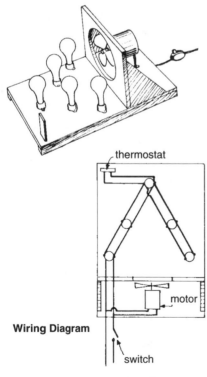

For this dryer buy porcelain fixtures with wire connectors mounted underneath. These can be installed on 4-inch shallow ceiling boxes.

Sun-drying is easy and practical only in those parts of the country where the air is dry and the sun is hot. It just isn't the thing for northern and damp areas, where you are lucky to have two sunny, dry summer days in a row. If you do sun-dry, however, use wooden frames with cheesecloth bottoms. Lay cheesecloth over the food to protect it from insects. Take the frames in at night before the dew falls or if it looks like rain. If bad weather persists, you can finish off in the oven at very low heat.

Electric dehydrators provide the quickest and easiest way to dry foods in any climate. The basic components of an effective dehydrator include a heat source, a fan to circulate the heat and remove the moist air, and trays for the food. Also helpful is a thermostat to regulate the temperature from a low of around 100°F. (for herbs) to a high of about 140°F. (for meats). You can make your own dehydrator or buy one of the many commercial models now available. These tend to be expensive, but are a worthwhile investment if you dry large quantities of food.

Oven-drying is practical if you are drying small quantities or experimenting with drying for the first time. Most people look upon drying as a supplement to other methods of food preservation, and they rely on it for special, lightweight foods or a change of taste or for snacks. For oven-drying, there is little or no initial investment. The only pieces of equipment needed are drying frames built to fit your oven, and cheesecloth (as in air-drying). You can use cookie sheets, or, simpler still, stretch cheesecloth over your oven racks for ready-made frames. But remember that drying is the process of removing water from the food *without cooking it,* so set your oven heat as low as possible, between 80° and 120°F. Leave the oven door ajar. It is possible to oven-dry in a gas stove with nothing more than the pilot light.

Stove-top dryers, another alternative, are best used with a wood stove. They can be homemade or mail-ordered. The principle behind them is simple and seems to work well. Water is heated in the bottom "box," which dries the food spread on top. Care must be taken to see that it doesn't burn out.

The household *microwave oven* cannot be used to successfully dry fruits and vegetables. Food cooks in a microwave in the following manner. Water molecules in food are set in motion by microwaves, causing friction, which in turn causes heat. The microwaves cause heating and cooking to occur internally, where the bulk of the water content is, before it occurs externally. Since fruits and vegetables have a high water content, these foods will cook and sometimes burn before they "dry." Microwave ovens, therefore, are not appropriate tools for drying anything other than herbs for home preserving (see page 101).

People air-dry fruits and vegetables successfully using no more than the heat from a furnace, a heat vent of the refrigerator, or a radiator heat register — but beware of dust and dirt. Improvise and use your imagination.

As important as the heat in the drying process is air circulation, which is aided if the dried food is spaced far enough apart so that air flows between the pieces. Sun-drying and dehydrators provide for circulation, but with an oven you have to leave the door ajar or completely open. You won't want to oven-dry on a hot summer day.

There's nothing complicated about drying fruits and vegetables. In general, cut or slice them into small pieces, spread them in thin layers over the drying trays and expose them to the sun, the heat of your oven (heat low and door ajar), or the warm air of a homemade or commercial dehydrator. Stir the food occasionally, so that it will all be ready to package at the same time.

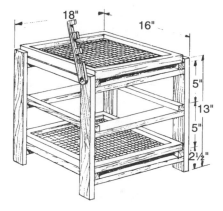

A homemade oven dryer.

Drying Vegetables

Start with the best of your crop, picking or buying vegetables when they are at their freshest, slightly under-mature, and most tender. Wash, peel, or shell them according to the chart on page 94. Some should be cut in thin slices or small pieces to expose as much surface to the air as possible, and thus allow them to dry more quickly. Others, such as peas and beans, can be dried whole. Whichever way, the pieces should be uniform in size for even drying. A single moist piece can cause an entire batch to mold.

Blanch the vegetable in boiling water or steam for the length of time listed on the chart for that vegetable. Drain, and if possible pat off water with paper towels. Don't dip the food in cold water after blanching, as you do in freezing, since the drying times are short enough to allow for the cooking that continues after the food is taken from the heat.

The reason for blanching before drying is the same as for freezing —to halt enzyme action and thus insure good storage quality. Blanching also prevents food deterioration during the drying process. It is especially important with the lengthy sun-drying, but is omitted by many who use a dehydrator.

Because they are low-acid, vegetables are more susceptible to decay than the high-acid fruits. Therefore, more moisture must be removed to insure safe storage. Spread the pieces in a thin layer on the trays and place in full sun or in the dehydrator warmed to 120°F. Dry the length of time recommended on the chart, cool and test a few pieces, then continue drying if necessary.

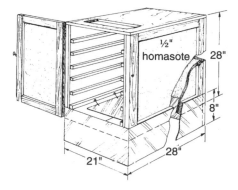

Times listed for sun-drying are for time in the sun. Trays must be taken inside at night so the food won't absorb the dew.

When dry, vegetables will be darker in color than when fresh, but should not be brown. Beans and peas should be hard enough to shatter or split when tapped with a hammer. Beans will be smaller but not shriveled. Leafy vegetables should be crisp enough to crumble.

Store dry vegetables in meal-size quantities in small jars or insect-proof containers. Use gallon glass jars, often available from restaurants, to store small amounts sealed in plastic freezer bags. Dried foods will absorb moisture each time a large container is opened, unless the food is wrapped in small packages.

Store containers in a cool, dry, dark place. An unused cabinet or closet shelf is ideal. Check the packages after a few days. Any condensation inside the jars or packages? If so — back to the drying trays with them.

Take your choice about soaking vegetables before using them. If

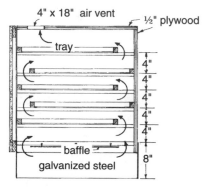

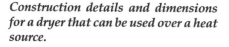

Construction details and dimensions for a dryer that can be used over a heat source.

Drying Vegetables

VEGETABLE	CUTTING	WATER BLANCH (minutes)	STEAM BLANCH (minutes)	DEHYDRA-TOR (hours)	SUN (days)	APPEAR-ANCE WHEN DRY	1 CUP DRY= CUPS COOKED	COOKING TIME (minutes)
Asparagus	½" slices	3	5	8-10	1-2	brittle	1½	30-40
Beans	shell	-	-	48	4-5	hard	2	120-180
Beets	cook, peel, slice	-	-	4-8	1-3	hard	2	30-40
Broccoli	split stalk, chop	2	3½	8-10	1-2	crisp	2	30-40
Brussels sprouts	halve	3-5	6-7	8-10	1-2	brittle	2	30-40
Cabbage	shred	1-2	2-3	12-15	2-3	brittle	1½	40
Carrots	slice, chop	2-3	3-4	12-18	2-3	leathery	1¼	35-45
Cauliflower	slice, chop	3-4	5	8-12	1-2	crisp	1½	20-30
Celery	trim, slice	-	-	12-18	2-3	crisp	1½	20-30
Corn	cut after blanching	1½	3	8-12	1-2	shriveled	2	50
Cucumbers	slice	-	-	8-10	1-2	crisp	-	-
Eggplant	slice, chop	-	3-4	18-24	2-3	leathery	1¼	soak, fry
Green beans	trim	2	4	12-14	2-3	leathery	2½	45
Greens	wash, trim	1½	3	8-12	1-2	crisp	½	15
Kohlrabi	trim, slice	2-3	3-4	18-24	2-3	crisp	1½	30-45
Mushrooms	slice	-	-	8-12	1-2	leathery	1¼	20-30
Okra	slice	-	-	8-12	1-2	brittle	1½	30-45
Onions	chop	-	-	12-24	2-3	papery	1¼	20-30
Parsnips	slice	2	3	8-12	1-2	crisp	1½	30-45
Peas	shell	2	3	12-18	2-3	wrinkled	2	40-45
Peppers	chop	-	-	8-12	1-2	leathery	1½	30-45
Potatoes	slice	5-6	6-7	18-24	2-3	brittle	1¼	45-50
Pumpkin	chop	1½	2-3	12-18	2-3	leathery	1	30-45
Sprouts	drain	-	-	8-12	1-2	crisp	-	-
Squash (summer)	slice	-	-	6-8	1-2	crisp	-	-
Squash (winter)	cook, slice	-	-	12-18	1-2	hard	1¼	30
Sweet potatoes	cook, slice	-	-	12-18	1-2	hard	1½	35-40
Tomatoes	slice	-	-	6-8	1-2	brittle	1½	30
Turnips	slice	3	4	12-18	2-3	crisp	1¼	35-40

1. Blanch washed, cut-up vegetables in steam or boiling water before drying. Fruits can be treated with an anti-oxidant, if desired.

2. Dry in the sun or in a dehydrator until leathery for fruits, or crisp-hard for vegetables.

3. Store in small, airtight containers and keep in the dark.

you do, cover them with water, then soak them 3 or 4 hours or overnight in the refrigerator, and use the soaking liquid in the cooking. Soaking cuts cooking times. The chart on page 94 lists cooking times without soaking.

Many vegetables are delicious eaten dry as a snack, such as beets, cabbage, and tomatoes. Some are used in salads, such as carrots, celery, Chinese cabbage, and radishes. Many make fine casserole toppings, such as celery, peppers, and tomatoes. And nearly all can be used in soups. Some of these are broccoli, cucumbers, onions, peppers, and tomatoes.

Drying Fruits

Fruits should be dried when they are fully ripe and at their most flavorsome — just before they become overripe. If they reach that overripe stage, they still can be used to make fruit leathers, which will be described later (page 97). For best flavor, allow fruits to ripen on the tree or vine.

Peel and cut them according to the directions on the chart (page 96). Some fruits can be dried whole, but fruits sliced as thin as possible or chopped in very small pieces will retain the best color, flavor, and nutritional value during drying. Cut pieces uniformly so they will dry evenly.

Some fruits tend to darken when cut up. Treating them with an anti-oxidant will prevent this, and will also reduce the amount of vitamin C lost during drying. See the accompanying chart (page 164) on how to treat the fruits. Both this step and sulfuring (page 97) are considered unnecessary by many who wish to dry fruits as naturally as possible.

TOMATOES IN THE WINTER

To have almost fresh-tasting tomatoes for your winter salads, reconstitute dried tomatoes by spreading the dried slices over a shallow plate and spraying them with warm water. Let set 15 minutes or so, then spray again. Repeat until tomato slices have plumped almost to the thickness of fresh tomatoes. This takes about 1 hour.

For a delicious fresh-tasting tomato juice or tomato sauce, place a stick of tomato leather (page 97) in warm water to cover and put in the refrigerator 24 hours, until softened and partially dissolved. Break up stick if necessary to cover with water. When softened, stir to dissolve or run through blender to complete reconstitution. The process can be speeded by dropping a piece of leather in boiling water and simmering 30 to 45 minutes, until dissolved. Thin with water for tomato juice.

For generations apples have been air-dried by being cut into wedges and strung, or cut into rings and dried on a pole over a fireplace or wood stove. Try cutting, peeling, and laying apple wedges, each separated from the others, on a cookie sheet in the sun. But remember that sanitary standards several generations ago were not the same as ours. If flies are a problem, cover your trays with cheesecloth. Flies carry germs and bacteria, detrimental not only to your foods, but to your health as well.

For a different taste treat, many people like the confection-like taste of fruit that has been dipped in a solution of 1 cup of sugar, 1 cup of honey, and 3 cups of warm water. Drain well before drying. A less sweet dip you might want to try is pineapple juice.

Fruits should be covered with a layer of cheesecloth before drying outdoors to protect them from insects and birds. Prop the cheesecloth up to keep it from touching the fruit and place the trays in full sun where there is good circulation of air. Take trays inside at night.

Fruits to be dried in a dehydrator can be sliced directly onto the dehydrator trays and dried at approximately 115°F. until there is no moisture in the center of the pieces. Stir pieces and rotate trays top to bottom and front to back once or twice during drying if necessary for even drying. At the end of the recommended drying time, cool a few of the pieces and cut or bite through the center. If they are not dry, continue drying another few hours.

When it is dry, the fruit should be cooled, then stored in plastic containers or small glass jars. Store containers in a cool, dry, dark place. In a few days, check for condensation on the inside of the container. If condensation is found, the fruit is not thoroughly dry and must be returned to the dehydrator. Dried fruit will keep well for a year or more in a dark place, but light will destroy its color and flavor.

Dried fruits can be eaten as snacks or soaked overnight in water to cover, then served as a cooked fruit.

Drying Fruits

FRUIT	CUTTING	DIPPING	DEHYDRATOR (hours)	SUN (days)	APPEARANCE WHEN DRY	1 CUP DRY= CUPS COOKED	COOKING TIME (minutes)
Apples	slice	ascorbic	6-8	2-3	leathery	1¼	30
Apricots	slice, chop	fruit juice, ascorbic	8-12	2-3	leathery	1½	30-45
Bananas	slice	fruit juice, ascorbic	6-8	2	crisp	1	eat dry
Berries	split skins	-	12-24	2-4	hard	1½	30-45
Cherries	pit, chop	-	12-24	2-4	hard	1½	30-45
Figs	pierce	-	36-48	5-6	wrinkled	-	-
Grapes	pierce	-	24-48	3-5	wrinkled	-	-
Peaches	slice, chop	ascorbic	10-12	2-3	leathery	1¼	20-30
Pears	slice, chop	ascorbic	12-18	2-3	leathery	1½	20-30
Persimmons	slice	-	18-24	3-5	chewy	1½	20-30
Pineapple	slice	-	24-36	3-4	chewy	1½	30-45
Plums	pierce	-	36-48	4-5	wrinkled	1½	20-30
Rhubarb	slice	-	8-12	1-2	hard	2	30-40
Strawberries	slice	-	8-12	1-2	hard	1¼	30-40

Fruit leathers are made by drying thin sheets of fruit purée. Almost any well-ripened fruit can be used, but it's a good opportunity to use overripe fruit.

Peel, core, and cut cooked or raw fruit in chunks and run through a colander, food mill, blender, or food processor until it forms a smooth purée.

Pour a small amount of this purée in the center of a tray or cookie sheet that has been covered with plastic wrap. Tilt the tray so that a very thin layer of the purée, about ⅛ inch deep, covers the plastic wrap almost to the edge.

Dry in full sun 2 to 3 days or in a dehydrator set at 120°F. for 6 to 8 hours, until the leather is sticky and can be pulled from the plastic wrap easily. Turn the leather over on the tray, pull off the plastic wrap, and dry another 4 to 6 hours. When dry, the leather will be pliable and easy to handle.

Just roll it up and enjoy. It's a delicious, natural treat. To store, wrap each roll in plastic wrap, or cut in smaller pieces if you wish and store in glass jars or plastic containers. Leathers will keep for several months (assuming no one else knows where they are).

Here are a few favorites:

Single-fruit leathers — bananas, peaches, prunes, apricots, cherries, apples, pumpkin, strawberries, or tomatoes.

Fruit-combination leathers — bananas and nuts, peaches and bananas, cherries and apples, strawberries and rhubarb, or applesauce with cinnamon.

SULFURING FRUITS

In the early days of drying foods in this country, sun was the source of heat and drying took several days. Result: fruit turned an unappetizing brown and often spoiled.

Then it was learned that this deterioration could be halted by treating the fruit with sulfur. Fruits most commonly treated by this method are apples, peaches, pears, apricots, and nectarines. Many of the fruits dried commercially are treated this way.

Proponents of this method of treating fruit before drying list the following advantages:

- The fruit dries faster after sulfuring.
- The color remains truer.
- Riper fruit can be used without fear of spoilage.
- Insects are not as bothersome around sulfur-treated fruit during the drying process.
- The loss of both flavor and nutrients is reduced.

The arguments against sulfuring are these:

VEGETABLE LEATHERS

Next time your favorite hiker heads for the trail, tuck one of these delicious, healthful, meal-in-a-stick snacks in his or her backpack.

2 cups chopped fresh
    tomatoes
½ green pepper, chopped
2 tablespoons chopped
    onion
½ cup chopped celery
2 medium carrots, sliced

Combine all vegetables. Add no water. Simmer over low heat, stirring occasionally to keep from sticking, for 20 to 30 minutes, until carrots and celery are tender. Run through a food mill or Squeezo Strainer to make a smooth pulp. Cover drying trays or cookie sheets with plastic wrap and spread ⅛ inch of this purée over the wrap. Dry in the sun or in a dehydrator until sticky and firm enough to pull away from the wrap easily. Turn over and remove plastic, then dry on the other side until firm enough to form a stiff roll. Wrap rolls in wax paper or plastic wrap.

- It alters the taste of the fruit.
- It can't be done indoors—the smell is too great.
- Chemical preservation is unnecessary if drying takes less than one day.
- Chemicals are unnatural and their safety questionable.

For those interested in trying this method, the following is the recommendation of the Extension Service at Utah State University. The accompanying list shows the recommended times for sulfuring various fruits:

Apples	1 hour for ⅛-inch rings or slices
Apricots	2 hours if quartered
Nectarines	2 hours if quartered
Peaches	1 hour if sliced, 2 hours if quartered
Pears	1 hour if sliced, 2 hours if quartered

As fruit is peeled, cored, or pitted, put it in a salt solution (4 tablespoons of salt to a gallon of water) to prevent discoloration. Remove from the saline solution and (without rinsing) drain thoroughly. Pat with a clean towel to remove surface moisture. The fruit is then ready for the sulfur treatment.

A sulfur box or compartment is necessary. This may be a large cardboard box, provided it is large enough to cover the drying trays and the container for the sulfur. It must be relatively airtight. A small opening must be provided near the bottom of the box for ventilation. Another small opening is necessary near the top of the box for exhaust, on the opposite side from the bottom opening.

The box should be tall enough to adequately cover the stacked trays and allow approximately 6 inches above the top tray — allow 1 to 1½ inches on three sides of the stack. It should also be large enough so that the sulfuring dish can be placed below, but in front of the stacked trays — not directly below them. The heat of the burning sulfur can requires space between it and the box sides and the first tray. There should be no less than 3 inches between the metal can holding the sulfur and the stacks of wooden trays, and between the can and the inside of the carton or covering.

1. Weigh the prepared fruit before placing it on trays. (For each pound of prepared fruit, use 1 teaspoon of sulfur.) Place fruit not more than one layer deep on wooden trays with wooden slats. Place the fruit with the skin side down to prevent the loss of juices. (Sulfur corrodes metal, so it is important that wooden trays are used.)
2. Blocks of wood or bricks placed on the ground can be used to support the trays. The lowest tray should be 6 or 8 inches from the ground.
3. Stack the trays filled with fruit one on top of the other, with blocks or spools between each two to allow for circulation between trays. They should be about 1½ inches apart.
4. Place the sulfur pan on the ground in front of the trays near the lower opening of the box. This pan should be a clean metal container such

---

DRYING EQUIPMENT

If you have a food dryer or an oven, or you live in a sunny location, there's little else besides the following items that you need to dry food.

- A thermometer that will read at least between 90°F. and 140°F. (An aquarium thermometer works fine.)
- Stainless steel knives.
- Non-toxic plastic wrap for drying runny mixtures such as soups and leathers.

You may need other things found in most kitchens, such as a meat grinder, a blender, a shredder, depending on what you plan to dry.

And no matter what you dry, you'll need containers. Plastic bags are good and so are glass and plastic jars. It's best to store small amounts in small containers. While it's possible to take portions of dried foods from a container, it's preferable to store the food in amounts that will be used all at once.

as a tin can, shallow, but deep enough to prevent overflow — 1 inch taller than the layer of sulfur. The burning time of the sulfur will vary with the ventilation, shape of container, weather conditions, and other factors.

5. Sulfur burns best when powder is in a smooth layer not more than ½ inch deep. The depth, not the total amount of sulfur, determines the rate of burning. Light the sulfur—do not leave burned matches in the container. Sulfur dioxide is created by the combustion of the sulfur. (Sulfur that is free from impurities is necessary for proper burning. Resublimed flowers of sulfur generally meet the standard of purity required. They can be purchased at a drugstore. Sulfur candles also can be used. They are pure sulfur formed into cakes with a short wick to start the melting process. Garden-dusting sulfur is not suitable.)

6. Cover the stack of trays with the box or compartment. Seal the bottom of the box by pushing dirt against the bottom edges.

7. Start counting sulfuring time after the sulfur has finished burning and both the air intake opening and the exhaust hole at the top have been tightly closed. The fumes must be given time to reach and penetrate the surfaces of the fruit on the stacked trays.

Drying Herbs

Herbs (and herb gardens) go back as far as the Pilgrims, when they were used to vary a monotonous diet, to camouflage odors, and to make medicines. They are easy to grow, often can be found in the wild (such as mints), and are easy to dry. Most are picked just before the flowers open or when the leaves are still young and tender. As the plants mature, the oils that produce the odors and flavors become less intense.

Herbs should be dried at cooler temperatures than fruits or vegetables to protect their delicate flavors and aromas. They should never be dried in full sun, but should be placed in the shade where there is good circulation of warm air, or dried in a dehydrator. Strong-flavored herbs should be dried separately from herbs that might pick up their flavors. Wash picked herbs only if they're dirty or have been treated with chemicals.

Herb seeds should be allowed to develop and partially dry on the plant. Do not allow them to dry completely, however, or the pod will burst, spilling out the seeds on the ground. To finish drying, remove the seeds from the plants, spread them in a thin layer on trays and dry them in the shade or in a dehydrator set at 95°F.

To dry *herb leaves*, spread them in a thin layer over drying trays and dry them in a shady area or in a dehydrator set at 95°F. or lower until leaves are crisp enough to crumble in the hands. Herb leaves also can be dried by tying stalks together with a string and hanging them upside down in a shady, well-ventilated area. This time-honored method is more picturesque, but there is some loss of flavor and aroma during the

SAVING HERBS

Sure, dry some of your herbs — but don't stop there. Try some of the many other methods that can be used to catch their flavors.

Freezing them is one of the easiest and most satisfactory methods of keeping herbs. Wash them well, then spread them out until they are dry and wilted. This may take several hours. Cut or chop them into the form you want for cooking, pack them in jars, and freeze them. With most herbs, flavor and color will be preserved. Try this first with chives and parsley, then move on to others.

Herb butters, too, can be made when herbs are most plentiful and frozen for later use. They are handy for adding flavor to vegetables as well as for the more conventional use with bread and rolls. Chop herbs very fine, then mix with butter or margarine on a ratio of one part herbs to two or three parts margarine, depending on your taste. Tarragon, chives, parsley, and rosemary are some to try, and combinations are recommended as you become more familiar with them.

The herbs and margarine should be blended with a fork and left in your refrigerator for a few days to permit the flavor to spread through the margarine. Then pack it for freezing. The plastic bowls in which some margarine is sold are handy for this.

Drying Herbs

HERB	PART DRIED	USE
Anise	Seed	Sweet rolls, salads, cookie batter
Basil	Leaves	Tomato dishes, soups, stews, meat pies
Bay	Leaves	Soups, stews, spaghetti sauce
Celery	Leaves	Soups, casseroles, salads
Chervil	Leaves	Egg, cheese dishes, salads
Chilies	Pods	Soups, stews
Chives	Leaves	Omelets, salads, casseroles
Cumin	Seed	Cheese spread, bread dough, sausage
Dill	Flowers, seed	Stew, cabbage, pickles
Fennel	Leaves, seed	Soup, casseroles, candies, rolls, cookies
Garlic	Bulb	Italian foods, omelets, chili
Marjoram	Leaves	Lamb dishes, sausage, stews
Mint	Leaves	Mint jelly, lemonade, roast lamb
Oregano	Flowers	Tomato dishes, spaghetti sauce, pork, wild game
Parsley	Leaves	Soups, sauces, vegetables
Rosemary	Leaves	Salads, lamb dishes, vegetables
Sage	Leaves	Sausage, cheese, poultry, omelets
Savory	Leaves	Bean dishes, stuffing
Tarragon	Leaves	Tomato dishes, salads, vinegar
Thyme	Leaves	Meat loaf, lamb dishes, onion soup

USING DRIED HERBS

"Dried herbs may be used without soaking. Simply add them to the food with which they are to be used. Keep in mind, however, that dried herbs have three to four times the potency of fresh herbs. Use them sparingly."

Phyllis Hobson
Drying Vegetables, Fruits and Herbs

longer drying time. The dried leaves should be removed from their stalks and left whole, and stored in small, tightly closed containers.

Jars or packages should be as small as possible to retain maximum flavor and aroma, but should be well filled to exclude air. Store in a dark, cool closet or cabinet. Dried herbs will keep their flavor for several months, but should be discarded after a year.

Use sparingly. You'll want about one-third the amount of dried herbs as fresh. When ready to use them, crumble them in your hands, or powder them with a rolling pin or mortar and pestle.

Most satisfactory, of course, is not to store herbs, but to have them fresh and ready for use. Every kitchen should have a pot or two or three of herbs. Start them outside in summer, then pot them up before the first frosts. The bigger the pot, the more productive will be the herbs. For starters, try parsley, chives, and basil. Give them as much sunshine as possible, keep them cut back regularly, and water them, and they will reward you with a constant supply of goodness.

MICROWAVE-DRYING HERBS

Your microwave oven will allow you to dry herbs in a matter of minutes, rather than the hours, days, or weeks previously required. There will no longer be the worry of dust contamination from hanging herbs to dry them. Best of all, you can do as much or as little as you are inclined to do. For instance, if you have over-picked a fresh herb to use in a dish, you can easily dry the remainder without wasting a bit of it.

Microwave-drying of herbs requires the same preparation as you would use to dry them in an oven or a dehydrator. If there is dirt on the herb you are drying, wash it carefully, being careful not to bruise the leaves, and dry thoroughly. You can use a salad spinner to dry large amounts of herbs at one time. Drying garlic or chilies in the microwave is not recommended, as both contain too much water to dry properly. All other herb seeds, leaves, and flowers can be dried by the following method.

Since the amount of herb you are drying will vary from time to time, there are no definitive guidelines as to time involved in drying. Once you have separated the leaves, seeds, or flowers from the stems and cleaned them, if needed, you are ready to begin. Dry one herb at a time. Spread a single layer on a double thickness of paper toweling and put it into the oven. Microwave on high power for 1 to 2 minutes at a time, redistributing the herbs for more even drying at each interval. After the second or third time, your herbs will be noticeably dryer. Continue this interval timing, but in ½- to 1-minute intervals, until the herbs are completely dry. Let them cool, and pack them into airtight containers.

HOW MUCH HERBS?

"When you begin to use fresh herbs in cooking, it is better to err on the side of too little rather than too much. Like salt and pepper, the quantity of culinary herbs to be used is a matter of taste, but it is generally safe to start with ¼ teaspoon of dried herbs or one full teaspoon of chopped fresh herbs to a serving for six persons."

Phyllis Hobson
Easy-to-Grow Herbs and How to Use Them

CHAPTER 8

Common Storage and Grains

C ommon storage is the oldest, easiest, and least costly method of keeping vegetables and fruits. It includes any method of storing produce that does not require processing — storing carrots in a root cellar, parsnips in the garden, or braids of onions in the pantry all are forms of common storage.

Crops that will store successfully are root vegetables, potatoes, winter squash, pumpkins, dry legumes, grains, green tomatoes, celery, cabbage, and (briefly) peppers. Among the fruits, apples and pears store the best. Grapes and citrus fruits will store for some time, given the right conditions.

There are many ways to store fruits and vegetables, including the "ideal" way and the "practical" way. The table on page 115 lists the ideal storage temperatures and humidity for a variety of crops, and if you have or can build the facilities to provide these perfect conditions, you should have little problem with storage. On the other hand, if you are like most of us and have to make use of space and temperatures already available, you will have better luck with some crops than others, and each year your experience may be different. The trick is to locate places in your home or outbuildings that are naturally suitable for storage and then hope for cooperation from Mother Nature.

You may be lucky enough to live in an older home that has a root cellar, or at least a basement that is cool (35°-50°F.) and damp. A basement with a dirt floor is best, especially when there is no furnace in the vicinity. Given these conditions, you can store potatoes (in simple bins or slatted boxes), root crops (in plastic bags or packing material), and fruit (in a separate area, in closed containers or plastic bags). There will be little need for alterations in order to be successful.

Upstairs or nearer the furnace there may be areas that are somewhat warmer (45°-65°F.) and drier, and more suitable for winter squash and pumpkins. Pantries, hallways, under the beds in cool bedrooms,

OUT OF THE ROOT CELLAR

Use vegetables and fruits as quickly as possible after taking them out of cold storage. They will not keep as long as freshly harvested produce. A warning signal is moisture condensing on the surface of produce when it is taken from the cold storage room. This "sweating" encourages decay. It can be avoided to some extent by allowing the produce to warm up gradually in a dry location.

Some years none of the squashes or pumpkins keep very well. Look for this, says master-gardener Dick Raymond, after an unusually warm autumn, which sets the vegetables to growing again. Watch your cold cellar carefully, and if there are signs of deterioration, process, freeze, or can the vegetables immediately.

STORING ONIONS

If your onions didn't keep well, they may not have been dried well enough after harvesting. That's the most common reason. Onions should be cured for several weeks in a warm, dry, and well-ventilated place. They're ready for storage when the skins rustle. After that the best place for them is a location that is barely above freezing, but where they will not freeze.

CARROT KEEPING

Garden Way gardener Dick Raymond recommends storing carrots in sawdust.

"I try to get fresh sawdust — the kind that is still light colored and unweathered," he writes in *Gardening Know-How*. "Then I take a regular cardboard box; put two or three inches of sawdust in the bottom; add a layer of carrots, making sure that the carrots are at least two inches from the sides of the box; and cover them with a half-inch layer of sawdust. I keep adding layers of carrots and sawdust until the box is full."

Raymond points out that if the boxes are to be kept in an unheated area, such as a garage, a large box should be used, permitting a layer of the insulating sawdust at least 5 inches thick around the bottom and sides. Turnips and apples can be stored this way, too.

closets, a big chest in the mud room, an attic room or garage that is partially heated — all of these areas can be used for some crops with varying success.

PRACTICAL STORAGE HINTS

Assuming you are going to try to store the "practical way" by using the places you have available, here are a few suggestions. These hints also apply to more scientific storage, which you may find you want to get into after a year or two. Experience in your own home and geographic area will be the best teacher.

1. Generally, later-maturing, longer-growing vegetables and fruits are the most suitable for storage. Harvest should be delayed until as late as possible in the fall when the weather has cooled, but before the first heavy frost.
2. Do not try to store immature vegetables. The obvious exception is green tomatoes, which ripen during storage. Winter squash are mature when your thumbnail cannot pierce their rinds, potatoes when a thumb pushed across them will not slip the skin. Onions with wide necks and green stalks will not store. Cabbage heads should be solid and heavy for their size. Root crops should have been in the ground long enough to mature, as indicated on the seed package. See Chapter 9 for detailed harvesting information on each vegetable crop.
3. Vegetables and fruits should be handled as little and as gently as possible. Those that are blemished or damaged in harvest will not store well. Washing before storage usually is *not* recommended and not necessary; instead, wash just before use. An inch or more of stem should be left on just about every vegetable and fruit that has one — especially squash, pumpkins, and beets. This helps keep juices in and infection out.
4. Crops should be cool and their surfaces dry before storing. For many crops, "curing" is necessary to dry and harden the skins before storing. Putting away vegetables fresh from the garden and covered with moist soil is a sure invitation to molds, disease, and insects.
5. Vegetables needing dry storage conditions (squash, pumpkins, onions) store best if kept up off the floor and not touching each other — so air can circulate freely around them. Onions can be braided or tied, then hung up. Large squash and pumpkins are more of a problem. If you're cramped for space, you may have to pile them up. If so, you should inspect them regularly and remove any that show signs of rot or mold. The mold on squash can double overnight if not kept in check. If mold appears, rubbing each squash with a cloth dampened with vegetable oil may help them keep.
6. Vegetables and fruits requiring moist conditions should be kept *in* something, rather than being exposed to the air. Roots traditionally are stored in fresh-cut sawdust, sand, or leaves. Plastic bags or linings for boxes, plastic garbage cans, metal cans lined with cardboard — these are all ways of keeping moisture in. Cut a few holes in plastic bags to allow some air circulation to avoid mustiness.

7. Strong-smelling vegetables such as cabbages should be wrapped closely in several layers of newspaper to keep in the odor as well as the moisture, or they can be stored outside in pits or a shed. Odors from vegetables can permeate fruits, which is probably why it is usually recommended that fruits and vegetables be kept separately.
8. Apples and potatoes cannot be stored near each other.
9. Boxes, shelves, and the area used for food storage should be cleaned and aired thoroughly before and after use. Molds and diseases can be harbored over the summer months, waiting to ruin your next year's harvest. Do not reuse packing material such as sawdust or cardboard boxes. Both can be put on the garden or compost pile.
10. Do not allow temperatures to go below freezing in your storage area, as this can ruin many crops. Also avoid fluctuations in temperature. Cool temperatures are needed for successful storage, so it is usually recommended to open windows or vents when it gets cold outside in the fall — unless you're going to forget to close them the next day when it warms up. It is better to have a closed room with constant temperature than irregular drafts of cold and warm air. Proper ventilation is part of the "ideal" method of storage, but may not always be practical.
11. Storage should be in the dark.
12. Protect your stored vegetables from rodents and dust. Mice will feast on potatoes and grain if given the chance. Keep them away by using a closed room or sealed containers when possible; or use traps or poison. Vegetables and canned foods stored in the open in a cellar gradually will become covered with grime. Covering them with newspaper or cloths will help.

Our experience one year with sunflowers provided a good example of how not to store. The sunflower heads were cut from the stalks and put immediately — warm and moist — into the root cellar, to avoid the birds. Within days they were covered with mold. We moved them outside on the lawn to dry out, and soon the crows were eating them and (worse) the neighborhood dogs were using them as markers. So we again moved them, this time to the floor of our tool shed. There they dried, protected from birds, dogs, and mold — and were completely eaten by mice!

The sunflowers would have been safer dried on the stalk, protected from the birds by cheesecloth or paper bags with holes cut in them for ventilation. Or they could have been cut and hung up out of reach in an airy shed.

Storage Containers

Any clean container, uncontaminated by previous use with diseased vegetables, can be adapted for storage. Vegetables and fruits requiring moist conditions can be kept in closed containers. Heavy-duty plastic trash or leaf bags or sheets of polyethylene can be used alone or inside most containers to maintain a moist atmosphere. Dry storage is best provided by containers that are open and airy. Some container suggestions include:

THE EASIEST VEGETABLE TO STORE

What's the easiest vegetable to store? We'll nominate the Jerusalem artichoke for the honor. This relative of the sunflower produces tasty tubers that can be used in many ways and are high in food value but low in calories. And this vegetable stores itself. You simply dig as many as you want when you want them. While they will keep well for a few days in the refrigerator, they're best kept in the garden.

Since the harvesting season is after the first frosts in the fall, the gardener may not use up this crop before the ground begins to freeze, making digging a chore. The solution is simple: Mulch the row heavily with leaves or spoiled hay. Then, during the winter, push back the mulch and dig as many as are needed. And, of course, the tubers will be there in early spring for use when there's little else in a garden but parsnips and perhaps a few dreams.

What happens if all the Jerusalem artichokes aren't harvested? They'll simply grow again, producing your crop for the next year.

STORING APPLES

"Apples freeze at about 28.5ºF. Hence it is necessary to keep them above this temperature. A storage temperature of 32ºF. is usually maintained in commercial storages. Ripening and softening of apples in storage is twice as rapid at 40ºF. as at 32ºF.; at 50º it is almost double that at 40º. Therefore, for extended storage, prompt cooling of picked apples is essential, since they will ripen as much in one day at 70º as they will in ten days at 30º. For the home grower without refrigeration the recommended 32-34º storage temperature is usually unattainable in the fall. The best alternative is to keep the apples as cool as possible in unheated basements, or specially built, insulated fruit storage rooms. By regulating openings to the outside, advantage can be taken of the cooling effect of night air."

Lawrence Southwick
Dwarf Fruit Trees for the Home Gardener

POTATO CELLAR-LOCKER

John Zircke has a simple way to keep potatoes at earth temperature throughout the winter. He buried a metal wall locker in the dirt floor of an old shed. The door faces upward to give easy access. An old rug or some straw is thrown over the top. Any cabinet or box would do as well. His potatoes keep fine this way.

- wooden barrels or nail kegs
- fruit crates
- cardboard boxes
- garbage or trash cans
- milk boxes
- mesh bags
- grain bags
- baskets
- simple bins made from slats of wood

Packing Root Crops and Fruits

Root crops and fruits can be packed in layers in:

- freshly cut sawdust
- clean, washed builders' sand
- dry leaves
- peat moss
- newspapers
- straw or hay
- burlap

Freshly cut sawdust can be hauled from a saw mill or lumber yard. It keeps vegetables especially well, for the same reasons that ice was preserved in it during the summer months in the days before refrigeration.

Sand or leaves may be easier to acquire and also work well, though sometimes sand lends an undesirable flavor to the vegetables. It should not be too moist (or the crops will root and grow) or totally dry (in which case they may wither).

For storage in a cool cellar or room. Put a 4-inch layer of packing material in the bottom of a container. We use fresh-cut sawdust and cardboard boxes, since they are light and easy to handle. Put in a single layer of root vegetables or fruit. The root crops should have been left out in the sun several hours, long enough for the dirt to dry and fall off. Cut their tops to about 1 inch from the root. The roots may touch each other, but do not wedge them tightly together. Leave 4 inches of room for sawdust all around the sides. Cover the vegetable or fruit layer with 2 to 3 inches of sawdust, then repeat. Fill in around the sides with sawdust, and over the top with 4 inches more. The box is ready to store in a cool place. When some carrots or apples or whatever are needed, dig down to a layer and remove, covering over what's left.

For storage where the temperature may dip below freezing occasionally, such as in a garage or shed. Use a bigger box and put in at least 6 to 8 inches of sawdust. Or pack the box as in the preceding paragraph, then place that box into a bigger one in which sawdust is placed 6 inches thick in the bottom, around the sides and over the top.

Boxes of root vegetables or fruit should not be stored directly on a concrete or dirt floor, since they might become too moist on the bottom. Set them on a shelf or lay several boards on the floor under them to allow air to circulate. If the boxes are stacked on top of each other, place boards in between.

BUILDING A ROOT CELLAR

The serious gardener who wants to achieve the best conditions for storage will want to build or improvise a root cellar. It can be a simple, small room in a corner of a cellar, or it can be an automatically ventilated, multi-chambered underground combination-root-cellar-and-emergency-shelter. We are including here plans for a simple root cellar. For more complex plans, contact the Extension Service at your state agricultural college, or send for Garden Way Bulletin A-22 on how to build a root cellar.

If your house has an unused outside stairwell or bulkhead into the basement, this area can be used for some storage with relative ease and small expense. Install an inside door to the steps to keep out basement heat; bank the doors to the outside with hay to prevent freezing cold or unseasonal hot sun from spoiling the stored food. If you want to create a larger storage area around the stairwell, build inward into the basement, taking care to insulate the extra space well. Temperatures in the closed stairwell will go down as you go up the steps (during cold weather). A little experimenting with a thermometer will help you determine the best levels for the different crops you are storing. If the air is too dry, set pans of water at the warmest level for extra humidity.

For small storage areas, window-area wells can be used by covering the well with boards banked with bales of hay. If basement windows

Storage of Common Apple Varieties

| | STORAGE PERIOD | |
VARIETY	NORMAL (months)	MAXIMUM (months)
Gravenstein	0-1	3
Wealthy	0-1	3
Grimes Golden	2-3	4
Jonathan	2-3	4
McIntosh	2-4	4-5
Cortland	3-4	5
Spartan	4	5
Rhode Island Greening	3-4	6
Delicious	3-4	6
Stayman	4-5	5
York Imperial	4-5	5-6
Northern Spy	4-5	6
Rome Beauty	4-5	6-7
Newton	5-6	8
Winesap	5-7	8

From Canada Department of Agriculture Publication 1532, *Storage of Fruits and Vegetables*, by S. W. Porritt, 1974.

open inward, access can be convenient and simple during the cold winter months.

A simple but effective root cellar was made by a friend of ours when he was building a new home. He chose the northeast corner of his basement, the coolest area, with no heating ducts running through it. If there had been, he would have insulated them.

He planned a 6-by-8-foot area, with an 8-foot ceiling. Using the corner gave him two concrete walls, which he did not cover; and he put up 2 x 4 studding for the other two walls which were made of homasote board, inside and out. These could have been further insulated with rolled fiberglass insulation. The ceiling was also insulated. A snug-fitting door completed the room, and movable shelves of rough, cheap lumber were built inside. An outside window, darkened, provided outside cooling and ventilation. Plans for a similar type of simple root cellar are shown below.

The layout of your basement will dictate the size and location of your root cellar. No matter what size it is, there are some guidelines that you will want to follow.

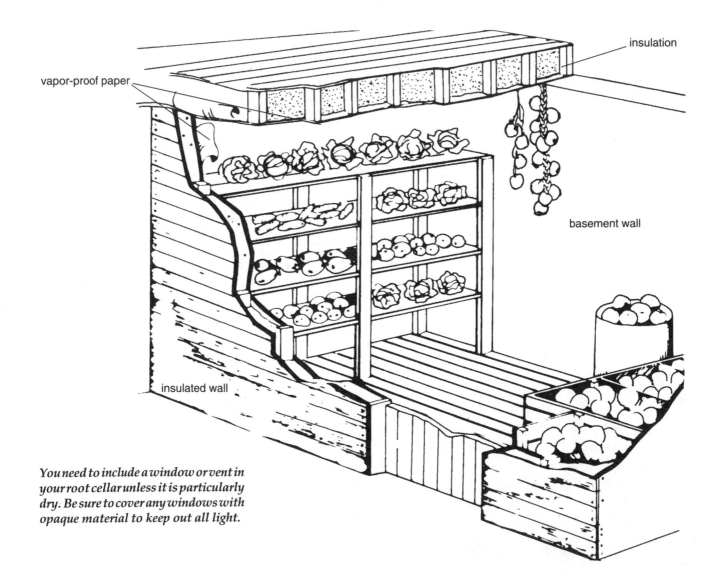

You need to include a window or vent in your root cellar unless it is particularly dry. Be sure to cover any windows with opaque material to keep out all light.

1. Locate the root cellar in the coldest area of the basement away from furnace and heaters. The north and east sides of the house are preferred.

2. If heat pipes or ducts cannot be avoided, insulate them carefully so heat will be kept out of the root cellar area.

3. Interior walls and the ceiling should be insulated to keep out basement warmth; the exterior wall(s) of concrete, block, or stone can be left uncovered so the coolness from the earth can penetrate.

4. Shelves built for the cellar should be in movable sections to make it easy to clean under and around them. Slatted rather than solid shelves provide the best air circulation.

5. The door to the root cellar should be insulated with a mouse-proof threshold, and wide enough to allow easy access to the room with large storage containers and crocks.

6. For added moisture the floor can be covered with sawdust or sand, and sprinkled with water. Or pans of water can be kept under the ventilator.

7. Ventilation to the room can be provided by means of a window or vent. If a window is used, it should be covered to exclude all light from the room. It can be boxed in, with the adjustable air flow directed to the floor to avoid cold drafts on the food.

8. With colder air entering and concentrating close to the floor, the temperature will be warmest close to the ceiling. With this in mind, plan your storage so that crops requiring the coldest temperatures are close to the floor, reserving the upper areas for those requiring warmer storage.

9. For scientific control of the temperature, two thermometers are helpful, preferably the kind that record minimum and maximum temperatures. Place one outdoors and the other in the coldest section of the root cellar. Regulate the indoor temperature by opening and closing the window or other opening used as the ventilator.

10. Outdoor temperatures well below 32°F. are necessary to cool storage air to near 32° and maintain that temperature. Once cooled to 32° the indoor temperature will rise again if ventilators are kept closed, even though the outside temperature is about 25°. Close ventilators tightly whenever the outdoor temperature is *higher* than the storage temperature. Both indoor and outdoor temperatures must be watched closely, and in most regions daily (or more frequent) adjustment of the ventilator is necessary. A brisk wind and very low temperatures could bring temperatures in the root cellar below the freezing point for the vegetables stored there.

KEEPING ONIONS

Stored onions can be decorative as well as useful if they are braided. When pulled in the fall, they should be dried in the garden for a few days. This cures them, and without this treatment they cannot be stored for many months. Use quickly (don't store) the thick-stemmed ones.

Braided onions will fall apart as the tops dry if the braid is not given some reinforcement. Cut 3 pieces of baler twine about 3 feet long. Tie them together at one end. Then braid twine and onion tops together, until within 6 inches of the end of the twine. Wrap one piece of twine fast around the onion stems, then tie to the other two, and hang in a dry, cool place. The onions can be clipped off with scissors as needed.

There's a practical advantage to braiding onions. A spoiled onion in a bag is a smelly nuisance, but it is a dried and hardly noticed part of a braid of onions.

OUTDOOR STORAGE

There are cheap and simple methods of outside storage that are useful for winter apples and pears, as well as for root crops, celery, and cabbage. However, they should not be attempted unless you live in a climate where the outdoor temperatures in winter average 30°F. or below.

Also, if you live in an area where the snow can get several feet deep, remember that shoveling snow will be necessary to get at your produce. Be sure to mark with high stakes where your vegetables are hidden so you can find them.

Mounds

A cone-shaped mound can be built on the ground in a well-drained location, or in a 6- to 8-inch-deep hole.

1. Spread a layer of straw, leaves, or other bedding on the ground, and spread a length of hardware cloth over that to deter winter feasting by rodents.
2. Stack the vegetables or fruits on the hardware cloth in a cone-shaped pile. Different types of vegetables can be stored together, separated by bedding, but do not store fruits and vegetables together.
3. Cover the pile generously with more bedding, and pack well.
4. Cover the whole pile with 3 or 4 inches of soil. Firm the soil to make the mound waterproof.
5. Cover everything with a thick layer of straw or hay to keep the soil from freezing too hard.
6. Dig a shallow drainage ditch around and sloping away from the mound.

Small mounds containing only a few bushels of vegetables or fruits will get sufficient ventilation if you let the bedding material that surrounds the produce extend through the top of the pile. Cover the top of the pile with a board or piece of sheet metal to protect the food from rain. A stone will hold the cover in place.

It may be difficult to dig out the produce from these mounds in cold weather, and once the mound is opened all the contents will have to be removed. Trying to rebuild the mound with frozen earth after exposing the contents to the cold air might do more harm than good. So it is better to have several small mounds than one large one.

When vegetables and fruits are brought into the house from outdoor storage, they first should be inspected for decay. Cut out any blemished areas and use that produce first. The rest should be put in plastic bags and stored in the refrigerator or a chilly area of the house until needed.

When spring comes, clean out the mounds, put the bedding on the compost pile or garden, and use a different place next year to avoid contamination.

Other Outside Storage

Another simple type of outdoor storage is a barrel covered with several layers of straw and earth. Cover the barrel opening with a lid or boards, and be sure the bedding is layered thickly on all sides.

If you have nine bales of hay or straw, you can build a storage pit with them. Arrange six of the bales in a rectangle as the walls of the pit. Line the pit with hardware cloth or store the produce in closed wooden boxes (leave some air holes for ventilation) to keep out the mice. Cover

KEG-OF-THE-MONTH PLAN

Ruth Harmon, a practical Kentucky gardener, harvests a keg full of assorted fresh vegetables every month throughout the winter. In the fall, she places a layer of straw in the bottom of a nail keg, then lays the keg on its side. She adds more straw, then half-fills it with white potatoes. Next come carrots, more straw, beets, and still more straw. Finally, she adds a layer of lettuce or another favorite vegetable — except any member of the cabbage family — and packs straw around it. She fills ten of these kegs, sets them all in a deep trench, and covers them with dirt.

the produce with loose bedding, and place the last three bales over the top.

Another method is to bury a box or other container in a pit dug in a well-drained area. An old refrigerator or freezer set in with its door facing upwards would work well. Or build a box to fit the size of the pit that is dug. The pit should be 2 to 4 feet deep, depending on the depth frost penetrates the ground in your area and how well you insulate your box.

To build the box, make a framework of rough lumber. Staple hardware cloth to the inside of this framework, then line the inside with styrofoam about 2 inches thick. The hardware cloth keeps out rodents and the styrofoam insulates. The top is finished with a solid wooden lid.

At harvest time, select the vegetables to be stored. Put a layer of clean, washed builders' sand or fresh-cut sawdust on the bottom of the box. Then place a neat layer of root vegetables or fruit in the pit and cover that layer with sand or sawdust. Handle the vegetables gently; do not just dump them into the box.

Continue in this manner until the box is filled. Making a map as you work can be helpful in finding the different vegetables later. Bales of hay or straw can be laid on the cover, and a plastic sheet can be thrown over them, weighted with stones, to keep off the snow. The insulation provided by the straw and styrofoam not only keeps vegetables from freezing in winter, but also keeps them cool during the warm days of Indian summer and early spring. When the weather becomes drier in the summer, the box should be thoroughly cleaned out, then left open to the fresh air and sunshine until fall.

A tile cylinder or piece of drainage pipe also can be used for in-ground storage. If a tile 18 inches in diameter and 30 inches high is buried upright in the soil, three bushels of vegetables or fruit can be stored in baskets in it. The tile should be located in a well-drained area, away from possible overflow from downspouts and eaves and where it will be shaded. Put a piece of hardware cloth across the bottom to keep out pests, and extend the tile slightly above ground and cap with a board to keep out rain and ground water. Cover with a deep mulch of straw, hay, or leaves.

STORAGE BIN

A 2-foot-deep storage bin can be built into the ground, preferably on sloping ground for good drainage. A covering of hardware cloth will keep out rodents, and a styrofoam lining will provide excellent insulation. Cover the top with boards and hay bales for easy access. Place sand between layers of vegetables.

GARDEN STORAGE

It is possible to leave some of your root crops in the ground where they grew until spring. When the ground begins to freeze in the late fall, cover such crops as carrots, turnips, and beets with a heavy (18-inch-thick) mulch of hay or straw. Except where the cold is severe (0°F. and below), you should be able to pull back the mulch and dig up the crops throughout the winter. Mark where you stop digging each time, so you will know where to start again.

If you are not sure about your climate, try leaving just a few roots in the ground, digging the rest in the fall to store elsewhere. That way some will be safe for sure, and if you are lucky you also will have fresh, crisp vegetables right out of the garden in mid-winter.

Traditionally, parsnips, horseradish, and salsify are best left in the ground long enough for thorough freezing, which improves their flavor. Harvested in the late winter or early spring, they provide a great taste treat. Be sure to harvest parsnips before they begin their second growth, because they become poisonous at that time.

Kale, a hardy green that is rich in vitamins A and C, withstands extremely cold weather. If the plants are mulched before snow falls, they will keep throughout the winter and be the first crop to grow in the spring. We have pushed snow and mulch aside from the kale and harvested a crop in late winter. This can be an important crop for your family's nutrition, since in late winter and early spring your root crops are beginning to lose large amounts of vitamin C.

Celery and Chinese cabbage plants of late-maturing varieties also can be stored in the garden for one or two months. Bank a few inches of soil around the base of the plants at the end of the growing season, then build the bank up to the top of the plants before severe freezing occurs. As the weather becomes colder, cover the banking with straw or corn stalks held in place with boards.

Celery and Chinese cabbage also can be dug up, keeping a good-sized clump of soil attached to the roots. Place these plants in a trench, a hot bed, a cold frame, or on a dirt or concrete floor in a root cellar. Provide protection from the weather and insulate with some kind of bedding for the outside storage, and you may have success keeping these plants until Christmas. Endive can be brought inside like celery with roots on and kept for a month or two. Tie the leaves together to help blanching. The celery and Chinese cabbage also will blanch in the dark.

Cabbages can be stored in mound-shaped or long pits. Their odor is penetrating, so store alone to avoid spoiling the flavor of other food. When stored this way, they should be dug up with their roots intact and placed head down in the mound and covered with bedding and soil.

Another way to store cabbage plants is upright in a shallow trench, covered by a framework made of boards and stakes driven into the ground, or a very thick covering of hay. Cabbages can also be hung up by their roots in a shed where they will not freeze, or kept wrapped in newspaper in the root cellar.

For healthy, large green tomatoes ready to harvest just before frost, take the suckers off new plants 2 to 3 weeks after planting in the spring. Put them in a glass of water for several hours and then plant, watering liberally. These late plants will produce tomatoes timed just right for cold storage.

SPRINGTIME PRESERVING OF STORED CROPS

After several months the quality of stored crops may begin to deteriorate, particularly when not stored under ideal conditions. As long as they are firm, crisp, and have good flavor and color, their nutritive value is close to that of the fresh crop. But when they begin to wither, their food value decreases.

The easiest place to store your garden produce is in the garden itself. Here are some vegetables that will withstand those first early frosts and go on giving you bountiful meals for many weeks: beets, broccoli, Brussels sprouts, cabbage, Chinese cabbage, cauliflower, Swiss chard, endive, kohlrabi, lettuce, mustard, onions, peas, radishes, and turnips.

Carrots, salsify, and parsnips are not bothered by heavy freezes, but can be difficult to dig from the frozen ground. Mulch them well with hay or a pile of fall leaves and they'll be available during much of the coldest winter.

To assure yourself of an ample supply of these frost-resistant vegetables, plant in midsummer so they will reach their peak in late fall.

Rather than letting these crops continue to deteriorate, you may want to preserve them in mid-winter or early spring by canning, freezing, or drying. The rush of the harvest season is over. There should be plenty of empty canning jars available now if you have been eating vegetables canned in the fall, and space in the freezer is opening up.

Now is the time to make and preserve strained pumpkin, squash, or turnip, applesauce, pickled beets, or what have you. Crops wintered in the garden or outside storage also should be preserved now. These winter vegetables and fruits then will be usable throughout the spring and summer — until the next harvest.

GRAINS

Grains such as wheat, oats, and corn are simple to store and will provide your family with an inexpensive source of nutritious food. Grains are high in protein, and when served in combination with another type of protein food, such as dairy products, nuts, dried legumes, or small amounts of meat, help provide the complete protein needed for body growth and maintenance. They are especially rich in the B vitamins. Baking bread from home-ground whole wheat flour is a labor of love that will give you satisfaction and your family good health.

Corn

Corn is the crop to try if you want to grow your own grain. It's easy to grow, simple to harvest, attractive while drying, and delicious when ground into cornmeal and used in a variety of dishes.

For best cornmeal, grow a variety of *flint corn* — Hard Northern Flint does well in the North. Plant it in rich soil after the last spring frost, and keep it well hoed. Delay harvesting until after the first fall frosts (you will know when the time comes because the bluejays will come to eat it), then pull back the husks and braid or tie the ears together. They can be hung up to dry in your home or any dry place where the mice or birds won't share your crop. It takes a long time to dry enough to grind. Usually don't shell it before February — it certainly will be dry in a year. Try a little in a hand grinder to see (this avoids gumming up your electric grinder). This corn keeps indefinitely in a cool, dry place. Freezing doesn't hurt it, and may even help by killing any bugs or eggs in it.

Corn-shelling is a good pastime to combine with conversation or TV-watching. Store the kernels in an airtight container. The corn is ready to be ground when needed.

Wheat

Flushed with the success of your flint-corn crop, you're ready to try another grain. Wheat can be grown in your garden, but be prepared for a little more work at the other end of the growing season.

Our neighbor, who has homesteaded for several years, has grown wheat on a small scale using two methods. One is to use a rectangle of

BASIC CORNMEAL MUSH

For each serving add about ¾ cup boiling water very slowly to ¼ cup freshly ground cornmeal, stirring rapidly. Cook for 2 to 3 minutes. The amount of water will depend on how thick or thin you like it. Serve as a hot cereal with cream and honey or as a side dish with salt, pepper, and butter. Or put mush into a soup or orange-juice can, cover, and chill. Then push out, slice, and fry the slices in butter.

GRINDING CORNMEAL

"For cornmeal, let the (sweet corn, yellow or white) ears dry until a kernel feels good and hard between your teeth. Remove the kernels (there are several hand-held shellers on the market now) and store in covered jars in a dry place. Then grind as you need white or yellow cornmeal. A grain mill is preferred, of course, but a kitchen blender will do a fine job if you grind small batches at a time.

John Vivian
Growing Corn for Many Uses

space, so that you have your own "amber waves of grain." The other — and use it if your garden tends to be weedy — is to grow the grain in wide rows, 5 feet or so, so that you can reach into the rows and pull out the weeds.

She says weather is the worst impediment. If the wheat ripens during a prolonged wet spell, you may have difficulty harvesting it.

Types of wheat. There are several different types of wheat. Hard red spring wheat is usually recommended for bread-making because it has the highest protein content, especially gluten, which is the sticky substance that holds bread dough together when it rises. Our neighbor likes to use hard white winter wheat with the spring wheat to make a softer, better loaf. She grinds the two together, 3 parts winter to 1 part spring, to make her flour for bread.

Harvesting. Wheat is ready to harvest when all but a few stalks have turned yellow and the grain will separate from its husks fairly easily when rubbed in your hand. The grain should not be thoroughly ripe or else it will scatter when cut. Test it daily by biting a kernel or two. They will be doughy at first. When they are hard, it's time to harvest. Any delay now and you risk losing your crop, since it will fall off the stalks onto the ground.

Use a sickle to cut the stalks. The old-style scythe with a cradle was fine for harvesting, since it not only cut the stalks, but laid them neatly on the ground, ready to be tied. But just try to find one of those today, outside of a museum. A scythe alone will cut the stalks, but they will fall helter-skelter, making the tying of them a slow job. If you use a sickle, you can hold a clump, cut it, then lay it in a pile, ready for tying.

Gather the stalks in a bunch about as large as you can surround with both hands. That's called a *sheave*. Tie it with string, or use the time-honored method of twisting several stems together, as you might with yarn, and tie the sheave with those stems. Stand about eight sheaves together, so they will hold one another erect. You've now created a *stook*. Tie a piece of cheesecloth over the stook to prevent birds from dining on the wheat. The stooks should stand in the garden for about 2 weeks to dry. The harvesting is best done during dry weather but a little rain will not hurt the crop.

The grain is removed from the stalks by threshing when both grain and stalks are completely dry. Clear a large area of floor and put down a canvas or plastic covering. Untie and lay out a bundle of stalks. Beat them with a flail or flexible stick until the grain breaks free. Remove the stalks and repeat until all the bundles have been threshed. Gather up the grain, which now must be *winnowed* to remove the chaff. To winnow the grain, pour it from one container to another on a windy day.

Storage. Wheat can be stored in clean, dry, airtight containers, such as plastic trash cans with lids or large glass jars. These containers should be kept in a cool, dry place. Do not store on concrete, especially if using metal containers, or they may sweat.

The drier the wheat, the better it will keep. Insects cannot reproduce in wheat with a 10 percent or less moisture content. But it is difficult

HARVESTING BLACK WALNUTS

"There are a number of ways for handling Black Walnuts in order to remove them from the husks, and you can take your choice. . . . Place the nuts on the driveway and drive the pickup truck over them slowly, forward and then back several times. If two people work at this and the second member of the team keeps shoveling the nuts (a square shovel is handy for this) under the wheels, the work goes faster. The abrasive action of the tires usually is sufficient. . . . After the hulls are off, the nuts should be thoroughly washed and spread out to dry away from direct sunlight for two or three weeks. The nuts then can be stored in a cool, dry place until needed."

Louise Riotte
Nuts for the Food Gardener

Storage of Vegetables and Fruits

COMMODITY	FREEZING POINT °F.	PLACE TO STORE	STORAGE CONDITIONS		
			TEMPERATURE °F	HUMIDITY	LENGTH OF STORAGE PERIOD
Vegetables:					
Dry beans and peas	-	Any cool, dry place	32° to 40°	Dry	As long as desired
Late cabbage	30.4	Pit, trench, or outdoor cellar	Near 32° as possible	Moderately moist	Through late fall and winter
Cauliflower	30.3	Storage cellar	"	"	6 to 8 weeks
Late celery	31.6	Pit or trench; roots in soil in storage cellar	"	"	Through late fall and winter
Endive	31.9	Roots in soil in storage cellar	"	"	2 to 3 months
Onions	30.6	Any cool, dry place	"	Dry	Through fall and winter
Parsnips	30.4	Where they grew, or in storage cellar	"	Moist	"
Peppers	30.7	Unheated basement or room	45° to 50°	Moderately moist	2 to 3 weeks
Potatoes	30.9	Pit or in storage cellar	35° to 40°	"	Through fall and winter
Pumpkins and squashes	30.5	Home cellar or basement	55°	Moderately dry	"
Root crops (miscellaneous)	-	Pit or in storage cellar	Near 32° as possible	Moist	"
Sweet potatoes	29.7	Home cellar or basement	55° to 60°	Moderately dry	"
Tomatoes (mature green)	31.0	"	55° to 70°	"	4 to 6 weeks
Fruits:					
Apples	29.0	Fruit storage cellar	Near 32° as possible	Moderately moist	Through fall and winter
Grapefruit	29.8	"	"	"	4 to 6 weeks
Grapes	28.1	"	"	"	1 to 2 months
Oranges	30.5	"	"	"	4 to 6 weeks
Pears	29.2	"	"	"	

From USDA Bulletin No. 119.

to tell just how dry the wheat is unless you buy it with a guaranteed moisture content, and even then it can pick up moisture from the air during wet weather. It should never be washed before storing, as this also increases the moisture content.

If you live in a humid climate or if you suspect insects are present, dry the grain before storing. Put it in shallow pans no more than ¾ inch deep and heat in a 130°-150°F. oven for 20-30 minutes. Leave the oven door ajar to allow air to circulate and prevent overheating. Stir occasionally to dry evenly. Do *not* heat wheat to be planted or sprouted.

Wheat is best aged at least a month before using, and then just the amount needed should be ground. Even a week's storage of the ground whole wheat flour will reduce its vitamin content, although refrigeration will help keep it fresh. Your home-ground flour has all the nutrients of the whole wheat, and you do not want to lose these by improper storage. Enriched white flour bought from the store will keep longer because the wheat germ has been removed (the same is true of store-bought cornmeal processed the "new" way, removing the germ to increase its storage life). Some vitamins lost with the germ and bran have been returned to the enriched flour, but not all the vitamins and not in their natural proportions.

If the wheat needs cleaning, sift it to remove dirt and debris, then wash it quickly in several changes of water. Dry thoroughly in the oven at 150°F. for 20 minutes if you are in a hurry. Then grind soon.

GRINDERS

There are many types of grinders available in a wide range of prices, both handcrank and electric. Not all are suitable for use with corn, so check before buying if you plan to make cornmeal. Some of the electric ones can be converted for use with a hand crank in the event of a power failure. The family that has a supply of wheat safely stored and the means to grind it can feel confident in any emergency.

SHORT-CUT WHOLE WHEAT BREAD

This bread tends to be heavy, but the flavor is delicious and it is quick to make.

7 cups wheat berries
5 cups hot water
⅔ cup melted butter, lard, or cooking oil
⅔ cup honey
4 teaspoons salt
3 tablespoons (packages) dry yeast

Grind 7 cups of wheat berries. Set an electric grinder on "fine"; by hand you may need to grind the wheat through three times to get it fine enough. You will produce 10-11 cups of whole wheat flour.

Put hot water, shortening, honey, and salt into a large bowl. A hand-turned bread-maker or electric mixer works well with this recipe. Add 6 cups of whole wheat flour and mix thoroughly. Add yeast and mix again. Then add the rest of the flour.

Mix for 10 minutes — this dough is too sticky to knead by hand. Then with oiled hands remove ⅓ of the dough at a time and form into loaves. Place in oiled bread pans and let rise in a warm place for 20 to 60 minutes or until doubled. A warm oven with a pan of hot water in the bottom is a good place to put the rising bread.

Place bread in a preheated 350°F. oven and bake for 45 minutes. Remove from pans and cool on a rack. For a crisp crust, brush with butter or oil. For a soft crust, cover with a towel while cooling.

Other Grains

Other grains such as oats, rye, barley, and buckwheat can be grown and harvested somewhat like wheat. Ask for advice on the type to use and the culture of all grains from your seed supplier or local Extension Service.

SPROUTING SEEDS

The seeds that you store, such as the grains and dried legumes, can be sprouted to provide fresh vegetables for salads, casseroles, and soups. Sprouts can be roasted, ground up, and used to enrich breads, cookies, and other baked goods. Sprouting greatly increases the food value of the seed and its digestibility, because some of the fats and starches are converted to vitamins and sugar. A dry seed becomes a homegrown vegetable in your kitchen any time of the year.

Sprouting is simple. We have found the easiest method is to put a few seeds into a clean, quart-size canning jar. Use about ½ cup of large seeds, such as beans, less of the small seeds like alfalfa. Cover the top of the jar with a piece of cheesecloth or fine screen wire, held in place by a screwband. Fill with water and soak overnight.

The next day pour off the water and rinse the seeds with cool, fresh water. The cheesecloth acts as a sieve on top of the jar. Pour off all water and put the jar in a dark place, such as a kitchen cabinet. The temperature should be warm but not hot; seeds may turn rancid at over 80°F.

Rinse the seeds several times a day with fresh water, always pouring it off, leaving the seeds damp but not soaking. In three or four days you will have nutritious sprouts ready to serve raw in salads or in cooked dishes. Store unused sprouts in the refrigerator to keep them fresh for several days.

Large bean sprouts such as kidney beans, soybeans, and garbanzos will need to be steamed for 10-15 minutes to tenderize them before using. Sprouted grains to be used in recipes such as breads can be roasted and ground before using.

Seeds will not sprout well if they have been heated at over 130°F. to dry or to destroy insects. If you intend to use some of your wheat or other grains for sprouting or for planting, do not use this heat treatment on them.

When buying seeds for sprouting, be sure that they are pure, untreated seeds suitable for eating. Many seeds sold for planting have been treated with fungicides that are poisonous.

PART II

Specific Instructions

CHAPTER 9

Vegetables and More

his chapter includes information on how to harvest and preserve all of the vegetables and a few non-vegetables commonly grown in the home garden. Where appropriate, we have suggested which preserving methods are most suitable for each vegetable. Cooking suggestions also are given where fitting.

Before going ahead with the preserving of any vegetable, please be sure to review the detailed how-to instructions in the chapters on freezing, canning, pickling, drying, curing with brine, and common storage. Also, if you live more than 1,000 feet above sea level, call your county Extension Service to find out what adjustments are necessary for canning vegetables at your altitude.

ASPARAGUS

Harvesting

Asparagus should be picked when 6 to 8 inches high and bigger around than a pencil. During harvesting, all shoots should be cut; leaving the smaller shoots to grow will shorten the harvest season. Harvesting can continue for 6 to 10 weeks in an established bed. The last stalks should be allowed to grow and go to seed. There are three ways to harvest asparagus:

1. Cut the stalk at ground level with a sharp knife.
2. Cut just below the ground. Use caution so as not to injure any shoots that may be growing up beside the one you are cutting.
3. Snap off the stalk, holding it midway from the ground. This method automatically breaks off the tender part of the stem, leaving the tough end in the ground.

Preparation

Wash asparagus and scrub with a vegetable brush. Trim off a few scales; if sand is present behind them, trim off the rest and wash again. If you have cut your asparagus, hold the piece at each end and snap — it will break where the tender part ends. Otherwise, trim off the tough ends. Sort for size or cut into pieces.

Pressure Canning

For spears, cut ¾ inch shorter than the jars. Or cut into 1-inch pieces.

Raw pack. Pack whole spears, tips up, tightly into clean, hot jars. Pack cut pieces as tightly as possible without crushing them. Leave 1 inch headroom. Cover with boiling water, leaving 1 inch headroom. Adjust lids. Process in a dial-gauge canner at 11 pounds pressure or a weighted-gauge at 10 pounds:

pints. . . . . . . 30 minutes
quarts . . . . . . 40 minutes

Hot pack. Stand whole spears upright in boiling water, covering all but the tips, or cover cut-up pieces with boiling water. Boil 2-3 minutes. Pack whole spears, tips up, in hot, clean jars, or pack hot pieces loosely to within 1 inch of top. Cover with boiling cooking liquid or fresh boiling water, leaving 1 inch headroom. Adjust lids. Process in a dial-gauge canner at 11 pounds pressure or a weighted-gauge at 10 pounds:

pints. . . . . . . 30 minutes
quarts . . . . . . 40 minutes

Freezing

Blanch for 2-4 minutes depending on the thickness of the stalks. Cool immediately in cold water. Drain. Pack into containers, leaving no headroom. For spears, alternate tips and ends. Seal and freeze. (See illustrated instructions on page 24.)

BEANS, DRY

Dry beans contribute both vitamins and protein to our diet, and can be grown easily by anyone who has a little extra garden space. Being legumes, the bean plants have low fertilizer needs because, if inoculated with nitrogen-fixing bacteria when planted, they will supply much of their own nitrogen rather than taking it from the soil. Cooking beans with animal foods (meat, cheese, or milk) or with grains or nuts completes the protein mix, so that they can supply the essential amino acids needed by the human body.

Harvesting

If planted early enough, the pods should be mostly dry on the vine by mid-fall. Harvest by pulling the entire plant (do not strain your back trying to pick each pod, as we did the first year), and *stook* them by making piles of the plants around posts, leaving them for a week or so. Then spread them out or hang them up in an airy shed or garage, and leave them for several weeks until pods and vines are completely dry.

The next step is to thresh the beans, which can be done a couple of ways:

1. Hold the plant by the roots upside down in a can or barrel, and bang it from side to side. The beans will fall out of the brittle pods.
2. Stuff the dry plants into sturdy burlap bags and close the tops securely. Then the fun begins! Invite as many children as you need to spend an afternoon jumping on the bags. Or, less joyfully, beat the bags with a stick. The pods will break with either treatment, and the beans will be freed. Turn the bag upside down and shake, then make a small opening and let the beans pour out.

Winnowing will remove the debris of broken vines and leaves that will be mixed with your beans. Pick a windy day and, using two buckets, pour the beans from one to the other from about 3 feet. The wind will carry away most of the chaff. (If you lack wind, a portable fan will do as a substitute.) The rest can be washed off just before using; but do not wash before storing.

Storage

The beans should be totally dry when stored. Use clean, dry containers that have tight-fitting lids, and seal them tightly to keep out worms and insects. Store filled containers in a cool, dry place. As with all dry foods, you will have the best results if you seal them on a dry day. Check the containers occasionally and if moisture appears on the lid or sides, or if there is a musty smell, remove the beans, spread them out in a warm, dry place and re-dry them, stirring occasionally. Re-pack in clean, dry containers.

Canning

Dry beans with sauce. Shell and wash dry beans, discarding discolored or withered ones. You can use the ordinary types (kidney, navy, or yellow eye) or the beans from snap bean or pole bean varieties that have gone unpicked. Cover beans with boiling water and boil 2 minutes. Remove from heat and soak 1 hour. Add more boiling water if there is not enough to keep the beans covered as they expand. Heat to boiling and drain, reserving the liquid for the sauce (see below). Fill jars ¾ full with hot beans. Add a small piece of salt pork, ham, or bacon. Cover with hot sauce, leaving 1 inch headroom. Adjust lids. Process in a dial-gauge canner at 11 pounds pressure or a weighted-gauge at 10 pounds:

> pints. . . . . . .75 minutes
> quarts . . . . . .90 minutes

Tomato sauce. Heat to boiling a mixture of 1 quart tomato juice, 3 tablespoons sugar or molasses, 2 teaspoons salt, 1 tablespoon chopped onion, and ¼ teaspoon mixture of ground cloves, allspice, mace, and

---

Wire baskets for blanching save time, insure against burns, and prevent overcooking those pieces that might escape.

cayenne. Or mix 1 cup tomato ketchup with 3 cups of liquid reserved from soaking beans, and heat to boiling.

Molasses sauce. To 1 quart liquid from soaking beans, add 3 tablespoons molasses, 1 tablespoon vinegar, 2 teaspoons salt, and ¾ teaspoon dry mustard. Heat to boiling.

Baked and Canned

Prepare and soak beans as above. Place beans in a pot or casserole. Cover with molasses sauce and bury a piece of salt pork, ham, or bacon in the beans. Cover pot and bake 4 to 5 hours at 350ºF. Add water as needed to prevent from drying out.

Hot pack. Pack hot beans into hot jars, leaving 1 inch headroom. Adjust lids. Process in a dial-gauge canner at 11 pounds pressure or a weighted-gauge at 10 pounds:

> pints. . . . . . .65 minutes
> quarts . . . . . .75 minutes

BEANS, GREEN AND WAX SNAP

Harvesting

The best quality will be achieved with young tender, crisp beans in which the bean seeds have only begun to form. Pick continually to prolong harvest. Remember to plant your beans at 2-week intervals in order to have fresh beans right up to the first frost and to spread out the period of preserving.

Preparation

If you are preserving by the bushel, try doing them in a variety of ways to avoid the cry of "not beans again!" Straight young beans can be canned whole, packed vertically in pint jars. For canning or freezing, they can be french-cut with a sharp paring knife or a "frencher," found on the end of some vegetable scrapers. Others can be cut into pieces, either straight across or on a slant, in varying lengths. More mature beans are best cut into ½-inch pieces, if you have the patience. The stem end should be removed from all beans; the blossom end can be left on or not, as you wish. On the older beans, be sure to remove the strings down the side, if present.

Pressure Canning

Raw pack. Pack washed, raw beans tightly into clean jars, leaving 1 inch headroom. Cover with boiling water, leaving 1 inch headroom. Adjust lids. Process in a dial-gauge canner at 11 pounds pressure or a weighted-gauge at 10 pounds:

> pints. . . . . . .20 minutes
> quarts . . . . . .25 minutes

✿ LEATHER BRITCHES

"Leather britches is a down-home name for dried green beans. String fresh green beans on white crochet thread, using a large-eyed needle. Hang on a clothesline in full sun for two or three days, taking them in at night. Once they're dry, slide them off the strings onto a cookie sheet. Warm up the oven, turn it off, and set the cookie sheet inside for five minutes. Store in glass jars. To cook, break beans, wash, and soak overnight in plenty of water. Pour off soaking water, add more, bring to a boil, and simmer all day. [For a change in flavor, add salt pork or bacon before simmering.]"

Dick Raymond
Down-to-Earth Gardening Know-How

Hot pack. Cover washed, cut beans with boiling water; boil 5 minutes. Pack hot beans loosely in hot jars, leaving 1 inch headroom. Cover with boiling cooking liquid, leaving 1 inch headroom. Adjust lids. Process in a dial-gauge canner at 11 pounds pressure or a weighted-gauge at 10 pounds:

> pints. . . . . . .20 minutes
> quarts . . . . . .25 minutes

Freezing

Blanch clean prepared beans in boiling water for 3 minutes. Cool immediately in cold water. Drain. Pack into containers, leaving appropriate headroom (see chart on page 170). Seal and freeze.

Drying

Refer to Chapter 7.

Pickling

See Dilly Beans, page 75.

Curing with Brine

See Sauer Beans, page 87.

BEANS, LIMA

Harvesting

Pick pods when fat and bulging. Most prefer the beans before they turn from green to tan.

Preparation

Shell, wash, and sort beans by approximate size.

Pressure Canning

Raw pack. Pack raw beans into clean jars. With small beans, leave 1 inch headroom for pints and 1½ inches headroom for quarts; with large beans, leave 1 inch headroom for pints and 1¼ inches headroom for quarts. Do not press or shake beans down. Cover with boiling water, leaving same headroom as listed above. Adjust lids. Process in a dial-gauge canner at 11 pounds pressure or a weighted-gauge at 10 pounds:

> pints. . . . . . .40 minutes
> quarts . . . . . .50 minutes

Hot pack. Cover shelled beans with boiling water and boil 1 minute. Drain and save cooking liquid. Pack hot beans loosely in clean, hot jars,

leaving 1 inch headroom. Cover with boiling cooking liquid, leaving 1 inch headroom. Adjust lids. Process in a dial-gauge canner at 11 pounds pressure or a weighted-gauge at 10 pounds:

> pints. . . . . . .40 minutes
> quarts . . . . . .50 minutes

Freezing

Blanch beans in boiling water for 2-4 minutes depending on size (2 for small, 3 for medium, 4 for large). Cool immediately in cold water. Drain. Put into containers, leaving appropriate headroom (see page 170). Seal and freeze.

Drying

Refer to Chapter 7.

BEETS

Harvesting

No matter how far apart beets are planted they will still have to be thinned, because the "seed" is actually a pod containing several tiny seeds that will germinate in the same spot. When thinning these plants, pull the largest and eat them fresh or preserve them as greens. Leave the tiny beets on the greens for a surprise taste treat. These can be either frozen or canned. The small plants left several inches apart in the row can be further thinned (and eaten) to leave plants about 8 inches apart to grow into full-sized beets.

The beets for storage should be harvested as late in the fall as possible before the ground freezes. For freezing or canning they can be picked whenever big enough. They have the best flavor when they are small (1-2 inches diameter) and can be preserved whole. Beets larger than 3 inches can be fibrous.

For storage, dig or pull the beets, and leave them in the sun for 2 hours, so dirt falls free of the roots. Cut the stems about 1 inch from the beet. Do not cut the root. Except for the gold varieties, beets will "bleed" away their color if cut into at all. Do not wash before storing.

Storage

Beets are best packed in fresh-sawed sawdust; sand or leaves can also be used. (See Chapter 8 for further information.) Store in a cold, moist place. In addition to being stored, pressure-canned, and frozen, beets can be pickled and used in relishes.

Preparation

Wash carefully, and leave on 1 or 2 inches of stem and the roots to prevent bleeding. Cover with boiling water and boil until the skins slip off easily, 15-25 minutes depending on their size. Dip in cold water to cool enough to handle, and slip off the skins. Trim off roots and stems. Baby beets can be left whole; larger ones can be cut into cubes or slices.

Pressure Canning

Hot pack only. Pack hot beets into hot jars, leaving 1 inch headroom. Cover with boiling water, leaving 1 inch headroom. Adjust lids, and process in a dial-gauge canner at 11 pounds pressure or a weighted-gauge at 10 pounds:

> pints. . . . . . .30 minutes
> quarts . . . . . .35 minutes

Pickled Beets

Pickled beets can be processed in a boiling-water bath rather than a pressure canner because of the acid in the vinegar. Prepare beets as for hot-pack canning. Pack hot beets into hot jars, leaving ½ inch headroom. Cover with boiling syrup (see below), leaving ½ inch headroom. Adjust lids and process in a boiling-water bath:

> pints. . . . . . .30 minutes
> quarts . . . . . .35 minutes

Pickling syrup. Mix and heat to boiling 3½ cups vinegar, 2 cups sugar, 2 sticks cinnamon (remove after boiling), 1½ teaspoons salt, 1½ cups water, and 1 tablespoon whole allspice. Yields approximately 6 pints.

Freezing

Freeze only very young, tender beets, as the texture and flavor of larger beets change during freezing. Prepare as for canning. Chill and pack prepared beets into freezing containers, leaving appropriate headroom (see page 170) if sliced or diced. No headroom is necessary for whole beets. Seal and freeze.

BROCCOLI

Broccoli, rich in vitamins A and C, is easy to prepare for eating and freezing. You can harvest it over a long period, well into frost. Early and late plantings of a few plants each will supply the average family with ample heads for eating fresh and preserving.

Harvesting

Broccoli will form a center cluster of green buds that should be harvested while the buds are shut and before any yellow flowers appear. These clusters should be cut with about 1½ inches of stem. Clusters may vary from the size of a small teacup to that of a large saucer. "Lateral" clusters of various sizes, but usually smaller than the center cluster, will

start forming on the sides of the plants after the center cluster has been harvested. These should be harvested every few days to prevent them from flowering. If allowed to flower and set seeds, the plants will stop producing new clusters; if kept picked, they will continue to produce through the fall until frosts are severe. Late-season broccoli is less likely to be infested with insects than that picked earlier.

Preparation

Freezing is recommended. Broccoli, as well as Brussels sprouts, cabbage, cauliflower, rutabagas, and turnips, becomes discolored and develops a strong flavor when canned.

Wash freshly picked broccoli and check closely for insects. Green cabbage worms are almost invisible in broccoli, so you may have to pull apart a stalk or two to locate them. If insects are present (and they most likely will be), soak the broccoli in salt water (1 tablespoon per quart of water) for 15 minutes. Check again for worms. The salt water may not reveal them; however, with cooking they turn white and can easily be found. Rinse well.

Pressure Canning

Hot pack only. Cut broccoli into serving-size pieces and boil for 3 minutes. Drain. Pack hot broccoli into hot, clean jars, leaving 1 inch headroom. Cover with boiling water, leaving 1 inch headroom. Adjust lids. Process in a dial-gauge canner at 11 pounds pressure or a weighted-gauge at 10 pounds:

> pints. . . . . . .30 minutes
> quarts . . . . . .35 minutes

Freezing

Blanch 3 minutes in boiling water. Cool immediately in cold water. Drain. Pack into containers, alternating heads and stems and leaving no headroom. Seal and freeze.

BRUSSELS SPROUTS

Harvesting

Brussels sprouts ripen from the bottom up and will appear all along the stem of the plant. They can be harvested as soon as they are about the size of a marble. Some may grow much larger. When the first sprouts on the bottom of the stem are harvested, break off the leaves around them and for 5-6 inches above them in order to encourage the stem to grow taller and to produce more sprouts. Repeat this process each time the sprouts are harvested. They can be cut off most easily if you follow the spiral formation in which they grow. The plants may grow as high as 3 feet and can be harvested throughout the winter in the South and, if covered, in the North.

Pressure Canning

Brussels sprouts, like broccoli, are inferior as a canned vegetable. However, to can them, discard the loose outer leaves, wash, then follow the directions for broccoli, page 128.

Freezing

Sort, peel off the outer leaves, then wash. Blanch for 3-5 minutes depending on size. Cool immediately in cold water. Pack into containers, leaving no headroom. Seal and freeze.

CABBAGE

Harvesting

Early varieties for summer use. Cut off the head when needed. If you leave two or three leaves on the stem in the ground, several smaller heads will usually grow later in the season as a bonus.

Late varieties for storage. Wait until the cabbage has fully matured and the weather is cool. Cut the heads off the plants, discarding loose outer leaves and any inner leaves that show signs of insect infestation. In wet weather you may find the cabbages are cracking. This is caused by the plant taking in water faster than it can be used. "Turn the water off" by twisting the cabbage one half turn, which breaks some of its roots.

Storage

Wrap each head in three newspapers, securing them tightly with string or large rubber bands. Store in a root cellar or any cool part of the house. Cabbage can also be pulled up by the roots and hung in a garage or shed if safe from freezing and where the temperature will remain fairly constant. They will, however, not keep as well as those wrapped in newspapers, especially if there is much fluctuation in temperature. Do not hang them in your cellar or in any other closed area, as the odor can become very strong.

Pressure Canning

Cabbage presents the same canning problems as broccoli, but if you like New England boiled dinners, a few jars of cabbage in the pantry will come in handy. Wash the cabbage, remove the loose outer leaves, and, if there are insects, keep removing leaves until there is no sign of them. Cut into wedges that will fit into your jars, and leave on enough of the core to hold the cabbage together. Cover with boiling water and boil for 3 minutes. Pack hot cabbage into clean, hot jars, leaving 1 inch headroom. Cover with boiling water, leaving 1 inch headroom. Adjust lids. Process in a dial-gauge canner at 11 pounds pressure or a weighted-gauge at 10 pounds:

RAISING BRUSSELS SPROUTS

"About the middle of September, pinch out the growing points in the top of each plant. The sprouts on the upper part of the plant promptly start to develop more rapidly and attain larger size."

Joseph Harris Company catalogue

"STORING" BRUSSELS SPROUTS

"They will stand many, many freezes during September, October, and November. Here in Vermont, I have picked Brussels sprouts as late as January. I had to dig in the snow for them."

Dick Raymond
Down-to-Earth Gardening Know-How

pints. . . . . . .45 minutes
quarts . . . . . .55 minutes

Freezing

Pick solid heads, cut off outer leaves. Cut heads as desired. Blanch shredded cabbage for 1½ minutes, wedges for 3 minutes in boiling water. Cool immediately in cold water. Drain and pack into containers, leaving appropriate headroom (see page 170). Seal and freeze.

Curing with Brine

See Sauerkraut, page 83.

CABBAGE, CHINESE

Harvesting

Chinese cabbage is a late fall crop, growing best in cool weather. It can be harvested throughout the winter in mild climates and through several hard frosts in the North. The bugs that might be a problem in summer cannot survive the cold and so are no problem to late plantings.

Storage

Storage is not feasible except for short periods refrigerated in plastic bags.

CARROTS

Harvesting

Carrots can be eaten whenever big enough to be enjoyed; the size and shape when mature (long or short, thin or thick, blunt or tapered) will depend on the variety planted. Tiny whole carrots are delicious frozen; "table size" — up to 6 inches long and no more than 1 inch in diameter at the widest point — are good for all uses. Great big, overgrown carrots tend to be tough and bitter, and are not desirable for eating.

Carrots planted early in the season should be harvested when ready for eating fresh, and any excess should be either frozen or canned. Always pull the largest carrots first; the smaller ones will fill in and catch up when given more space. The largest can be identified by looking for the tops that are darkest green; follow these down to the ground to pull the carrot.

Storage

For storage, plant carrots later in the season, allowing time for them to mature before frost. They will keep in the ground after frosts, but should be dug before the ground freezes if they are to be stored in the root cellar. If heavily mulched, they can be kept in the ground through the winter and dug when needed. These will be sweet and delicious, but must be used immediately after digging.

After digging carrots for storage, leave them in the sun for 2 hours until the dirt dries enough to fall off them. Trim the stem close to the carrot, and pack in freshly cut sawdust, or other packing material. (See Chapter 8 for more storage information.) They also can be kept in plastic bags with a few holes for ventilation to prevent rot. Carrots do best stored in a cold, moist place.

Pressure Canning

Carrots can better than they freeze, and they are useful as a vegetable to be served alone or to be used in stews, soups, and mixed-vegetable dishes. Small ones can be canned whole; larger ones are either sliced or diced.

Wash thoroughly and scrape the skin; or parboil long enough for the skins to slip off.

Raw pack. Pack raw prepared carrots tightly into clean jars, leaving 1 inch headroom. Cover with boiling water, leaving 1 inch headroom. Adjust lids. Process in a dial-gauge canner at 11 pounds pressure or a weighted-gauge at 10 pounds:

> pints. . . . . . .25 minutes
> quarts . . . . . .30 minutes

Hot pack. Cover washed, skinned, and cut-up carrots with boiling water and boil for 1 minute. Drain, reserving the cooking liquid. Pack hot carrots into hot jars, leaving 1 inch headroom. Cover with boiling cooking liquid, leaving 1 inch headroom. Adjust lids, and process in a dial-gauge canner at 11 pounds pressure or a weighted-gauge at 10 pounds:

> pints. . . . . . .25 minutes
> quarts . . . . . .30 minutes

Freezing

For freezing, use only very tender, tiny young carrots, as the texture of larger ones changes with freezing. Freeze whole little carrots for soups and stews.

Remove tops, wash and peel or scrub hard with a vegetable brush. Blanch whole carrots in boiling water for 5 minutes — 2 minutes for diced, slices, or strips. Cool immediately in ice cold water. Drain. Pack into freezer containers, leaving appropriate headroom (see page 170). Seal and freeze.

Drying

Refer to Chapter 7.

ˇ₰ BAKED CHINESE CABBAGE

Wash the head, cut into small pieces, and cook in enough salted water (1-1½ teaspoons to a quart of water) to barely cover the cabbage. Boil for about 7 minutes, or until tender. Drain and place 4 cups of cabbage in a greased baking dish and season with a sprinkling of paprika. Combine 2 beaten eggs with 2 cups of milk and add ¼ teaspoon of salt. Pour this mixture over the cabbage, and place the baking dish in a pan of hot water. Bake at 350°F. for about ¾ hour, or until it is firm.

ˇ₰ CARROTS

"Have you tried leaving your carrots in the ground during the early winter months to save storage space in the house? They can be kept there, covered with a heavy mulch of some kind. Many people prefer them to the frozen or shipped stuff you get at the supermarket."

Stu Campbell
The Mulch Book

CAULIFLOWER

Harvesting

Cauliflower is ready to harvest when the "curds" or florets are well formed, but before they shoot up and flower. The full-grown head may vary in size from several inches to a foot across. When the heads have begun to form (about 4 inches across), they must be blanched, or shaded from the sun, in order to be white and tender. This can be done by tying the leaves over the head (not too tightly or in damp weather they will rot). A better method is to partially break several of the large side leaves, pull them over the top and tuck them under the cauliflower head on the far side. The leaves will shed rain, lessening the chance of rot. The head should be ready to harvest about a week later.

To harvest, cut the head off above the leaves (no new head will form, so the space can be given up for lettuce or another quick-growing crop). The florets are delicious raw and served with dips, or cooked. The best method of preserving is freezing; canning is a poor second best as cauliflower will develop a strong flavor and change color when canned. Cauliflower can be used in pickled mixed vegetables. (See Mustard Pickles, page 74.)

Pressure Canning

Cut the cauliflower into individual flower stalks and pressure-can following the directions for broccoli, page 128.

Freezing

Choose firm, tender heads. Break or cut into florets. Soak for ½ hour in a solution of 1 tablespoon salt to 1 quart water if necessary to remove insects. Drain and rinse. Blanch the cauliflower for 3 minutes in a boiling solution of either 4 teaspoons salt or the juice of 1 lemon to a gallon of water. This will help prevent it from darkening when frozen. Cool immediately in ice cold water. Drain and pack into freezer containers, leaving no headroom. Seal and freeze.

CELERY

Harvesting

The outer stalks can be cut off whenever they are long enough. They will be dark green and strongly flavored unless bleached by placing soil or boards around the stalks up to the leaves. Celery can be harvested until a hard frost if heavily mulched.

Cold Storage

Celery will not keep long in storage. The best results are achieved by washing, putting into plastic bags, and storing in the refrigerator or a very cool cellar.

Preparation

Wash and cut off tough and discolored spots. Celery that has been blanched in the garden will make the most tender product. If necessary, remove tough strings and cut celery into strips or pieces.

Pressure Canning

Celery that has been canned is convenient for use in soups and stews, as well as in vegetable combinations. It also can be canned with tomatoes or other vegetables. (See directions under Mixed Vegetables, page 139.)

Hot pack. Cover cut-up celery with boiling water and boil 3 minutes. Drain. Pack hot into clean, hot jars, leaving 1 inch headroom. Cover with boiling water, leaving 1 inch headroom. Adjust lids. Process in a dial-gauge canner at 11 pounds pressure or a weighted-gauge at 10 pounds:

> pints. . . . . . .30 minutes
> quarts . . . . . .35 minutes

Freezing

Wash and cut. Blanch for 3 minutes in boiling water. Cool immediately in cold water. Drain. Pack into containers, leaving appropriate headroom (see page 170). Seal and freeze. Celery freezes best in combination dishes.

SWEET CORN

Harvesting

Check your sweet corn often as it approaches ripeness, so you can enjoy this garden favorite as early as possible—and before raccoons find it (if your garden is unfenced). We often find the first ripe ears in the center of the rows, so don't be misled by immature ears at the ends.

There are several ways to tell when sweet corn is ripe. First look at the silk, which will darken and dry out as the ears mature. Then feel the top of the ear by pinching through the husk (without opening it). The end of the ear should be blunt rather than tapered as the kernels fill out near the top. When an ear looks and feels right, the final test is to pull down part of the husk and press a kernel with your fingernail. If the corn is perfectly ripe, the sweet juice will spurt out. You can also bite into a raw ear. A sweet juicy ear is a ripe one.

Pick as close to processing time as possible, since the sugars quickly turn to starch. Keep the ears cool. For preserving, plan to plant some corn that will mature 2 or 3 weeks before frost, so it will not stay in your freezer longer than necessary.

Preparation

Husk corn, remove silk (a vegetable brush helps here), and wash. Blanch 3 minutes in boiling water.

CELERY

"Some say celery should not be undertaken by the home gardener. Others say try it; you may be successful. Celery does like rich soil and a lot of moisture. It also needs coolish nights. If you can provide these necessities, then give it a whirl. The big question with this vegetable seems to be blanching. I say yes, it is necessary to blanch so that the stalks are not tough and stringy. But blanching is not that difficult a proposition. When your celery gets tall, just lay light boards along either side, on an angle of an inverted V. This will cover the stalks sufficiently and will save you the work of hilling. Pascal and Fordhook are good growers, and a ten-foot row should be sufficient unless you are avid celery eaters. You don't need to wait for full maturity to pick this plant; the stalks can be used from the time the plants are half grown."

Marjorie Page Blanchard
Home Gardener's Cookbook

CORN CUTTERS

Corn cutters come in several varieties but after trying all of them, we feel nothing improves on a sharp knife. The corn cutters are wasteful and have caused more than their share of gouged knuckles.

PARCHED CORN

"Be sure to let some of your large-eared yellow and white corns stand on the stalks until they dry. Remove them before frost and check for proper drying. The kernels of sweet corn shrivel up considerably with age. If you bite a drying kernel and feel it 'give' a little, it is good for parching. Remove the kernels, keep in a covered container in the refrigerator (for several months if you wish). Then to parch, proceed as with popping corn, using a small amount of cooking oil in the popping pan, and stirring until kernels turn light brown. They half-pop into a chewy but tasty treat to go with the Thanksgiving cider."

John Vivian
Growing Corn for Many Uses

Canning Whole-Kernel Corn

Cut off the kernels with a sharp knife. Avoid cutting the cob itself.

Raw pack. Pack corn into clean jars, leaving 1 inch headroom. Do not shake or press down. Cover with boiling water, leaving 1 inch headroom. Adjust lids. Process in a dial-gauge canner at 11 pounds pressure or a weighted-gauge at 10 pounds:

> pints. . . . . . .55 minutes
> quarts . . . . . .85 minutes

Hot pack. To each quart of cut corn, add 1 pint of boiling water and heat to boiling. Drain, reserving liquid. Pack hot corn into hot jars, leaving 1 inch headroom, and cover with the boiling cooking liquid, leaving 1 inch headroom. Or fill to 1 inch of top with undrained corn and liquid. Adjust lids. Process in a dial-gauge canner at 11 pounds pressure or a weighted-gauge at 10 pounds:

> pints. . . . . . .55 minutes
> quarts . . . . . .85 minutes

Freezing Whole-Kernel Corn

Heat ears in boiling water for 4 minutes. Cool immediately in cold water. Drain. Cut off the kernels, but avoid cutting the cob itself. Pack into containers, leaving appropriate headroom (see page 170). Seal and freeze. (See page 25 for illustrated instructions.)

Freezing Corn-on-the-Cob

Many people feel that corn-on-the-cob is a questionable use of freezer space unless you have lots of room to spare. The quality doesn't compare with whole kernel, but the treat of corn-on-the-cob in mid-winter is worth the space, and it's a special treat for children. Use freezer bags for packaging.

Blanch small ears 7 minutes, medium ears 9 minutes, large ears 11 minutes. Cool immediately in ice water. *Drain well* and pat dry with towels. Pack into containers, expelling as much air as possible. Or wrap each ear tightly in freezer wrap or aluminum foil. Seal and freeze.

Optional. Use seal-and-freeze bags. Here corn doesn't come in contact with water during reheating and stays crisper. Try including a little butter in the bags before sealing.

To cook. There are several schools of thought, but we have found that taking the corn straight from the freezer and putting it into cool water, then raising it to a boil until done, works best. A tablespoon of sugar added to the water will improve the flavor. Corn in seal-and-freeze bags should be placed frozen (bag and all) in boiling water and boiled for 15 to 25 minutes, depending on the size of the ears. Some blustery winter evening, when there's a fire in the stove or fireplace, try roasting the frozen corn, wrapped in foil, on the hot coals.

CREAM-STYLE CORN

Use well-matured but still sweet ears, rather than the earliest ones that usually disappear at the picnic table.

Preparation

Husk and remove all silk. Wash. Cut down through the tops of the kernels with a sharp knife. Then turn the knife on its side and scrape down the sides of the cob to draw out the "cream" and insides of the kernels left on the cob. Or you can use a table knife for this step. Do not use quart jars for canning cream style, since the length of processing time would be so long that the flavor and food value would be destroyed.

Canning Cream-Style Corn

Raw pack. Pack corn and cream into clean jars, leaving 1 inch headroom. Do not shake or press down. Cover with boiling water, leaving 1 inch headroom. Adjust lids. Process in a dial-gauge canner at 11 pounds pressure or a weighted-gauge at 10 pounds:

    pints. . . . . . .95 minutes

Hot pack. To each quart of creamed corn, add 1 pint boiling water. Heat to boiling. Pack hot corn and juice into hot jars, leaving 1 inch headroom. Adjust lids. Process in a dial-gauge canner at 11 pounds pressure or a weighted-gauge at 10 pounds:

    pints. . . . . . .85 minutes

Freezing Cream-Style Corn

Heat ears in boiling water for 4 minutes. Cool immediately in cool water and process as above. Pack into containers, leaving appropriate headroom (see page 170). Seal and freeze.

Drying

Refer to Chapter 7.

EGGPLANT

Harvesting

Pick when the eggplant has a glossy shine. The size will vary from several inches to a foot or more, depending on the variety, climate, and soil conditions.

Preparation

Eggplant darkens in color as do potatoes when canned or frozen but is useful for Italian eggplant-and-tomato casseroles. Optional: treat

> ### 🍃
> ### WHEN TO PICK EGGPLANT
>
> "Admiration of the beauty of the fruit should not delay harvesting. When fruit is large and shining, cut it from the plant. If fruits are left until they lose their gloss, the taste will suffer and the plant will stop producing."
>
> Roger Griffith
> *Vegetable Garden Handbook*

with an anti-oxidant (see page 164). Wash, pare, and slice small eggplants or cube large eggplants.

Pressure Canning

Hot pack only. To remove some of the moisture from the eggplant, sprinkle it with salt, cover with cool water, and let stand for 45 minutes. Drain, cover with boiling water, and boil for 5 minutes. Drain and hot-pack into clean, hot jars, leaving 1 inch headroom. Cover with boiling water, leaving 1 inch headroom. Adjust lids. Process in a dial-gauge canner at 11 pounds pressure or a weighted-gauge at 10 pounds:

> pints. . . . . . .30 minutes
> quarts . . . . . .40 minutes

Freezing

Best results are obtained with small, tender eggplants. Pare and cut into slices ½ inch thick. Do just enough for one blanching at a time to avoid discoloration. Blanch 4 minutes in a gallon of boiling water to which ½ cup lemon juice has been added. Chill quickly, pat dry. Put freezer wrap between the slices, pack, and freeze.

Or, prepare your favorite eggplant casserole, cook until almost done in a dish lined with aluminum foil, cool, and freeze. When solid, remove the dish and leave the casserole wrapped in foil or freezer wrap. When ready to use, unwrap, put back into original dish, and bake until done.

GARLIC SPRAY

"Grow your own garlic and try this recipe. Take 3 to 4 ounces of chopped garlic bulbs and soak in 2 tablespoons of mineral oil for one day. Add a pint of water in which 1 teaspoon fish emulsion has been dissolved. Stir well. Strain the liquid and store in a glass or china container, as it reacts with metals. Dilute this, starting with 1 part to 20 parts of water and use as a spray against your worst insect pests. If sweet potatoes or other garden plants are attracting rabbits, try this spray. Rabbits dislike the smell of fish, too. Garlic sprays are useful in controlling late blight on tomatoes and potatoes."

Louise Riotte
Carrots Love Tomatoes

GARLIC

Harvesting

Garlic requires a long growing season in well-aerated soil to achieve maximum size. It should be harvested late in the fall before the ground freezes, or when the tops have died completely if that is sooner. As with onions, bulbs must be dried in the sun for 2 or 3 weeks, or until the roots are completely dry and dead, before storing.

Storage

Garlic can be stored like onions. When thoroughly dry, braid the tops together or put the garlic in a mesh bag. Then hang it close to the ceiling in an airy, cool, dry, dark place.

GREENS

Harvesting

Kale is a hardy green that grows well in the fall and tastes better after the first frost. It can be harvested even under snow in the winter. Harvest the leaves when big enough to eat, discarding large, tough leaves and stems. Very young leaves are good raw in salads.

Collards are grown mainly in the South and have a mild cabbage-like flavor. They can be frozen or canned successfully. In mild climates they can be harvested from the garden throughout most of the winter. Harvest the outer, lower leaves as soon as they mature, so that they don't have a chance to get too large and tough. For fresh eating, harvest when very green and small.

Swiss chard is a sturdy cousin of spinach, slower growing but much more durable. In fact, one or two rows of chard will provide all the cooked greens you can eat during the summer and fall up until severe freezing weather, plus supplying leaves for freezing or pressure canning.

Whenever there is a lapse between other crops during the summer and after most others have gone by, Swiss chard appears on our table. The very tender center leaves are good in salads, but the larger ones are too tough. Swiss chard takes longer to cook than spinach, but it shrinks less, so not nearly as much need be picked for a meal.

When chard reaches 6-8 inches high (45-55 days from planting), it can be harvested like spinach. Cut off the whole plant about 1 inch above the ground, which will give you a mix of large and small leaves. The plant will recover, and soon new leaves will be large enough to harvest. You also can cut just the larger outside leaves, leaving the inner ones to grow. Chard rarely bolts, so it does not make a lot of difference how you harvest it — our only problem is having more than we can use!

When allowed to grow extra large, the leaves develop a thick white stalk (red in rhubarb chard), which some people enjoy cooked and served like asparagus.

Spinach can be harvested as soon as the leaves are big enough to eat. For preserving, let them attain enough size so that you do not have to fuss with hundreds of tiny leaves. To harvest spinach, cut the entire plant off at about 1 inch above the ground, so that you will get the tender little leaves in the center of the plant as well as the more mature leaves on the outside. This will help prevent the seed stalk from growing, which causes the plant to "bolt," or go to seed. Unless the weather is hot, there should be at least one more full growth of leaves on each plant, and often more than that before the plant bolts. If the seed stalks form, they need not go to waste, as they are edible, too.

Since spinach grows poorly in hot weather, plant it very early in the season and also late in the summer for a fall crop. Be sure to allow enough time for it to mature before the first expected frost. The plants can stand light frost, but will not grow much thereafter. Planting spinach in wide rows will save time and space in the garden, as well as being easier to harvest. Freezing and canning are both successful methods of preserving spinach.

New Zealand spinach, which is not a true spinach, is harvested differently. Just pick the leaves that are large enough, from the vines on which they grow.

Mustard can be grown and harvested year round in the South. As soon as the leaves are large enough to eat, they can be harvested by cutting the entire plant off about 1 inch from the ground.

DANDELIONS

"To avoid an unpleasant flavor to your dandelion greens, pick them young before the flowers blossom, and if possible get them from a field rather than your own lawn. If you are initiating your family into the practice of trying wild greens, start slowly with a few leaves or some tender roots, tossed with the usual lettuce salad. Or you may make the dressing [on page 136]."

Marjorie Page Blanchard
Home Gardener's Cookbook

SPINACH

"If you let spinach get three or four inches high and then cut down the whole row to a height of one inch, you can cut it several more times before it 'bolts' and goes to seed. If you just pick at it, one leaf at a time, you won't harvest much."

Dick Raymond
Down-to-Earth Gardening Know-How

Preparation

The most important thing to remember is to use only fresh, tender, young greens that have been thoroughly washed in several rinse waters, lifting them from the rinse water each time, and picked over to remove wilted leaves, tough stems, and weeds. Strong-flavored greens, such as wild dandelions, should be cooked in several changes of water before canning.

Pressure Canning

(See illustrations on page 46.) Spinach and other mild greens can be steamed in a basket or cheesecloth bag for about 10 minutes to wilt, or can be heated in a little water until wilted. Do small quantities at a time (½-1 pound) so that the greens will be evenly cooked.

Hot pack only. Pack hot spinach or other greens loosely in hot jars, leaving ½ inch headroom. Cut through the greens at right angles with a sharp knife. Cover with boiling water, leaving ½ inch headroom. Adjust lids. Process at 11 pounds pressure for a dial-gauge canner and 10 pounds for a weighted-gauge:

pints. . . . . . . 70 minutes
quarts . . . . . . 90 minutes

Freezing

Blanch dandelion greens 1½ minutes. Blanch spinach, New Zealand spinach, kale, chard, mustard greens, turnip greens, and fiddleheads 2 minutes. Blanch collards 3 minutes. Cool immediately in cold water. Drain. Pack into containers, leaving appropriate headroom (see page 170). Seal and freeze.

HORSERADISH

Horseradish grows like a weed, so plant only a few roots for your seasoning needs.

Harvesting

Horseradish roots can be dug as needed when the plants are dormant in the fall, winter, or early spring, or they can be dug up in the fall and stored like other root crops. Leave enough root in the ground for the next year's crop.

Prepared Horseradish

Wash and pare the horseradish root, and shred, or cut into small pieces. To each cup of horseradish add 3-4 tablespoons water and 1-2 tablespoons of vinegar and chop fine in a blender or food processor. For a color change, add a few pieces of raw beet to the horseradish before chopping.

This spicy relish will keep a long time in the refrigerator, where it will be on hand to pep up stews and clear your sinuses! It does lose its potency in time.

KOHLRABI

Harvesting

Kohlrabi is best eaten fresh. It can be harvested when the bulb-like stem just above the ground is 2 or 3 inches in diameter.

Freezing

Trim, peel, and wash kohlrabi, then cut crosswise into ¼-inch slices. Small bulbs can be left whole. Blanch slices 2 minutes, whole bulbs 3 minutes. Cool immediately in ice cold water. Drain. Pack into containers, leaving appropriate headroom (see page 170).

MIXED VEGETABLES

Pressure Canning and Freezing

Some vegetables go well together and can be preserved in the same canning jar or freezing container — such combinations as succotash (limas and corn), tomatoes and celery, or a mixed assortment of whatever is ripe and ready at the same time in the garden and that appeals.

Use your imagination and try a few combinations to spice up the winter menu. Just don't use leafy greens in a mixed-vegetable combination. Prepare the vegetables by washing and cutting as you like them.

Pressure Canning

Hot-pack and process in the pressure canner using the longest time required for any of the vegetables included. If there is a big time difference, one vegetable will be overdone, so you might prefer to can the vegetables separately and mix them at the time of eating.

Freezing

Blanch each vegetable separately if the recommended times are different. Then chill, drain, and pack into freezer containers, leaving appropriate headroom (see page 170). Seal and freeze.

MUSHROOMS

Be sure to use only mushrooms that you know are edible!

HORSERADISH

Gardeners find horseradish a crop that is easier to grow than to stop growing. The harvested part of the plant is the root, which consists of one main root and several smaller ones branching off from it. If any of these smaller roots are lost during the harvesting, they will produce yet another mighty horseradish plant the following summer. Horseradish is as strong as its flavor, and given the opportunity, will take over major portions of a garden.

KOHLRABI

"The best ones are those that have grown quickly; those that grow slowly are usually tough and woody. A side dressing of fertilizer will help to speed up growth."

Dick Raymond
Down-to-Earth Gardening Know-How

"Although turnip shaped, it has a far more delicate and enjoyable flavor. Finely shredded over a salad it adds vitamins and variety or it can be cooked as fritters, purée, au gratin or boiled and finished off by sauté in butter."

Thompson & Morgan catalogue

Pressure Canning

Cut off bad spots and tough ends of stems. Brush off dirt if necessary, or soak in cold water for 10 minutes to remove dirt. Wash in clean water. If badly soiled, they can be peeled.

Cut large mushrooms into pieces; small ones can be left whole. Cover with water and boil 5 minutes.

Hot pack only. Pack hot mushrooms in hot half-pint or pint jars, leaving 1 inch headroom. For better color, add ⅛ teaspoon of ascorbic powder, or a 500 mg. tablet of vitamin C. Add boiling hot cooking liquid or water to cover mushrooms, leaving 1 inch headroom. Adjust lids and process in a pressure canner at 11 pounds pressure for dial-gauge or 10 pounds for weighted-gauge:

half-pints and pints. . . . 45 minutes

Freezing

Sort and clean mushrooms. Cut according to taste, trimming ends and bad spots. For "fresh" use, blanch in boiling water 5 minutes for whole, 3 minutes for sliced. Cool immediately in ice cold water. Drain. For use cooked, heat in a frying pan with butter or fat until done. Cool by placing pan in a bowl of ice cold water.

Pack into containers, leaving appropriate headroom (see page 170). Seal and freeze. Optional: treat with an anti-oxidant before freezing (see page 164).

Drying

Refer to Chapter 7.

OKRA

Harvesting

Pick pods when 2-3 inches long and harvest continually. Plant in conditions suitable for sweet corn. Okra is good dried.

Preparation

Wash and cut off stem, but don't cut into pod. Sort. For use in gumbo, cut the okra crosswise in slices after removing both stem and blossom ends.

Pressure Canning

Hot pack only. Cook in boiling water for 2 minutes. Pack hot okra in hot, clean jars, leaving 1 inch headroom. Cover with boiling water, leaving 1 inch headroom. Adjust lids. Process in pressure canner at 11 pounds pressure for dial-gauge or 10 pounds for weighted-gauge:

```
pints. . . . . . .25 minutes
quarts . . . . . .40 minutes
```

Freezing

Blanch in boiling water for 3-4 minutes depending on size. Cool immediately in cold water. Drain. Pack into containers, leaving appropriate headroom (see page 170). Seal and freeze.

ONIONS

Harvesting

Onions for use fresh can be harvested green whenever needed, from the scallion or green-top stage right through the formation of a large bulb.

For winter storage, onions should be harvested when 95 percent of the tops have turned brown and died, or late in the fall before the ground is frozen even if the tops have not died. Bending the tops over in the early fall helps encourage the plant to funnel all its energy into enlarging the bulb rather than the top. Be sure all seed pods are picked off as soon as they appear so the onion will not wear itself out making seeds rather than a big bulb.

Curing

After pulling onions for storage, you must cure them. This means allowing them to dry out for about 2 weeks so the skins become paper crisp and roots completely dead, shriveled, and wiry. If the weather is dry and warm, the onions can be spread out on gravel or other dry area, turned occasionally and protected from animals and other hazards. An alternative is to spread them out on the floor or on newspapers in a dry, well-ventilated garage or shed.

Storage

When the onions feel crisp and dry, they can be put into mesh bags, or their tops braided or tied together, and then hung in a dry, cool, dark place that is well-ventilated. This can be at the ceiling level of a cellar storage room or in an attic, a spare room, or garage. As with all stored vegetables, one of the most important factors is consistency of temperature — when the temperature fluctuates between extremes, the onions may rot. Slight freezing of stored onions will not ruin them unless they are handled while frozen or are thawed out and refrozen, or there is a long delay after being frozen before they are used. Bermuda-type onions generally cannot be stored for any length of time.

Canning

Not recommended, except in pickle combinations. (See Chapter 5 on pickling.)

USING OKRA

In addition to being stored for later use, usually in gumbos, okra can be boiled and served with a hollandaise sauce. It's a pleasing dish, nutritious — and slightly slippery.

LOOKING AHEAD WITH ONIONS

Storage of onions takes lots of planning. The right varieties must be planted and must be planted at the right time. The gardener who plants onion sets is limited to a few varieties; select one advertised as a "keeper," and plant it relatively late, so that it will be full-sized at the very end of the growing season.

The better method is to start onions from seeds, so that the best keepers can be selected. Three of these are Yellow Globe, Southport, and Ebenezer. There's a relationship between the taste and the keeping qualities of onions, with the milder varieties, such as Sweet Spanish, not keeping well. And, no matter what variety, the thick-stemmed onions should be culled from the keeping crop and eaten early.

Freezing

Onions can be frozen in small quantities for a quick source of diced onion to put into sauces and casseroles. This is a good way to keep the Bermuda variety that does not store well. Peel, wash, and dice onions. Pack into small freezer containers, leaving appropriate headroom (see page 170). Seal and freeze.

PARSLEY

Although used mostly for decoration and flavoring, parsley is a powerhouse of vitamins and minerals. Ounce for ounce it contains more vitamin C than oranges, more iron than spinach, and nearly as much vitamin A as carrots.

Parsley can be harvested throughout the season whenever there are enough leaves to cut. For winter use, plants can be lifted and potted to grow inside on a sunny windowsill. Parsley can be preserved by freezing or drying.

Freezing

Cut leaves with stems several inches long. Tie gently in bunches, shake in cold water to wash, drain. Place in freezer bags (several bunches to the bag) or containers and freeze. If in bags, store where they will not be crushed by other packages. Parsley can be blanched before freezing, which will help it retain its color, nutrients, and flavor over a longer storage period. To blanch, dip the washed bunches into boiling water for ½-1 minute, then cool rapidly in ice water, drain, and freeze.

Drying

Refer to Drying Herbs, page 99.

PARSNIPS

Harvesting

Parsnips develop their distinctive sweet flavor after freezing in the ground, and are best left in the ground and harvested when the ground can be dug fall and spring. If mulched heavily, the ground should be soft enough to dig them throughout the winter.

Any parsnips left in the spring should be dug before top growth begins, because they become poisonous when they start growing again. This is the best time to harvest them for freezing or canning rather than during the busy fall harvest season.

If preferred, parsnips can be harvested in the late fall and stored in the root cellar, or canned or frozen, with freezing yielding the most superior results.

☙ PARSLEY

Parsley can be frozen or dried for winter use, but why bother? Have it fresh all winter, and enjoy a friendly, perky plant in a sunny window in your kitchen.

In mid-summer, soak parsley seed (it's extremely slow to germinate unless you do) and plant a short row in your garden. Well before frost, dig up several individual plants, and give each its own roomy pot. It will thrive in the kitchen if kept well watered, and doesn't resent being clipped for the many uses you will find for its tasty foliage.

Because parsley is a biennial, it turns to seed production the second year. Thus, for best parsley, start new plants each year.

☙ PARSNIP SEEDS

Some seeds can be saved over a season and planted the following spring. But not parsnip seeds. At their freshest best, they are slow to germinate. Using outdated seeds will only make this problem more acute, since many will never germinate. The mark of a good gardener is a row of parsnips unblemished by lengthy and soil-wasting gaps.

Other seeds not recommended for storing beyond the current season are onions and leeks, parsley, and salsify.

Storage

Store as you would carrots. (Refer to Chapter 8.)

Pressure Canning

Thoroughly wash, scrape, and wash again, then slice parsnips or leave whole if small. Cover with boiling water and boil 3 minutes.

Hot pack only. Pack hot into hot jars, leaving 1 inch headroom. Cover with boiling water, leaving 1 inch headroom. Adjust lids. Process in a pressure canner at 11 pounds pressure for dial-gauge or 10 pounds for weighted-gauge:

> pints. . . . . . .30 minutes
> quarts . . . . . .35 minutes

Freezing

Use only tender, small, top-quality parsnips. Remove tops, wash and peel, and cut into ½-inch cubes or slices. Blanch in boiling water 2 minutes. Cool immediately in cold water. Drain. Pack into containers, leaving appropriate headroom (see page 170). Seal and freeze.

PEAS, FIELD

Harvesting

Harvest field peas for fresh use or preserving when the pods are well-filled with tender peas. For dry peas, harvest as you would dry beans. The fresh field peas can be either pressure-canned or frozen.

Pressure Canning

Raw pack. Shell peas, discarding any that are hard. Wash and pack loosely into clean jars, leaving 1 inch headroom. Do not shake or press peas down. Cover with boiling water, leaving 1 inch headroom. Adjust lids and process in a pressure canner at 11 pounds pressure for dial-gauge, 10 pounds for weighted-gauge:

> pints and quarts . . . . . .40 minutes

Hot pack. Cover shelled and washed field peas with boiling water and bring to a rolling boil. Drain and pack hot peas in hot jars, leaving 1 inch headroom. Do not shake or press peas down. Cover with boiling cooking liquid, leaving 1 inch headroom. Adjust lids and process in a pressure canner at 11 pounds pressure for dial-gauge, 10 pounds for weighted-gauge:

> pints and quarts . . . . . .40 minutes

PARSNIPS

Here's a vegetable that demands special treatment — to be virtually ignored for months, then treated with kindness in the kitchen.

In the garden the parsnips want room (at least 4 inches between plants), a loose soil, and peace, until after the first heavy frost. From then until spring (if they are heavily mulched so they can be dug), they are available, and good.

For too many years they have been treated as the poor relative of the root family, eaten only when nothing else was available, and treated by the cook in ways that only increased the unpopularity of this plant.

In her book, *Home Gardener's Cookbook,* author Marjorie Page Blanchard suggests a more kindly and understanding approach:

"Treat parsnips as you would a sweet potato, adding apples or onions, brown sugar and nutmeg or cinnamon to slices of cooked, peeled parsnips, and baking all together to amalgamate the flavors. Or mash them and add some of the natural juices of a roast, especially a pot roast which has been cooked in strong black coffee or a spicy combination of horseradish, cranberries and allspice."

Freezing

Shell, sort, and wash field peas. Blanch in boiling water for 2 minutes. Chill immediately in ice cold water. Drain. Pack into freezer containers, leaving appropriate headroom (see page 170). Seal and freeze.

PEAS, GREEN

Harvesting

To eat or preserve, fresh peas should be picked when tender and sweet, before fully mature, when their sugars start to turn to starch. Watch the pods carefully as they ripen, and pick when enough are about three-quarters full of ripe peas. Taste is the best test — and the most enjoyable!

Speed is essential to capture the sweet, fresh flavor, so peas should be picked and preserved within as short a time as possible. If it is necessary to hold them several hours before use, they should be refrigerated.

There are several different machines for shelling peas, some of which work best when the peas have been picked several hours before shelling. Considering the time saving involved in doing a large quantity by machine, it may be worth it to sacrifice that first hour of freshness.

Sugar (or edible-pod) peas are harvested before the peas form in the pod, and when the pods are still tiny. They can be used fresh — raw in salads or as a quick-cooked vegetable — or frozen. The pods become tough and stringy when the peas mature, but they still can be harvested and shelled for the peas if they get by you.

With all peas, the freshest flavor is preserved by freezing, though pressure canning is another successful method. Fresh peas also can be dried (see Chapter 7). Or dry the peas on the vine, and harvest and pressure-can as you would dry beans, page 123.

Pressure Canning

Shell and wash fresh peas, and sort for size if there is much difference.

Raw pack. Pack peas loosely into clean, hot jars, leaving 1 inch headroom. Do not shake or press peas down. Cover with boiling water, leaving 1 inch headroom. Adjust lids, and process in a pressure canner at 11 pounds pressure for dial-gauge, 10 pounds for weighted-gauge:

pints and quarts . . . . . . .40 minutes

Freezing

Shell and wash fresh peas, and sort for size. Large and small peas should not be mixed in freezing, because they will cook unevenly when used. Blanch peas in boiling water for 1½ minutes. Chill immediately in ice cold water and drain. Pack peas into freezer containers, leaving appropriate headroom (see page 170). Peas can also be flash-frozen by placing blanched, cooled, drained peas on a cookie sheet and freezing them. Seal and freeze.

PEAS, SUGAR SNAP

Sugar snap peas — a delight to eat raw or just barely cooked — aren't ideal for canning, but they can be fast-frozen and used later in heated dishes, in which the loss of crispiness won't be noticed.

To freeze them, first "string" them, by pinching the tip of the pea, pulling the string up, pinching off the stem end, then pulling the rest of the string off the other side of the pod. Next, blanch them in boiling water for 2 or 3 minutes. Don't blanch them longer than this, or they will lose texture and flavor. Figure on using 6 quarts of water for each pound of peas. When the water is boiling, put peas in a wire basket and submerge them. Begin timing when water again reaches a boil. Shake basket during blanching so that heat penetrates all of the peas. Lift peas from boiling water, and put them at once into a pan of ice water for 3-5 minutes.

Lay pods separately on trays and freeze them immediately. When they are thoroughly frozen, break them down into batch sizes, and store them in plastic bags.

Whether fresh or frozen, these peas require only 2 minutes to cook. Thus, they can be added to cooked dishes only minutes before serving.

PEPPERS, HOT AND SWEET

Harvesting

Pick at any size, but remember the more you pick, the more the plant will continue to set fruit. Any pepper, whether hot or sweet, will turn red if left on the plant long enough. Sweet red peppers make especially attractive additions to relishes. Grow sweet peppers far from hot varieties to avoid a mix-up.

Preparation

Wash and cut into desired pieces, removing seeds and stems. Use caution in handling hot peppers — always wear plastic gloves and be careful not to touch your eyes.

Pressure Canning

Peppers should be canned only in half-pint or pint jars.

Hot pack only. Cut to preference and then boil for 3 minutes. To peel (if desired) dip hot in cold water and strip skins. Drain and pack into hot jars, leaving 1 inch headroom. Add ½ teaspoon salt *and* 1 tablespoon

---

PLANTING PEAS

"Some years, I have planted peas in patches that were as large as 12 feet square. I am often asked, 'How do you get in to harvest them in a patch so large?' Easy. I take a stool, go out in the patch, sit down, reach out for the peas around me, and pick a peck. Then I move the stool, and do it again. You may raise so many peas you can't stay ahead of them!"

Dick Raymond
Down-to-Earth Gardening Know-How

PLANTS OR PEPPERS?

Some gardeners believe that since a little nitrogen is good for their gardens, twice as much is twice as good. They shouldn't raise peppers.

Their pepper plants will be the best in town, with but a single fault — few peppers.

Give pepper plants a warm soil (they'll only sit and shiver in temperatures under 55°F.), a lot of moisture, a good compost base, and a mulch only when the soil is well warmed, but go light on the lime — and hold the nitrogen. Peppers thrive when they are crowded and placed in your poorest soil.

DRYING PEPPERS

"Small, hot peppers may be strung whole on twine by threading with a large-eyed needle. Large, sweet peppers may be washed, cut in half and seeded, then strung in the same way. Both may be hung on a clothesline or in any sunny, airy spot."

Phyllis Hobson
Drying Vegetables, Fruits and Herbs

vinegar to each pint. Cover with boiling water, leaving ½ inch headroom. Adjust lids. Process in a pressure canner at 11 pounds pressure dial-gauge or 10 pounds weighted-gauge:

half-pints and pints. . . . 35 minutes

Freezing

Although not quite like fresh, peppers freeze beautifully and don't need blanching. Sweet peppers to be used in cooked dishes can be blanched to get more into a container. If desired, blanch in boiling water for 2-3 minutes.

Pack into containers, leaving no headroom if unblanched, or ½ inch headroom if blanched. Try flash-freezing diced peppers: spread them out on a tray to freeze, and put in containers when frozen. These can be used a little at a time, as they come apart easily.

Curing with Brine

Refer to Chapter 6.

Drying

Refer to Chapter 7.

Approximate Yield of Canned Vegetables

These are approximate yields and should be viewed as guidelines only. The actual number of jars will depend on the size and condition of the produce and the way an individual prepares and packs the produce in the jars. The weights of bushels, lugs, and boxes are regulated state by state, not by national guidelines. The yields are for seven quart jars or nine pint jars, the normal canner's capacity for one full batch.

VEGETABLE	QUANTITY	YIELD
Asparagus	24½ lb.	7 quarts
	16 lb.	9 pints
	31 lb. crate	7-12 quarts
Beans, dry	5 lb.	7 quarts
	3¼ lb.	9 pints
Beans, green and wax snaps	14 lb.	7 quarts
	9 lb.	9 pints
	30 lb. bushel	12-20 quarts
Beans, lima	28 lb.	7 quarts
	18 lb.	9 pints
	32 lb. bushel	6-10 quarts
Beets	21 lb.	7 quarts
	13½ lb.	9 pints
	52 lb. bushel	15-20 quarts
Carrots (without tops)	17½ lb.	7 quarts
	11 lb.	9 pints
	50 lb. bushel	17-25 quarts

VEGETABLE	QUANTITY	YIELD
Corn, cream style	20 lb. (in husks)	9 pints
	35 lb. bushel	12-20 pints
Corn, whole kernel	31½ lb.	7 quarts
	20 lb.	9 pints
	35 lb. bushel	6-11 quarts
Greens	28 lb.	7 quarts
	18 lb.	9 pints
	18 lb. bushel	3-9 quarts
Mushrooms	14½ lb.	9 pints
	7½ lb.	9 half-pints
Okra	11 lb.	7 quarts
	7 lb.	9 pints
	26 lb. bushel	16-18 quarts
Peas, green (in pods)	31½ lb.	7 quarts
	20 lb.	9 pints
	30 lb. bushel	5-10 quarts
Peppers, hot and sweet	9 lb.	9 pints
	25 lb. bushel	20-30 pints
Potatoes, sweet	17½ lb.	7 quarts
	11 lb.	9 pints
	50 lb. bushel	17-25 quarts
Potatoes, white	35 lb.	7 quarts
	22½ lb.	9 pints
	50 lb. bushel	8-12 quarts
Pumpkins and winter squash	16 lb.	7 quarts
	10 lb.	9 pints
Tomatoes (whole or quartered) hot pack	21 lb.	7 quarts
	13 lb.	9 pints
	53 lb. bushel	15-21 quarts
Tomatoes raw pack	22 lb.	7 quarts
	14 lb.	9 pints
	53 lb. bushel	17-20 quarts
Tomatoes juice	23 lb.	7 quarts
	14 lb.	9 pints
	53 lb. bushel	15-18 quarts
Tomatoes sauce, thin	35 lb.	7 quarts
	21 lb.	9 pints
	53 lb. bushel	10-12 quarts
Tomatoes sauce, thick	46 lb.	7 quarts
	28 lb.	9 pints
	53 lb. bushel	7-9 quarts

These figures are from the USDA guidelines.

Use pimientos that are ripe, crisp, and thick-walled.

Preparation

Wash first, then to peel, roast in a 400°F. oven for 3 to 4 minutes. Rinse off the charred skins in cold water. Remove seeds, stems, and blossom ends. Flatten whole pimientos.

Pressure Canning

Pack flattened pimientos into clean, hot jars, leaving 1 inch headroom. Add ¼ teaspoon salt and ½ tablespoon vinegar to half-pints, or ½ teaspoon salt and 1 tablespoon vinegar to pints. Do not add water. Adjust lids and process in a pressure canner at 11 pounds pressure dial-gauge or 10 pounds weighted-gauge:

> half-pints and pints. . . . 30 minutes

Freezing

Pack prepared pimientos into containers, leaving appropriate headroom (see page 170). Seal and freeze.

POTATOES, SWEET AND YAMS

There are two types of sweet potato—the dry meated and the moist or yam. Sweet potatoes are more delicate than white potatoes and are more difficult to store. Canning is the preferred method of keeping.

Harvesting

For summer eating, dig as needed when large enough. For storage, harvest when the plants are dead and the potatoes well matured. Avoid damaging with shovel or fork when digging, and handle gently. They should not be air-dried like white potatoes, so pack them directly into storage containers when harvesting.

Curing

Sweet potatoes will not keep well unless cured properly. They should be held for about 10 days under moist conditions at 80°-85°F., if possible. Cover the storage containers with paper or heavy cloth to keep up the humidity, and find a warm place (near a furnace or stove, for example) to cure them. If the temperature is below 75°F., the curing should last 2-3 weeks.

Storage

After curing, the sweet potatoes, like pumpkins and winter squash, should be stored in a moderately warm (55°-60°) and dry place. Avoid

---

☙ PIMIENTOS

Most people know the pimiento only from the near end of a stuffed olive. It is, however, a distinct type of heart-shaped sweet red pepper that is grown largely in California and warmer climes. Where grown, it often is used just as bell peppers are — stuffed, in strips in salads, or cooked with meat and egg dishes. The leading varieties of pimientos are Perfection, Tru-hart, and Panama.

☙ SWEET POTATOES

"You can dig sweet potatoes as soon as there is anything big enough to eat. Storing them well is something of a problem — for me, at least. To keep really well, they should be put in a very warm and humid place for eight to ten days before they go into the root cellar. I find it easier to can or freeze them."

Dick Raymond
Down-to-Earth Gardening Know-How

temperatures below 50°F. A closet or under a bed would make a better storage place than a cold cellar. (See Chapter 8.)

Pressure Canning

Choose small to medium potatoes. They should be mature, but not fibrous. They should be canned within 1-2 months of harvesting.

Hot pack. Wash and boil or steam potatoes for 15-20 minutes (until slightly soft). Do not mash or purée pieces. Pack hot sweet potatoes into hot jars, leaving 1 inch headroom. Cover with boiling water or light or medium syrup (see below), leaving 1 inch headroom. Adjust lids, and process in a pressure canner at 11 pounds pressure dial-gauge or 10 pounds weighted-gauge:

>   pints. . . . . . .65 minutes
>   quarts . . . . . .90 minutes

Syrup.
>   Light — 2 cups sugar and 4 cups water.
>   Medium — 3 cups sugar and 4 cups water.
>   Combine sugar and water and heat until dissolved.

Freezing

Use medium to large sweet potatoes that have been cured. Sort and wash. Cook until tender in water, steam, or oven. Let cool at room temperature. Peel, cut into slices or mash, or use whole. Optional: to prevent darkening, dip whole or cut-up sweet potatoes in a solution of ½ teaspoon lemon juice to 1 quart water for 5 seconds. Mix 2 tablespoons lemon or orange juice with each quart of mashed potatoes. Pack into containers, leaving appropriate headroom (see page 170). Seal and freeze.

Syrup pack. Sweet potatoes can be covered with cold syrup made of equal parts of sugar and water before freezing. Leave ample headroom (see page 170), seal, and freeze. Or simply roll pieces of sweet potato in sugar before packing and freezing.

POTATOES, WHITE

Harvesting

Potatoes can be harvested anytime after they start to form around the roots of the plants—just dig down next to the plant and take as many as you need, then cover the roots back up and leave the plant to grow more. This is accomplished most easily when potatoes are planted on the ground under a thick covering of hay, rather than in the soil. Tiny new potatoes are a special treat in mid-summer. Try them with fresh peas or beans and cream and butter. With a loaf of fresh french bread, a better dinner cannot be found!

THE BEST POTATOES

If you are the industrious-ant type, you will grow a bountiful crop of potatoes, wait until the tops are all dead, then store them by the bushel. But if you live more for today, you will sacrifice part of that crop, and enjoy far better eating.

When the tops are well up, run an inquisitive hand under the mulch or into the potato hill, depending on the method of growing you use, and seek out potatoes that have reached the size of golf balls. Pick enough for one meal, and plan on at least three or four per person. Sure, you'll be sacrificing what could be much larger potatoes if harvested later, but you'll also be enjoying the best potato-eating of your life.

FREEZING FRENCH FRIES

Here's a way to freeze oven french fries that will delight all members of your family. It's a method suggested by the Extension Service of Pennsylvania State University and tried with great success in the Garden Way kitchens.

Pare medium to large potatoes. Cut lengthwise into uniform strips about ⅜ inch thick. Rinse quickly in cold water to remove starch. Dry thoroughly.

Arrange in a shallow baking pan. Brush generously with melted fat. Bake in preheated oven at 450°F. until they begin to brown, turning occasionally. Remove from oven, cool in refrigerator as quickly as possible, and pack in moisture-vapor-proof containers. Label and freeze.

To serve, spread frozen fries on shallow baking pan and bake in preheated 450°F. oven until thawed and golden brown. Turn occasionally, season to taste.

The cooks at Pennsylvania recommend keeping these frozen for no more than a month.

For storage, potatoes are best harvested late in the fall when the tops are all dead and a skin has formed on potatoes that cannot be slipped or broken when you push your thumb across it. Late-maturing potatoes are the best for storage. Early varieties may begin to rot in the ground if left until fall, and the weather may be too warm to store them if dug sooner.

To harvest potatoes for storage, dig them up in the late fall on a dry day, being sure to dig deeply around every plant to get all the potatoes. There may be no more than one or two potatoes, or as many as a dozen at each plant. The potatoes should be spread out on a dry surface until the dirt has dried and fallen off them. Do not leave them out in the sun for any length of time, however, because they will turn green when exposed to light. This indicates the presence of solanine, which is poisonous if eaten in any quantity. Use up any potatoes damaged in harvesting, saving only the soundest for storage.

Storage

Potatoes will store moderately well under most conditions for the first few months, when they are normally dormant anyway — as long as they are kept in the dark. For longer storage, and to prevent rotting, softening, or early sprouting, try to achieve these more ideal conditions:

- Store potatoes under moderately moist conditions in the dark, at 35°-40°F.
- Store the potatoes in a slatted bin or big mesh bags, kept 1 or 2 inches off the floor. They need some air circulation, so pile them no more than 12-18 inches deep.

Pressure Canning

To common-store the potatoes is more sensible than canning, but there are times when it is convenient to have some already clean and peeled in a canning jar to be used at a moment's notice. Small ones can be canned whole; larger ones can be cubed.

Wash, peel, and wash again. Cut up if desired. Cubes can be dipped into a brine made of 1 teaspoon salt to 1 quart water to prevent darkening. They can also be placed in an ascorbic-acid solution (see page 164). Drain. Cover with boiling water and cook 2 minutes for cubes and 10 for whole potatoes. Drain.

Hot pack only. Pack hot potatoes into hot jars, leaving 1 inch headroom. Cover with boiling water, leaving 1 inch headroom. Adjust lids and process in a pressure canner at 11 pounds pressure dial-gauge or 10 pounds weighted-gauge:

> pints, whole or cubed. . . . .35 minutes
> quarts, whole or cubed . . . .40 minutes

Drying

Refer to Chapter 7.

PUMPKIN AND WINTER SQUASH

Harvesting

Harvest before the first severe frost, leaving an inch or so of stem on. If your thumbnail can penetrate a winter squash, it isn't suitable for root cellaring. It should be eaten soon or processed.

Storage

Pumpkins should be left in the sun to cure for a week before storing. They can be kept in a cool room where the temperature stays constant and the humidity is fairly low for most of the winter.

Preparation

The best cooking varieties are the little round sugar pumpkins, which have the thickest flesh. For making pies and puddings, it is convenient to have the pumpkin partially cooked, either cubed or strained. For cubed squash or pumpkin, wash and cut open, removing seeds and stringy insides. Pare and cut into 1-inch cubes. Add just enough water to cover and bring to a boil. Drain and reserve cooking liquid.

Pressure Canning

Hot pack only. Pack hot cubes into hot jars, leaving 1 inch headroom. Cover with boiling cooking liquid, leaving 1 inch headroom. Adjust lids. Process in a pressure canner at 11 pounds pressure dial-gauge or 10 pounds weighted-gauge:

pints. . . . . . .55 minutes
quarts . . . . . .90 minutes

Freezing

Wash pumpkin or squash and cut open. Remove seeds and stringy insides. Cut into large pieces and steam until soft, or cut in half if small enough and place face down in a shallow pan of water. Bake at 350°F. until soft. Scrape soft insides from rind and put through a food mill or strainer. Place the fine, fiber-free pulp in a pan placed in a larger bowl of cold water to cool. Stir occasionally. Pack into containers, leaving appropriate headroom (see page 170). Seal and freeze.

RUTABAGAS

Harvesting

Rutabagas, like turnips, are harvested for fresh use as soon as the roots are large enough; for storage they should be harvested as late in the

ANOTHER REASON FOR PUMPKINS

Most of us raise pumpkins for eating or for jack-o'-lanterns. But there's another reason for them, and that's the nutritious seeds they contain.

Many people don't like to eat them because of the bother of shelling them, but here science has come forward with a hand. The new Lady Godiva pumpkin is fat with seeds, and they can be eaten just as they come from the pumpkin, as they are naked (without hulls). These seeds can be eaten raw or roasted, and they're high in protein. But don't count on using the pumpkin as well, since it ranks low for table use.

BAKED RUTABAGAS

"Bake the rutabagas whole for about an hour or a little more in a 375° oven and serve them right in their skins with lots of butter, salt and pepper."

Marjorie Page Blanchard
Home Gardener's Cookbook

fall as possible before the ground freezes. In areas without severe winter weather they can be mulched and left in the garden for winter use.

Dig or pull the rutabagas, and leave them in the sun for a couple of hours until the soil dries and falls off. Trim off the stems to within about 1 inch of the top; do not cut the roots off.

Storage

To store the rutabagas, pack them in freshly cut sawdust or in sand. They should be kept in a cold place. (See Chapter 8 on common storage.)

Rutabagas can be frozen satisfactorily, but canning is undesirable because they discolor like turnips and develop a strong taste.

Freezing

Cut off the tops of tender young rutabagas. Wash and peel. Cut into cubes. Blanch for 2 minutes in boiling water. Cool immediately in ice cold water. Drain. Pack into containers, leaving appropriate headroom (see page 170). Seal and freeze.

For mashed rutabagas, continue cooking until tender, then mash. Cool by placing the pan in a bowl of cold water. Stir occasionally to speed up the cooling. Pack into containers, leaving appropriate headroom (see page 170). Seal and freeze.

SALSIFY

Salsify is the unsung hero of the vegetable garden, and it's difficult to explain the silence. Here's a plant that is easy to grow (you can almost plant and forget it), easy to harvest and store (leave it in the garden until you want it), and delicious (much like oysters in flavor, which accounts for its other name, *oyster plant*).

Harvesting

Salsify can be used anytime after it is half grown.

Storage

Treat like other root crops. At least an inch of stem should be left when the tops are cut off to help prevent the root from shriveling. Storage works well in an outdoor pit or where it grew in the garden.

SHALLOTS

The shallot is a mild-breathed member of the onion family, widely used in French *haute cuisine*, but certainly not a familiar figure in the American kitchen. This is a pity, considering its flavor, which is milder than onions, and has a hint, but not the muscle, of garlic.

Expensive in grocery stores, shallots are as easy to grow as their relatives. They are started from either seeds or the cloves themselves, as with garlic. Excellent "keepers," shallots will, like garlic, be in perfect condition for a year or more. Those for storage are pulled up only when the tops have turned brown, and the bulbs are then dried and separated. But they can be used, too, while still green. In this case, don't throw away the tops — cut them up for a delicious addition to salads.

Harvesting

Shallots taste like a delicate cross between onions and garlic. They grow in clusters of many separate cloves attached at the roots. For use in summer salads, the clusters can be pulled as needed.

Storage

For winter storage, treat like onions. We usually plant, harvest, and store them right along with the onion crop.

SOYBEANS

The soybean is the one vegetable that is a complete protein; that is, it contains all the essential amino acids needed by human beings. It is, however, low in one of them (methionine), so for completely balanced meals some animal protein (milk or cheese, for example) should be cooked or served with it.

Harvesting

Soybeans can be picked while green and the beans eaten as a fresh vegetable, or they can be allowed to mature until most of the pods are dry. In the fall when the plants are dying, pull the entire plant and stack them to dry out completely, as you would dry beans. Some varieties of soybeans are harder to remove from the shell than most other beans, and you may have to shell many of them by hand. This is done when they are dry and brittle, and it makes a good occupation for cold evenings in front of the fire. It will go quickly if many hands help.

Other varieties open readily and can be harvested and threshed like other dry beans. Be sure to harvest before they open naturally and spill your beans in the garden!

Storage

Store soybeans as you would other dry beans (see page 123).

Freezing

Pick beans while they're still in the green stage. Boil pods 5 minutes, blanching them and at the same time softening pods, so that, when cool, beans can be squeezed out of pods like toothpaste out of a tube. Rinse

THE RIGHT SOYBEANS

Gardeners impressed with the high food value of soybeans often run up against a practical problem in growing them, particularly if their gardens are in the northern section of the country.

The problem is finding a bean that will mature within the growing season of that region. Many of the common varieties take 100 or more days. Kanrich, a popular bean, is listed as 103 days, and it must not be planted before the date for the average last frost of the spring.

There are two approaches. One is to extend the season by starting beans indoors, using peat pots, or by covering the rows with Hotkaps, plastic, or cold frames. The second is to find seed companies that have specialized in short-season soybeans. Two of these are Stokes (Box 548, Buffalo, N.Y. 14240) and Johnny's Selected Seeds (Albion, Maine 04910).

and drain. Put into containers, leaving appropriate headroom (see page 170). Seal and freeze.

Cooking

To use the dried soybeans, wash and sort, then cover them with plenty of boiling water and let soak for several hours. Use them sparingly, as 1 cup dry will make about 3 cups when soaked. Drain and cover with fresh water (or use soaking water) and simmer for 2 to 3 hours, adding more water if they start to dry out.

A pressure cooker can be used to speed up the cooking of soybeans. Rinse the dry beans in cold water. Put 3 to 4 times as much water as dry beans in the pressure cooker and bring to a boil. Add the beans, lock cover, and bring to 10 pounds pressure. Cook for 20 to 25 minutes. Cool cooker under running water.

Other vegetables, seasonings, or salt pork or bacon can be added during the last hour of conventional cooking to overcome the uninteresting, "raw" flavor of the beans, or the plain cooked beans can be used in mixed casseroles or loaf dishes. Soybeans are delicious baked like other dry beans.

Pressure Canning

Use green soybeans. Prepare as for hot-pack lima beans (see page 125). Process in a pressure canner at 11 pounds pressure dial-gauge or 10 pounds weighted-gauge:

> pints. . . . . . .55 minutes
> quarts . . . . . .65 minutes

Soy Flour

Soy flour is a protein- and vitamin-rich supplement that can be added to other flour when making bread, cookies, and other baked goods. Use in small quantities because it will affect flavor and rising qualities. To make soy flour, freeze the dried beans, then run them through a hand or electric grain grinder. Their oil content may cause them to glaze the stones of a grinder if milled unfrozen.

SQUASH, SUMMER

Harvesting

Pick squash when very young with tender skins and immature seeds. They should be sliced but not peeled. If necessary, the slices can be halved or quartered so that they are all of uniform size. Older squash also can be used but only the firm flesh. These must be peeled, seeded, and the soft core removed before cutting the flesh into cubes. The blossoms can be sautéed for use in casseroles or soups when they are about 2 inches long and before they open. Zucchini can also be pickled if you have an overabundance. (See Chapter 5 on pickling.)

NANCY MERRILL'S BLUE RIBBON AWARD-WINNING ZUCCHINI BREAD

3 eggs
2 cups sugar
2 cups grated zucchini
1 cup vegetable oil
2 cups flour
¼ teaspoon baking powder
¼ teaspoon baking soda
1 teaspoon salt
3 teaspoons cinnamon
1 cup chopped nuts
3 teaspoons vanilla

Beat eggs. Add sugar, zucchini, and oil and mix. Sift all dry ingredients together and add to mixture. Add chopped nuts and vanilla. Bake in 350°F. oven for 1 hour and 15 minutes. Makes two small loaves.

Pressure Canning

Hot pack only. Cover washed and cut-up squash with boiling water and bring to a boil. Drain and reserve cooking liquid. Pack hot squash loosely into hot jars, leaving 1 inch headroom. Cover with boiling cooking liquid, leaving 1 inch headroom. Adjust lids and process in a pressure canner 11 pounds pressure dial-gauge or 10 pounds weighted-gauge:

> pints. . . . . . .30 minutes
> quarts . . . . . .40 minutes

Freezing

Prepare squash as for canning. Blanch in boiling water for 3 minutes. Cool immediately in cold water and drain. Pack into freezer containers, leaving appropriate headroom (see page 170). Seal and freeze.

Summer squash tends to be pretty rubbery when frozen this way. Try cooking and mashing it before freezing, or cook and put through a food mill or blender to purée. The squash purée can be used as a base for thick soups or combined with tomatoes for a thickened tomato sauce. Pack in appropriate containers, leaving ample headroom for wet pack (see page 170). Seal and freeze. Extra zucchini can be grated, squeezed dry, and frozen without blanching. Good in bread if used within a couple of months.

Drying

Refer to Chapter 7.

TOMATOES

Almost everyone who has a garden grows tomatoes, our most versatile fruit. Even a few plants placed in flower borders or in buckets on an apartment patio can produce enough tomatoes to preserve. During the season large quantities can be bought fresh at a farmers' market or picked yourself at a truck farm for reasonable prices to be put up at home.

The tomato has come a long way since the time it was called the "love apple" and was grown for its shiny appearance while being considered unfit to eat. Fortunately someone realized its potential as a food, and its many uses were developed: sliced, stuffed, stewed, juiced, and made into sauces.

Tomatoes are important as a source of vitamins A and C, having approximately one-tenth the vitamin A of an equal amount of carrots, and the juice having about one-third as much vitamin C as an equal amount of orange juice.

To ensure safe acidity for canning whole, crushed, or juiced tomatoes, you can add acid. Three kinds of acid are recommended: pure

---

LINDA'S SUMMER SQUASH CHOWDER

This is a delicious soup that will help you use up that extra zucchini and summer squash. Make it from fresh squash and freeze the soup, or use your frozen squash.

> 15 or 20 small squash, cut up
> 1 stick butter or margarine (½ cup)
> 2 cups chicken bouillon
> 1 large onion, chopped
> 1 package frozen chopped broccoli
> 2 cups milk
> flour and water for thickening

In a large pot, cook squash in ½ stick butter until just beginning to get tender. Add bouillon, onion, and broccoli. Cook until tender. Add 2 cups milk and cook a few minutes more. Add remaining ½ stick butter. Make a thin paste of flour and water. Stir into soup, and continue stirring until thickened and smooth. Add salt and pepper to taste. Makes about four quarts.

The danger of contaminated food is well known, but one other danger exists in home food-processing that is consistently overlooked—and it is one over which you have much control. That is burns. Every summer many people receive minor burns and some even need treatment in a hospital. Few other cooking procedures require such volumes of boiling water and steam.

So be careful! Keep small children from under foot when juggling large kettles of boiling water. Always wear shoes — a small spill on bare feet can be a forerunner of a much larger burn if you should then drop a kettle of water. Always open a pressure canner away from you to avoid a rush of steam in your face. Never use a damp towel or pot holder to lift a hot kettle, as the dampness conducts heat rapidly.

If you *are* burned, immediately immerse the burned area in cold water to reduce the amount of blister.

crystalline citric acid, bottled or fresh lemon juice, and white distilled (not cider) vinegar. None of these will affect the flavor of the tomatoes, as cider vinegar will.

Here are the recommended amounts:

Citric acid
      ¼ teaspoon per pint
      ½ teaspoon per quart

Lemon juice
      1 tablespoon per pint
      2 tablespoons per quart

White distilled vinegar
      1 tablespoon per pint
      2 tablespoons per quart

Place on top of the tomatoes in the canning jar; then adjust lids and process.

Tomatoes can be canned or frozen. We think the canned product has superior flavor, texture, and versatility. Once processed and stored on a shelf, it is ready to be used at a moment's notice for stewed tomatoes or as the base of a sauce. Frozen tomatoes tend to separate, making them less attractive for stewing. But if you are putting up small quantities, have space in your freezer, and prefer not to can them, then frozen tomato sauces and juice are fine. Also, you may prefer freezing mixtures of tomatoes and low-acid vegetables or meats to canning them, because they must be processed in a pressure canner.

Harvesting

Tomatoes are ripe and ready to harvest when they are a uniform red color (except, obviously, the yellow varieties). For best flavor and texture, be sure they are ripe but still firm before canning. If not, there will be tough spots that will end up as waste and the skins will be more difficult to peel. Tomatoes can also be used in an unripe, green state for pickles, relishes, mincemeat, and marmalade. Some recipes for green tomatoes are included in Chapters 5 and 6 on pickling and curing with brine.

Canning

Ripe tomatoes are canned whole or cut up (usually peeled) for use as stewed tomatoes or sauce, or they are cooked briefly and strained for juice, or cooked more for sauce and a lot more for paste. There may be no seasoning added, or some salt, or a variety of spices and herbs. If a low-acid vegetable is added, such as onion, green pepper, or celery, it is necessary to pressure-can your sauce (see Mixed Vegetables, page 139). Ketchup and chili sauces are exceptions, because the large amount of vinegar used increases the acidity enough to allow safe processing in a boiling-water bath.

Ripe tomatoes bruise easily, which spoils their flavor. So be careful when you pick, pack, and carry them. They should be stacked not more than two layers deep in box or basket, unless they are to be removed immediately.

Many bacteria harbored in the soil are carried into the kitchen. So wash tomatoes, utensils, canning jars, work areas, and hands thoroughly with detergent immediately before canning. Cut away any hint of decay from the fruit; do not use any that are more than slightly cracked or otherwise damaged or diseased. Use only firm, just-ripe tomatoes. Take no short-cuts. And before tasting or eating tomatoes, boil vigorously in an open pan for 15 minutes.

These directions call for peeling the tomatoes, but this can be omitted if you expect to cook them further and put them through a food mill. Some people use them in stews, skins and all, and say that by the time you are ready to serve, you hardly know the skins are there.

Tomatoes peel easily if scalded for ½-1 minute in boiling water, then chilled in ice water. We use a blanching kettle to scald the tomatoes, keeping them in the steaming basket for chilling and draining.

Remove the tomatoes from the cold water after a minute. Do not allow them to soak longer, or they will become soggy and lose nutrients. Pull off the skins with a paring knife and cut out the stem and core, removing any blemishes, green spots, or bruises.

Raw pack. (See page 37 for illustrated directions.) Wash the tomatoes thoroughly with lots of water and a vegetable brush to remove soil and any pesticide residues. Peel.

If the tomatoes are too large to fit into your jars easily, cut them into quarters. The time required for processing them is so long that even if you leave them whole they will not retain a firm round shape. Pack the tomatoes tightly into clean canning jars, pushing down on them to force their juice to run out and cover them. Leave ½ inch headroom over juice and tomatoes.

A frequent mistake made with tomatoes is to plop too few into the jar, press gently and seal, only to find after processing a small concentration of tomatoes floating near the top of the jar and a lot of juice below. So do not hesitate to squeeze in as many tomatoes as you can, and if they are very juicy you may find there is enough extra juice from several quarts to pour off for either drinking fresh or canning separately.

Add acid, if desired, according to directions on page 156. Adjust lids and process in a boiling-water bath:

> pints. . . . . . .40 minutes
> quarts . . . . . .45 minutes

Remove when done and cool on a rack or towel. Check for a good seal, remove bands, wash jars, label, and store in a cool, dark place. Tomatoes will darken if stored in the light.

Preferred method — hot pack. Tomatoes can also be preserved by the hot-pack method, which makes a more solid pack.

Wash, peel, and quarter tomatoes; put them in a kettle and bring to a boil, stirring to prevent sticking. Ladle them boiling hot into clean, hot jars, leaving ½ inch headroom. Add acid per instructions on page 156. Adjust lids and process in a boiling-water bath:

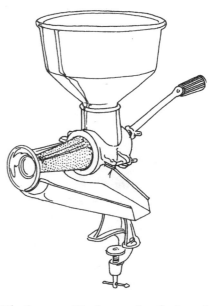

The Squeezo Strainer makes fast work of removing skins and seeds from tomatoes, providing a thick, delicious purée.

BASIC TOMATO KETCHUP

8-10 pounds very ripe to-
matoes (35-45 medium)
1-2 ripe sweet red pep-
pers (use all green if red
are unavailable)
1-2 sweet green peppers
4-5 onions
3 cups cider vinegar
1-3 cups sugar or honey
3 tablespoons salt

Tie in a cheesecloth bag:

½-1½ teaspoons
whole allspice
½-1½ teaspoons
whole cloves
½-1½ teaspoons bro-
ken stick cinnamon

Quarter tomatoes, removing blossom and stem ends and blemishes. Seed and cut up peppers; dice onions. Mix all vegetables and cook until tender (15 to 30 minutes). Put through a food mill. (Or raw vegetables can be put through a blender, ¾ full at a time, and then cooked down.) Add all remaining ingredients, except vinegar. Simmer uncovered, stirring often, until thick. Add vinegar and cook an additional 15 minutes. Remove bag of spices; ladle into clean, hot pint jars. Adjust lids and process in a boiling-water bath for 15 minutes. Yields four or five pints.

pints . . . . . . .40 minutes
quarts . . . . . .45 minutes

Cool and store as for raw-pack tomatoes.

Pressure Canning

Process for the recommended times and pressures below:

Dial-gauge pressure canner

pints	15 minutes	6 pounds
quarts	10 minutes	11 pounds

Weighted-gauge pressure canner

pints	15 minutes	5 pounds
quarts	10 minutes	10 pounds

All canned tomatoes should be boiled 15 minutes in an open pan before tasting or using. They can be used for stewed tomatoes, adding a favorite seasoning with croutons, or as a base for chili con carne and other tomato dishes. For a smooth sauce, put the tomatoes through a food mill to remove seeds and skins. You also can put them through a blender, which breaks all parts down, making a good base for soups and spaghetti sauce. For a different breakfast or lunch dish, try canned tomatoes served on waffles, topped with grated cheese.

Freezing

Frozen tomatoes are particularly good for casseroles, but they are not as convenient to use as canned, since they must be defrosted before using.

Wash fresh, ripe tomatoes. Blanch for ½ minute in boiling water, chill in cold water, peel, and quarter. Cool in a pan set in cold water. Stir occasionally. Or cook further, then cool. Pack into containers, leaving ample headroom for wet pack (see page 170). Seal and freeze.

Freezing stewed tomatoes. Cook peeled tomatoes with peppers, celery, and onions to taste. Simmer for 10 to 20 minutes. Place cooled container in ice water and stir occasionally. Pack into containers, leaving ample headroom for wet pack (see page 170). Seal and freeze.

Salad tomatoes. You can try freezing a few small tomatoes whole or cut into wedges for use in salads. Success will depend on careful handling, very fast freezing, and storage for only a few months. They should be thawed only partially before being used, leaving some ice crystals in the tomatoes for good texture. Using small, firm, ripe tomatoes, scald briefly, ¼-½ minute, dip briefly in cold water, peel, and core. Quarter or leave whole, pack loosely in freezer containers, leaving no headroom, seal and freeze in the coldest part of the freezer (turned down to -19° or -20°F., if possible). Use within 2 or 3 months in salads.

Storage

Green tomatoes can be stored for 1 or 2 months, depending on their ripeness when brought in and the storage temperature. Our last one is usually ripened and gone by the end of November, and it always amazes us how good they taste compared to "fresh" ones bought in the stores at that time of year.

We cover our tomato plants in the garden with heavy cloths when the first light frosts come, but when a severe frost is warned we bring in all the tomatoes left on the vines, except those that are diseased or very small. Tomatoes will ripen, but will not grow any larger in storage than they were when picked, so only sound, full-sized fruit need be brought in. Tomatoes planted late, or varieties that require a longer growing time, will provide the best green tomatoes.

Sort the tomatoes according to ripeness, and store spread out on newspapers on shelves or floor. Cover with more newspaper to keep them dark, and the air around them moist; otherwise, they will shrivel up. Do not put them in the sunlight to ripen; it tends to rot them instead. The tomatoes can be washed before storing, or not; but do not try to wipe off soil because it will cause sand-scarring, which can lead to decay.

The warmer tomatoes are, the more quickly they will ripen. At 65°-70°F. the mature green tomatoes (those that have started to turn red or are whitish at the blossom end) will ripen in about 2 weeks. At 55° it will take up to 4 weeks. The less-mature tomatoes will take longer to ripen. If too moist, they may rot first; if too dry, they may shrivel up and never ripen. Check the tomatoes every week or so to remove those that have spoiled as well as the ripe ones.

Tomatoes also can be brought in on the vine. The plants are pulled, roots and all, and hung up in a warmish shed or cellar. The tomatoes will gradually ripen right on the vine. Some are bound to get bruised between garden and cellar, and the debris that drops to the floor makes a mess. However, if you're in a hurry to beat Jack Frost, this method is worth a try.

Drying

Refer to Chapter 7.

TOMATO JUICE

This healthful drink can be easily produced and preserved at home. It can be chilled and drunk as it is, or doctored to make a tomato juice cocktail. It also can be used as a base for soups, or cooked down for sauce when needed. It is quick and easy to make, requiring little cooking time before canning. In fact, the less time, the better, to preserve the most vitamin C, which is destroyed by overcooking and by exposure to air.

Ripe, juicy tomatoes fresh from the garden make the best juice. Pick tomatoes in their prime (firm and not overripe), and wash thoroughly. Cut into quarters and remove every blemish and hint of rot, green and white spots, and blossom and stem ends. We go so far as to taste each one, because one tomato with an off-flavor will spoil a whole batch.

Put the tomatoes in a kettle (enamelware or stainless steel, preferably) and simmer over medium heat, stirring often to prevent sticking. Do not boil. Cook just long enough for the tomatoes to be soft and juicy.

CHILI SAUCE

Follow the basic ketchup recipe on page 158, adding 1 or 2 hot chili peppers or ½ teaspoon ground red peppers. Peel tomatoes and cut the vegetables up fine. Cook down without putting through a food mill.

Variations to basic chili sauce. For a different flavor try adding any of the following seasonings to your chili sauce: celery or celery seed, basil, bay leaf, apples or applesauce, mustard seeds or dry mustard, peppercorns.

1. Sort, wash, and cut up red, ripe tomatoes. Put in a kettle and simmer over medium heat, stirring often. Cook until soft and juicy.

2. Put hot tomatoes through a food mill, press, or sieve.

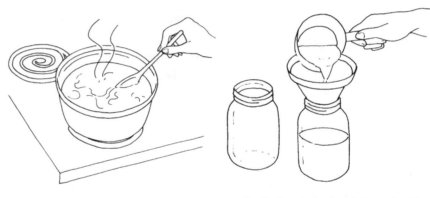

3. Put juice back into kettle and reheat just to boiling.

4. Ladle hot juice into clean, hot jars, leaving ½ inch headroom. Adjust lids. Process in a boiling-water bath for 35 minutes for pints and 40 for quarts. Remove jars.

Put them through a food mill, food press, or sieve. The finer the sieve, the finer the pulp of the juice will be and the less it will settle out after processing. There should be little waste, mostly seeds and skins, if the tomatoes are ripe enough.

Pour the juice back into the kettle and reheat just to boiling. Ladle the hot juice into clean, hot jars, leaving ½ inch headroom. Add acid per instructions on page 156. Adjust lids and process in a boiling-water bath:

pints......35 minutes
quarts......40 minutes

Remove from hot water as soon as time is up in order not to overcook. Cool and store as for canned tomatoes.

TOMATO SAUCE

You can put up tomato sauce with no seasoning or just salt, waiting until you are ready to use it to add appropriate seasonings. Or you can add spices and sugar before canning. Chili sauce and ketchup are, of course, seasoned first.

One advantage of canning sauce rather than juice or whole tomatoes is that you cook out much of the water and thus reduce the number of jars and the amount of space needed.

To make a plain tomato sauce, follow the directions for making juice, except the tomatoes must be cooked (either before or after straining) for 1 to 2 hours, or as long as it takes to reduce the water and thicken them as much as desired. Then proceed to can the sauce as you would juice. To reduce the cooking time, turn the tomatoes into a fine strainer to drain off the watery liquid, saving it to drink or for soups. The remaining pulp will cook down quickly.

For ketchups and other seasoned sauces, add onions and peppers when cooking begins and before putting through a food mill. Then add other seasonings. For a chunkier chili sauce, peel and cut up vegetables before cooking and do not put through food mill. The vinegar in ketchups and chili sauces raises the acidity of the total mixture enough so that they can be processed in a boiling-water bath despite the addition of the low-acid vegetables.

TOMATO PASTE

Traditionally tomato paste was a dried product, cooked until thick and spread on boards or paper to dry in the sun. It then was rolled into balls, dipped in oil, and stored.

Nowadays we cook it down over low heat to a thick paste, stirring frequently to prevent scorching. A large, heavy skillet will produce the best results by providing more surface area for heating and evaporating the fluid. Avoid using iron, however, since the acid in tomatoes causes a chemical reaction with the metal.

Prepare tomatoes as for tomato juice. Cook 1 hour and put through a food mill or sieve. Measure and add ½ teaspoon citric acid (or 2 tablespoons lemon juice or distilled white vinegar) for every 4 cups of sauce. Continue cooking until thick.

When the paste is the desired consistency, pack it hot into small (half-pint) jars, leaving ½ inch headroom. Adjust lids and process in a boiling-water bath for 35 minutes. Remove jars.

TURNIPS

Harvesting

Turnips are used for both the roots and the greens. For greens choose a variety that is especially good for that purpose. The greens are

TURNIPS

There's a cycle of unpopularity surrounding the turnip, and you can break it by not ignoring this blue-collar member of the gardening family. Turnips get planted and weeded—and then ignored until they have grown big and strong. Eventually someone remembers that the turnips should be picked, and they are harvested and cooked, and there's general agreement not to grow turnips again because they are too woody and too bitter, no matter how they are cooked. Break this chain of events by harvesting the turnips *before* they are full grown, while they are small and tender —and good to eat.

ready about 30 days after planting, when the leaves are big enough to cook. Harvest them then, by cutting off all but a few of the smallest ones, which should be left on the plant to support the growth of the root. As the plant matures, the leaves become tough and bitter and not good for eating. Turnip greens can be preserved like spinach and other greens. (Refer to Greens, page 136.)

The turnip root should be harvested as late in the fall as possible before the ground freezes. Pull or dig up the roots, and leave them in the sun for several hours until the soil dries and falls off them.

Storage

Trim the stems to within about 1 inch of the turnip; do *not* cut off the roots. Pack in fresh-sawed sawdust or sand and store in a cold, dark place. The ideal storage temperature is as close to 32°F. as possible with a moist atmosphere. (For further details on root crops, see Chapter 8.) Turnips also can be waxed. Trim roots and stem, wash or wipe clean, and apply a thin coat of melted paraffin with a brush.

Canning

Pressure-canning turnips is possible but undesirable because they develop a strong flavor and off-color when canned.

Freezing

Turnips can be prepared as for serving and frozen. Cut off tops of young, tender turnips. Wash and peel. Cut into cubes. Blanch for 2 minutes in boiling water. Cool immediately in ice cold water. Drain. Pack into containers, leaving appropriate headroom (see page 170). Seal and freeze.

Curing with Brine

Refer to Sauerruben, page 87.

CHAPTER 10

Fruits and Berries

ewer people grow their own fruit than grow their own vegetables. Fruit trees take time to care for, and often they take years to bear. Many berry fruit crops require more space than the average home gardener has available. But this need not discourage the home canner. Co-ops offer excellent buys on fruit by the bushel. Local farms often invite public picking of strawberries, apples, cherries, blueberries, plums, tomatoes, and even raspberries. (Be sure to pick with care and according to directions. Abuse of carefully nurtured trees and plants is one reason more growers don't let the public pick.) Roadside stands often have high-quality fresh fruit at reasonable prices. Even foraging for wild berries can provide a pleasant family expedition.

As with other produce, pick or buy only the best. Unripened fruit is lower in flavor and sugar content. Cherries, plums, and berries, especially, should be firm, never overripe or bruised. To ensure the best quality of apricots, nectarines, peaches, pears, and plums, allow them to ripen for one or more days between harvesting and processing.

Many fruits, with the exception of applesauce, pears, plums, and peaches, freeze more easily than they can and retain a better color and shape that way. If you prefer to can, however, the basic procedure is the same for all fruits, since they are all high in acid and can be safely processed in a boiling-water bath instead of a pressure canner. The specific directions for preserving each fruit by whatever methods are appropriate are given later in this chapter. As we said in the previous chapter, if you live more than 1,000 feet above sea level, call your county Extension Service to find out what pressure is needed for canning at your altitude.

It is imperative for safety to sterilize empty jars to be used for any fruit, jam, jelly, or pickled product processed in a boiling-water bath for 10 minutes or less. To sterilize empty jars, put them right side up on the rack in a boiling-water canner. Fill the canner and jars with hot (not boiling) water to 1 inch above the tops of the jars. Boil 10 minutes at altitudes less than 1,000 feet. At higher elevations, boil 1 additional minute for each additional 1,000 feet elevation. Remove and drain hot, sterilized jars one at a time. Save the hot water for processing.

Chill the fruit first, and then wash it *gently*; this can't be overemphasized, unless you've seen valuable raspberries go to pieces under a heavy stream of water. Don't let fruits sit in water.

If you want a firm product that retains its shape, raw packing is a necessity. Also, a *tight* pack will prevent shrinkage that allows the fruit to float to the top of the jar — which won't affect the keeping qualities of your product, only the esthetic ones.

With most hot packs and all raw packs, a syrup or fruit juice will be needed to can fruit. This addition does not prevent spoilage of these foods, rather it helps the fruit retain its color, flavor, and shape. Cover the fruit completely to prevent darkening.

Syrups are made from water and sugar, heated and brought to a boil before using. The table on page 169, taken from the most current USDA guidelines, offers a syrup for every use. Syrups vary in sugar content from "very light," which most closely approximates the natural sugar content of many fruits, to a "very heavy" syrup to use with sour fruits. Many fruits that are typically packed in heavy syrup are excellent when packed in lighter syrups. It is recommended that you use the lightest syrup possible as it contains the fewest calories from added sugar. Honey or corn syrup can be substituted for half the sugar in a recipe, or more if you like the flavor. If the honey is strong, be cautious, lest it overpower the fruit.

Canning fruits with sugar syrups is a long-accepted practice. However, if you are concerned about adding extra calories or processed sugar to your freshly harvested fruits, you may want to try using fruit juice to can your fruits.

Bottled or canned juice, or frozen juice reconstituted with water, can be used in this process. Boil the juice in an enameled or stainless pan and pack fruits in the hot juice. A number of different juices can be used, depending on your personal taste and preference. Try several combinations. Cranberry juice and apricots, peaches, or pears make a beautiful addition to a Christmas compote, not to mention how pretty the jars look lined up on the shelf. Apple juice works well with sour or sweet cherries. Pineapple juice or white grape juice is delicious with pears, peaches, or nectarines.

The juices used in canning fruits have the advantage of not having to be drained off and discarded as do the heavier sugar syrups. They can be chilled and used to drink or cook with. You may find it necessary to

USING AN ANTI-OXIDANT

Discoloration is common with some fruits — especially apples and peaches — and a few vegetables. Work quickly and in small batches, and treat them with any of the following anti-oxidants.

1. A commercial preparation such as Fruit Fresh can be used according to label directions.
2. Add 1 teaspoon ascorbic acid (vitamin C) to a cup of water. Dip the fruit in as you go along. Or add ¼ teaspoon ascorbic acid as you pack the fruit into jars if you didn't soak them beforehand. Ascorbic acid in a crystalline form can be obtained at drugstores.
3. Regular 500 mg. vitamin C tablets are economical and easily found. Crush and dissolve 6 tablets per 1 gallon of water as a treatment solution.
4. A solution of 2 tablespoons salt and 2 tablespoons vinegar can be added to 1 gallon cold water to slice fruit into before packing. Work quickly and drain thoroughly, since food values will deteriorate after 10 minutes in this solution.
5. Substitute 4 teaspoons of citric acid or 5 tablespoons of lemon juice per gallon of water for the salt and vinegar in number 4.

dilute the juice slightly with water for drinking, as it may be a little more concentrated than it was when you started.

After packing your fruit and adjusting the lids, process all fruit in a boiling-water bath for the time called for in the specific directions. Remember to begin timing only when the water has reached a rolling boil.

Store all your jars in a cold, dry, dark place. Red berries, especially, will fade when exposed to light.

Approximate Yield of Canned Fruits

These are approximate yields and should be viewed as guidelines only. The actual number of jars will depend on the size and condition of the produce and the way an individual prepares and packs the produce in the jars. The weights of bushels, lugs, and boxes are regulated state by state, not by national guidelines. The yields are for seven quart jars or nine pint jars, the normal canner's capacity for one full batch.

FRUIT	QUANTITY	YIELD
Apples	19 lb.	7 quarts
	12¼ lb.	9 pints
	48 lb. bushel	16-18 quarts
Applesauce	21 lb.	7 quarts
	13½ lb.	9 pints
	48 lb. bushel	14-19 quarts
Apricots	16 lb.	7 quarts
	10 lb.	7 pints
	50 lb. bushel	20-25 quarts
Berries, whole	12 lb.	7 quarts
	8 lb.	9 pints
	24 lb. crate	18-24 quarts
Cherries	17½ lb.	7 quarts
	11 lb.	9 pints
	25 lb. lug	8-12 quarts
Grapefruit and orange sections	15 lb.	7 quarts
	13 lb.	9 pints
Grapes, green seedless	14 lb.	7 quarts
	9 lb.	9 pints
	26 lb. lug	12-14 quarts
Nectarines, peaches, and pears	17½ lb.	7 quarts
	11 lb.	9 pints
	48-50 lb. bushel	16-25 quarts
Pineapple	21 lb.	7 quarts
	13 lb.	9 pints
Rhubarb	10½ lb.	7 quarts
	7 lb.	9 pints
	28 lb. lug	14-28 quarts

APPLES

Wash, pare, core, and cut into pieces. (If you like apple jelly, save the cores and peels to boil down for jelly.) Use of an anti-oxidant is optional but recommended (see page 164).

Boiling-Water Bath

Hot pack. Prepare as above. Boil 5 minutes in thin syrup, juice, or water. Pack hot fruit into hot, sterilized jars. Cover with hot, thin syrup, leaving ½ inch headroom. Adjust lids. Process in a boiling-water bath:

> pints and quarts . . . . 20 minutes

Freezing

Wash, peel, core, and slice apples. For appropriate headroom, see chart on page 170.

Syrup pack. Put into a rigid container and cover with a medium syrup, allowing appropriate headroom. Seal and freeze.

Sugar pack. To each quart of prepared apples, add ½ cup sugar and stir. Pack into containers, leaving appropriate headroom. Seal and freeze.

A tip. Freeze unsweetened or presweetened apple slices (treated with an anti-oxidant) in a pie tin until solid. Then remove the pie tin and wrap apple slices in freezer paper. The pie-shaped apples are ready to slip into a pie crust later.

Drying

Refer to Chapter 7.

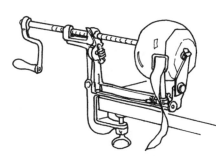

The old-fashioned apple parer that screws onto a table will quickly peel apples with a few turns of the hand crank. A simple coring knife also is helpful at apple-harvest time, as are gadgets that section and core an apple in one push.

APPLESAUCE

Wash and quarter sound apples. Don't remove skins, as they provide color. Put in a kettle with 2 inches of water. Cover and cook until soft, stirring occasionally to prevent scorching. Put through a food mill or press, adding sugar and cinnamon to taste (these can be added later if desired).

Boiling-Water Bath

Hot pack. Pack hot applesauce into hot, clean jars, leaving ½ inch headroom. Adjust lids and process in a boiling-water bath. (See illustrated instructions on page 167.)

> pints . . . . . . 15 minutes
> quarts. . . . . . 20 minutes

CANNING APPLESAUCE

1. *Cut up apples and place in a kettle with enough water to prevent burning. Cover. Stir often. Add a stick of cinnamon if desired.*

2. *When apples are soft, put them through a food mill or strainer. If desired, add sugar or other sweetener to taste, up to 1 cup per dozen apples.*

3. *Heat applesauce just to boiling, stirring often.*

4. *Pour into hot, clean jars, leaving ½ inch headroom. Wipe rims with a damp cloth. Adjust lids and process in a boiling-water bath for 15 minutes for pints and 20 minutes for quarts.*

Freezing

Cool prepared applesauce and pack into rigid containers, leaving appropriate headroom (see page 170). Seal and freeze.

Remember, thawing applesauce takes some time. If you will be using it often at the last minute, can it.

APRICOTS

Boiling-Water Bath

Ripened apricots can be canned whole or the pits can be removed from fruit that is harvested before it is completely ripe. Treat with an antioxidant (page 164) if desired.

Raw pack. Wash, sort, and cut into halves. Peel if desired. Pit. Pack into hot, clean jars, leaving ½ inch headroom. Cover with hot medium or thin syrup or juice, leaving ½ inch headroom. Adjust lids. Process in a boiling-water bath:

> pints . . . . . . 25 minutes
> quarts. . . . . . 30 minutes

Hot pack. Wash and scald apricots. Slip skins and remove pits. Cook apricots, a few at a time, in a thin or medium syrup or fruit juice of your choice until heated through. Pack hot into hot, clean jars, leaving ½ inch headroom. Cover with boiling syrup, leaving ½ inch headroom. Adjust lids. Process in a boiling-water bath:

> pints . . . . . . 20 minutes
> quarts. . . . . . 25 minutes

Freezing

Wash, halve, or slice. Pit. If not peeled, place in boiling water for ½ minute to keep skins tender. Cool immediately. See page 170 for appropriate headroom.

Syrup pack. Pack apricots in containers. Optional but recommended: add ¾ teaspoon crystalline ascorbic acid to each quart of medium syrup. Cover with syrup, leaving appropriate headroom. Seal and freeze.

Sugar pack. Add ½ cup sugar to each quart prepared fruit. Stir to dissolve. Pack into containers, leaving appropriate headroom. Seal and freeze.

Purée or crushed. Peel fully ripe apricots by dunking them in boiling water and cooling them immediately in cold water. Peel, slice, and pit. Crush with a masher for crushed, or use a food processor, food mill, or blender for purée. Add 1 cup sugar to 1 quart fruit. Optional: add ¼ teaspoon crystalline ascorbic acid dissolved in ¼ cup water to fruit before adding sugar. Pack into containers, leaving appropriate headroom. Seal and freeze.

AVOCADOS

Few of us are lucky enough to grow our own avocados or live where they are grown, but they are on special sale occasionally. Some like them puréed for milkshakes and ice cream, but we love guacamole salad or dip for chips.

Peel the avocado. Then mash soft but not mushy. Add ⅛ teaspoon crystalline ascorbic acid or 2 tablespoons lemon juice to 1 quart of purée. Pack into containers, leaving appropriate headroom (see page 170). Seal and freeze. When thawed, season the guacamole with chopped onion, tomato, and hot pepper.

Preparing and Using Syrups

| SYRUP TYPE | APPROX. % SUGAR | FOR 9-PT LOAD* | | FOR 7-QT LOAD | | SUGGESTED USE |
		CUPS WATER	CUPS SUGAR	CUPS WATER	CUPS SUGAR	
Very light	10	6½	¾	10½	1¼	Approximates natural sugar level in most fruits and adds the fewest calories.
Light	20	5¾	1½	9	2¼	Very sweet fruit. Try a small amount the first time to see if your family likes it.
Medium	30	5¼	2¼	8¼	3¾	Sweet apples, sweet cherries, berries, grapes.
Heavy	40	5	3¼	7¾	5¼	Tart apples, apricots, sour cherries, gooseberries, nectarines, peaches, pears, plums.
Very heavy	50	4¼	4¼	6½	6¾	Very sour fruit. Try a small amount the first time to see if your family likes it.

Procedure. For raw packs, heat water and sugar together; bring to a boil and pour over raw fruits in jars. For hot packs, bring water and sugar to boil, add fruit, reheat to boil, and fill into jars immediately.

* This amount is also adequate for a 4-quart load.

BERRIES

Most berries can be categorized as either firm or soft and processed accordingly. Blueberries, elderberries, currants, gooseberries, and huckleberries are firm berries; blackberries, dewberries, loganberries, raspberries, and youngberries are soft. Fresh raspberries are almost a vanishing fruit for most families, so if you can buy, pick, or grow them, appreciate them.

Don't overlook picking from the wild. Elderberries for wine, blackberries, and black raspberries, small blueberries, and even cranberries (page 171) are often found growing wild, and the picking makes a memorable event for families. Confirm your identification with a good field guide before tasting if you are unsure.

Boiling-Water Bath

Raw pack. Recommended for soft berries and blueberries. Carefully wash berries and drain. Fill jars, shaking down gently, leaving ½ inch headroom. Cover with hot thin or medium syrup or fruit juice, leaving ½ inch headroom. Adjust lids and process in a boiling-water bath:

pints . . . . . . 15 minutes
quarts. . . . . . 20 minutes

Hot pack. Most of the firm berries listed above make a better canned fruit when hot-packed. Wash and sort. *Slowly* bring to a boil, treating the fruit as carefully as possible. Shake the kettle to prevent sticking rather than stirring the berries.

Fill hot, clean jars with berries and a thin syrup or fruit juice to cover, leaving ½ inch headroom. Adjust lids. Process in a boiling-water bath:

pints and quarts . . . . . . 15 minutes

Freezing

It is possible to freeze berries to be used for making jellies or jam at your leisure. Be sure to label them with how much sugar has been added and adjust your jelly or jam recipe accordingly.

All berries. Wash, sort, drain. Optional: steam firm berries 1 minute to tenderize skins, cooking immediately.

Individually frozen. Place clean, sorted berries on a cookie sheet in freezer and freeze until firm. Pack into containers and keep frozen.

Syrup pack. Pack berries into containers, covering with medium syrup, leaving appropriate headroom (see page 170). Seal and freeze.

Sugar pack. Recommended for pies. Add ½ cup sugar to each quart of fruit, and mix thoroughly. Pack into containers, leaving appropriate headroom (see page 170). Seal and freeze.

Unsweetened pack. Pack berries into containers, leaving appropriate headroom. Seal and freeze.

Crushed or puréed. Crush by using blender or food mill. Stir in 1 cup sugar to each quart fruit. Pack into containers, leaving appropriate headroom (see page 170). Seal and freeze.

Drying

Refer to Chapter 7.

CHERRIES

Use tree-ripened cherries. Stem, sort, and wash. Drain and pit. Pitting can be done with a commercial cherry pitter or a sharp paring knife (with some loss of shape). Or unbend a paper clip so you have two U's and use the U on either side as a pitter. Cherries are tasty canned with apple juice or white grape juice.

Boiling-Water Bath

Raw pack. Prepare as above. Fill jars compactly with cherries. Cover with thin syrup, water, or juice, leaving ½ inch headroom. Adjust lids.

Process in a boiling-water bath:

      pints . . . . . . 20 minutes
      quarts. . . . . . 25 minutes

Hot pack. Prepare as above. Add ½ cup water, juice, or syrup for each quart of drained fruit. Slowly bring to a boil, adding water if it sticks. Boil covered. Pack hot into hot, clean jars. Shake down, cover with syrup, leaving ½ inch headroom. Adjust lids. Process in a boiling-water bath:

      pints . . . . . . 15 minutes
      quarts. . . . . . 20 minutes

Freezing

Red cherries are usually best. Process quickly. Some people find freezing with the pit in gives an off-flavor, but we haven't found this to be so. Pitting can be very tedious, so if you have picked quarts, think about freezing some with pits in, to be pitted when used. If pitted when semi-frozen, they do nicely. See page 170 for appropriate headroom.

Sugar pack. Prepare as above. Add ¾ cup sugar to 1 quart fruit. Mix well until dissolved. Pack into containers, leaving appropriate headroom. Seal and freeze.

Syrup pack. Prepare as above. Pack into containers, covering with medium or heavy syrup, leaving appropriate headroom. Seal and freeze.

Puréed. Crush prepared cherries. Heat to boiling, cool, and press through a food mill or blender. Add ¾ cup sugar to 1 quart fruit. Pack into containers, leaving appropriate headroom. Seal and freeze.

Crushed. Prepare as above. Crush, adding ¾ cup sugar to 1 quart fruit. Mix well. Pack into containers, leaving appropriate headroom. Seal and freeze.

Drying

Refer to Chapter 7.

CRANBERRIES

Buy cranberries when on sale and save for sauce or breads.

Boiling-Water Bath

For cranberry sauce, prepare as follows:

      1 quart cranberries
      1 cup water
      2 cups sugar

Wash and sort berries, adding water and cooking until they are soft and pop. Press through a sieve, adding sugar, and boil for 3 minutes.

Pour into clean, hot jars, leaving ½ inch headroom. Adjust lids. Process in a boiling-water bath. Yields two pints.

pints . . . . . . 15 minutes
quarts. . . . . . 20 minutes

Freezing

Freeze directly in the box or bag from the store. After thawing for use, wash and sort. Or prepare cranberry sauce according to directions above, cool, and pack into containers, leaving appropriate headroom (see page 170). Seal and freeze.

GRAPEFRUIT AND ORANGES

Grapefruit and oranges, in season, are often good buys and can be purchased by the bushel through a co-op. Their season, late winter, is when the freezer is getting low.

Use extra-meaty fruits. Wash and peel, cutting out membrane and seeds. Save juice.

Syrup pack. Pack into containers. Cover with the juice or a medium syrup. Leave appropriate headroom (see page 170). Seal and freeze.

Grapefruit and orange sections can also be canned. The flavor of orange sections is best if they are canned with equal parts of grapefruit. Grapefruit can be canned without oranges.

Raw pack. Wash and peel fruit, cutting out membrane and seeds. Save juice. Prepare a very light, a light, or a medium syrup and bring to a boil. Fill sterile jars with sections and hot syrup, leaving ½ inch headroom. Adjust lids and process:

pints and quarts . . . . . . 10 minutes

GRAPES

New varieties of green seedless grapes are being grown more and more, even in colder climates. Choose unripe, tight-skinned, green seedless grapes, preferably harvested 2 weeks before they reach optimum eating quality. These are best canned with white grape juice or a very light or light syrup. Stem, wash, and drain grapes.

Raw pack. Fill jars with grapes and hot syrup or juice, leaving 1 inch headroom. Adjust lids and process:

pints . . . . . . 15 minutes
quarts. . . . . . 20 minutes

Hot pack. Blanch grapes in boiling water for 30 seconds. Drain and proceed as for raw pack, using sterilized jars:

pints and quarts . . . . . . 10 minutes

MELONS

Few of us in the North raise enough melons to freeze, but occasionally they are on sale, and they are excellent frozen. Serve plain or in a mixed fruit or salad dish.

Cut ripe melons in half, scooping out seeds; peel and slice or dice. Pack into containers, covering with thin syrup. Leave appropriate headroom (see page 170), seal and freeze.

MIXED FRUITS

For fruit salad or compote, combine any combination of fruits except oranges and bananas. Remember, color makes a dish, so let your imagination loose. Mixed fruits are just right for those odd lots of fruit not large enough to freeze separately.

Boiling-Water Bath

Raw pack. Prepare as in specific directions for each fruit. Pack into clean, hot pint jars and cover with hot medium syrup or fruit juice, leaving ½ inch headroom. Adjust lids. Process in a boiling-water bath for the time required by the fruit having the longest processing time.

Freezing

Prepare each fruit according to specific directions. Cover with medium syrup or juice after packing into containers. Leave appropriate headroom (see page 170). Seal and freeze.

NECTARINES

Canning

Can as you would peaches (page 174).

Freezing

Freeze as you would peaches. Overripe fruit may have a disagreeable flavor when frozen.

PEACHES

Nothing is more satisfying than peaches, so if you are wondering where to start with fruit, look no further. Check your local quality, however. Shipped peaches are picked unripened and are often sadly lacking in flavor and texture.

GRANDMA THURBER'S PICKLED PEACHES

These peaches are delicious with any meal, and make a much appreciated holiday gift.

1 peck (12 pounds) peaches, with "pink cheeks"
7 pounds sugar
2 quarts vinegar
4 sticks cinnamon and 2 tablespoons whole cloves, tied in a cheesecloth bag additional cloves

Combine sugar, vinegar, and spice bag, and bring to a boil. Be sure to use a large kettle, as this boils over quickly.

Scald peaches in boiling water just long enough to loosen skins; dip in cold water and peel. Put 4 whole cloves into each peach, and drop a few at a time into boiling syrup. Cook until tender and translucent, then put into sterilized canning jars. When jars are all filled, add boiling syrup to cover, leaving ½ inch headroom. Wipe rims carefully, adjust lids, and finish in a boiling-water bath. Makes 4-6 quarts.

pints and quarts . . . 5 minutes

To peel, scald briefly by dipping into boiling water. Cool quickly in cold water, and the skins will slip off easily.

Boiling-Water Bath

Hot packs make a better-quality canned product. Wash, peel, and section; peach halves may retain air bubbles in the packing. Optional but recommended: treat with an anti-oxidant (see page 164).

Hot pack. Boil for 3 minutes in a medium syrup or fruit juice. Pack into hot, clean jars, leaving ½ inch headroom. Add additional hot syrup if necessary to cover, leaving ½ inch headroom. Adjust lids. Process in a boiling-water bath:

> pints . . . . . . 20 minutes
> quarts. . . . . . 25 minutes

Raw pack. Pack sections into hot, clean jars. Fill with medium syrup or fruit juice, leaving ½ inch headroom. Adjust lids. Process in a boiling-water bath:

> pints . . . . . . 25 minutes
> quarts. . . . . . 30 minutes

Freezing

See page 170 for appropriate headroom.

Syrup pack. Pack prepared fruit into containers and cover with medium syrup. Optional but recommended: add ½ teaspoon crystalline ascorbic acid to 1 quart syrup. Press fruit down, using a crumpled wad of wax paper to keep fruit below surface of syrup. Leave appropriate headroom. Seal and freeze.

Sugar pack. Add ⅔ cup sugar to 1 quart fruit. Mix well. Pack into containers, leaving appropriate headroom. Seal and freeze. Optional: sprinkle ¼ teaspoon crystalline ascorbic acid mixed with ¼ cup water over fruit.

Purée or crushed. Prepare as above. Crush coarsely. For purée, heat for 4 minutes in just enough water to prevent scorching. Mix 1 cup sugar to 1 quart fruit. Pack into containers, leaving appropriate headroom. Seal and freeze. Optional: add ⅛ teaspoon crystalline ascorbic acid to 1 quart purée.

Drying

Refer to Chapter 7.

PEARS

Firm pears are necessary. Bartletts are best, but try Seckel for spicing. Pears are best when picked slightly underripe and just turning yellow. Wrap each one in paper and store at room temperature for 2 or

3 weeks. Check them often. They will ripen evenly and be delicious. Wash, peel, cut, and core. An anti-oxidant is optional but recommended (see page 164). Pears are best canned with apple juice, pineapple juice, white grape juice, or a very light, light, or medium syrup.

Boiling-Water Bath

Raw pack. Pack prepared fruit into hot, clean jars, leaving ½ inch headroom. Add boiling thin or medium syrup or juice, leaving ½ inch headroom. Adjust lids. Process in a boiling-water bath:

> pints . . . . . . 25 minutes
> quarts. . . . . . 30 minutes

Hot pack. Prepare as above. Boil briefly in syrup or juice. Drain, saving liquid. Pack hot into hot, clean jars, leaving ½ inch headroom. Add hot liquid, leaving ½ inch headroom. Adjust lids. Process in a boiling-water bath:

> pints . . . . . . 20 minutes
> quarts. . . . . . 25 minutes

Freezing

Wash, peel, and core pears. Place them in an anti-oxidant (page 164). They can be left as halves, or sliced or quartered. Prepare a syrup by mixing 3 cups of sugar to 4 cups of water. Boil this, then let cool. Drain pears and blanch them 2 minutes. Cool immediately, and pack in containers, leaving appropriate headroom (see page 170). Cover with cool syrup. Seal and freeze.

CINNAMON PEARS

14 pounds pears
1 teaspoon stick cinnamon
1 teaspoon whole cloves
1 quart cider vinegar
6 pounds honey

Peel pears. Put spices in cheesecloth bag. Heat vinegar and honey to boiling, adding spice bag and pears. Cook until pears are tender. Remove pears and spices. Boil syrup until thick. Pack pears into hot, clean jars, leaving ½ inch headroom. Cover with hot syrup, leaving ½ inch headroom. Adjust lids. Process in boiling-water bath. Makes 6 quarts.

pints and quarts . . . . . 20 minutes

PINEAPPLES

Few of us live where pineapple is native, but it is a good buy from time to time and worth putting up. Uncooked pineapple cannot be used in gelatin salads or desserts, as the acid in the fruit prevents jelling.

Boiling-Water Bath

Hot pack. Wash, slice, and peel pineapple, removing eyes and core. Slice into rings or wedges. Boil in pineapple juice or medium syrup for 5-10 minutes. Pack into hot, clean jars, leaving ½ inch headroom. Adjust lids. Process in a boiling-water bath:

> pints . . . . . . 15 minutes
> quarts. . . . . . 20 minutes

Pineapple (and other juicy fruits) can be canned in its own unsweetened juice rather than in a sugar syrup. Cut up and crush the ripest parts of the pineapple. Simmer (185°-210°F.) until the juice runs freely. Strain through a jelly bag or several layers of damp cheesecloth. Use this juice in place of the sugar syrup called for in the canning recipe.

Freezing

Wash, slice, and pare ripe pineapples and cut according to preference.

Syrup pack. Pack tightly into containers, covering with thin syrup (made with juice or water). Leave appropriate headroom (see page 170). Seal and freeze.

Unsweetened pack. Pack into containers, leaving appropriate headroom; seal and freeze.

PLUMS AND PRUNES

Use ripe, firm fruit. Sort, wash, pit, and cut according to preference. If you are canning plums whole, prick the skins with a needle to prevent bursting.

Boiling-Water Bath

Raw pack. Prepare as above. Pack into hot, clean jars, leaving ½ inch headroom. Add boiling fruit juice or very light, light, or medium syrup, leaving ½ inch headroom. Adjust lids. Process in a boiling-water bath:

      pints . . . . . . 20 minutes
      quarts. . . . . . 25 minutes

Hot pack. Add plums to hot juice or syrup and boil 2 minutes. Cover pan and let stand 20-30 minutes. Fill jars with hot plums and cooking liquid, leaving ½ inch headroom. Process in a boiling-water bath:

      pints . . . . . . 20 minutes
      quarts. . . . . . 25 minutes

Freezing

Syrup pack. Prepare as above. Pack into containers, covering with medium syrup. Optional: add ½ teaspoon crystalline ascorbic acid to 1 quart syrup. Leave appropriate headroom (see page 170). Seal and freeze.

Unsweetened pack. Prepare as above. Pack into containers, leaving appropriate headroom. Seal and freeze.

RHUBARB

Harvesting

As soon as the stalks are as thick as your thumb, they can be harvested. There are red and green varieties, so the color is not important. To pick, twist off (don't cut) the outside stalks. Be sure to cut

---

🌱 GROWING RHUBARB IN THE WINTER

If you're fortunate enough to have an excess of rhubarb crowns, dig up a few (two-year-olds are best) any time after the first heavy frosts of the fall. They will provide a taste of summer in the winter.

With each crown, dig up as much of the roots as possible in one clump, and pot each crown in a roomy container with rich soil or compost. Store in a cold, dark place. A month before rhubarb is wanted, move the pot into a warm, dark location. (Temperature of 60°F. is ideal.) Soil should be kept moist for maximum growth. As much as 2 pounds of rhubarb will be produced by each crown.

out the seed pods as they form in the center of the plant in order to keep the plant producing stalks.

Preparation

Whether rhubarb is technically a fruit or vegetable is for the horticulturists to decide. Low on the pH scale, it is processed as a fruit. Wash and cut off both ends (don't peel them), then cut into 1-inch pieces. The leaves contain oxalic acid, which is poisonous, so warn children. Consider putting up rhubarb as a dessert sauce or stretching strawberries by making strawberry-rhubarb pie or jam.

Boiling-Water Bath

Add ½ cup sugar to each quart. Let the fruit stand for several hours to draw out the juice. Boil for 1 minute. Pack into hot, sterilized jars, leaving ½ inch headroom. Cover with hot juice, leaving ½ inch headroom. Adjust lids. Process in a boiling-water bath:

pints and quarts . . . . . . 10 minutes

Freezing

Unsweetened. Pack tightly into containers, leaving appropriate headroom (see page 170). Seal and freeze.

Syrup pack. Optional: put rhubarb into boiling water for 1 minute, cooling it quickly in cold water. Pack into containers and cover with medium syrup, leaving appropriate headroom. Seal and freeze.

STRAWBERRIES

Harvesting

Strawberries should be picked as soon as they are ripe, red, and juicy. Keep them picked every couple of days, so the plant will put its energy into ripening more fruit.

Freezing

Strawberries should be frozen or made into jellies or jams; canning is not recommended. See illustrations, page 19. Sort and wash ripe, red strawberries; remove hulls and wash again. See page 170 for appropriate headroom.

Syrup pack. Put berries into containers and cover with a cold heavy syrup, leaving appropriate headroom. Seal and freeze.

Sugar pack. Add ¾ cup sugar to 1 quart fruit and mix thoroughly. Pack into containers, leaving appropriate headroom. Seal and freeze. Strawberries frozen this way can be whole, sliced, or crushed.

Unsweetened. Pack into containers, leaving appropriate headroom (see page 170). Seal and freeze. Optional: add 1 teaspoon crystalline ascorbic acid to 1 quart water and pour over berries. Pack into containers, leaving appropriate headroom. Seal and freeze.

Flash-freezing. Use only perfect, large berries. Place them on a metal sheet and freeze until solid. Then transfer them to freezer containers. Seal and freeze. These are ideal for decoration on cheesecakes or strawberry shortcakes, especially when used semi-thawed so as to retain their shape.

Purée. Prepare strawberries, then press through a food mill or run through a blender. Add ⅔ cup sugar to 1 quart berries. Mix well and pack into containers, leaving appropriate headroom. Seal and freeze.

Canning and Freezing Fruit Juices

Fruit juices are quick and easy to make. They are a practical use for extra fruit and for misshapen or slightly bruised fruit that would be unattractive preserved whole. Good-quality juice requires fruit with a full, ripe flavor and from which all signs of rot or blemish have been carefully cut.

If storage or freezer space is limited, you may hesitate to fill it with juice, which is, after all, largely water. But weigh against this the many ways home-canned juices can be used. They can be iced for a healthful beverage, used for leisurely jelly-making when the crush of the harvest season has passed, or made into syrups to brighten breakfast pancakes or dinner desserts. Fruit juices can provide the liquid base for homemade gelatin desserts and salads. Several varieties can be blended for a special Christmas punch. Or serve them steaming hot on a cold winter afternoon with a stick of cinnamon. In summer children love popsicles of sweetened berry juice frozen in molds or improvised from ice trays or paper cups into which a stick is put.

Fruit juices will retain their fresh flavor if heated as little as possible during preparation, and for freezing they should be chilled as rapidly as possible. Processing in a 5-minute boiling-water bath is recommended for most of the fruit juices to ensure safe storage.

Equipment Needed

Kettles and bowls should be made of stainless steel, glass, plastic, or unchipped enamelware. Aluminum pans are safe to use, but the acid in the fruit juice will cause unattractive pitting in the pan, and aluminum salts dissolved in the juice may cause unpleasant color or flavor changes. A double boiler is used for gentle heating of the juice to simmering for hot-pack canning, or an asbestos pad can be used under a pan if the juice is heated directly over the flame.

The jelly bag should be made of tightly woven muslin or canvas for the clearest juice. You will need cheesecloth, or clean paper coffee filters for straining pressed juice. Cheesecloth should be washed and rinsed before use to avoid imparting off-flavors to the juice. To be sure the temperature of the juice does not exceed that recommended, a thermometer is helpful but optional.

For canning. Standard canning jars should be thoroughly washed and sterilized. Leave them in simmering water (or hot in dishwasher with sterilizing cycle) until ready to use. Lids should be prepared according to manufacturer's directions, or wash and cover with boiling water. Leave in water until ready to use. A water-bath canner or large kettle with a rack is needed for a boiling-water bath.

For freezing. The best containers to use are rigid plastic freezer containers. Freezing jars with wide mouths and tapered sides with no shoulders can also be used. Other standard canning jars can be used only if recommended by the manufacturer for freezing as well as canning. Be sure enough headroom is left (see chart on page 183), so that the glass will not break when the juice expands during freezing. Containers should be thoroughly washed in hot soapy water, rinsed, and scalded with boiling water.

Ascorbic Acid

Crystalline ascorbic acid can be added to juices to help preserve color and flavor, as well as adding supplementary vitamin C. This can be bought at drugstores. To citrus juices, ¾ teaspoon can be added per gallon of juice; add 1 teaspoon to a gallon of other types of juice.

Sweetening

Natural, unsweetened fruit juices are delicious and healthful, but sugar can be added if desired. One cup of sugar to a gallon of the sweeter juices is usually enough. About half as much mild-flavored honey can be used instead. If the juice is to be used for jelly, omit the sugar; or label the jar with the amount of sugar used and adjust the jelly recipe accordingly. For people on sugar-restricted diets, a sugar substitute that is recommended by your doctor may be used as the sweetener but should be added after opening a container of unsweetened juice; artificial sweeteners added to heated juice before processing may give the juice an off or unpleasant taste. The use of sugar depends on personal preference and is not necessary for preserving the juice.

Preparation of the Fruit

Use ripe, fresh, flavorful fruit for the best juice. Juice for jelly-making should be made of the type of fruit recommended in the jelly recipe. Sort and wash the fruit, and remove blemishes, stems, pits, or what have you. Some fruits are cut up and heated slightly (in enough water to prevent sticking, if necessary) to start the juice flowing. Juicy fruits are cut up, crushed, and the juice squeezed from them without heating. Apples for cider are crushed and pressed without heating; for apple juice, water is added to cut-up apples and they are simmered until soft. Orange, grapefruit, and lemon juices are squeezed from the fresh fruit and heated only enough to be hot-packed into canning jars; for

---

NO-SUGAR CANNING AND FREEZING OF FRUIT

If you are looking for sugar-free directions for dieting or diabetic reasons, Kerr Glass Manufacturing Corporation has some good guidelines.

Fruit can be canned safely without sugar. For hot pack, preheat fruit over low heat in a small amount of water. Then pack fruit into jars, covering with juice from the kettle, and process according to the specific directions. For raw pack, pack the fruit into jars raw. Add fruit juice obtained by crushing completely ripe fruit and boiling it over low heat. Then strain the juice through a clean cloth and fill to within 1½ inches of the top of the jars. Process according to specific directions.

To use artificial sweeteners, check the directions for each and consult your doctor before using. More information can be obtained by writing to the American Diabetic Association, Inc., 18 East 48th Street, New York, NY 10017.

To freeze without sugar, prepare according to individual instructions. Use either 3 tablespoons of lemon juice to 1 gallon of water or ascorbic acid as an anti-oxidant as explained on page 164. Process quickly and freeze, leaving appropriate headroom (see page 170).

freezing, no heat is applied. Light cherries and white grapes also are not heated except enough to hot-pack for canning.

A blender can be used to break down the fruit without heat, and an electric juicer will quickly separate juice from the pulp of most fruits. The juicy pulp from the fruit can be squeezed through a jelly bag, and for a clearer juice re-strained through 4 layers of damp, washed cheesecloth. Sugar and ascorbic acid can be added if desired, and the juice is ready for processing.

Freezing

Pour the prepared juice into clean containers, cool it rapidly (if hot) in the refrigerator or packed in ice, label it, and put it into the coldest part of the freezer to freeze. Be sure to leave adequate headroom in standard canning jars (see page 183).

After the juice has been frozen in the coldest part of the freezer, it can be moved for storage to any part of the freezer where the temperature is 0°F. or less. Under these conditions, frozen citrus juices should be good for 3-4 months, other juices for up to 8 months.

CANNING FRUIT JUICES

Reheat the prepared juice to simmering (190°F. for most juices; 165°F. for citrus juices), and pour immediately into hot, sterilized canning jars, leaving appropriate headroom. Adjust lids, and process in a boiling-water bath for 10 minutes according to the specific instructions (pints and quarts).

To keep the total heating time of the juice to a minimum, have the water just below boiling when the jars are placed in the kettle. Start timing as soon as the water reaches a full boil, and as soon as the time is up remove the jars.

Set on a rack or towel in a draft-free spot, and allow to cool completely. Check for a good seal, remove screwbands, label, and store in a dark, cool place. The jars can be wrapped in paper or cloth to exclude the light if the storage area is not dark. Color and certain vitamins may be lost by exposure to light.

When the directions call for a hot-water bath instead of a boiling-water bath, follow the directions above *except* do not allow the water to exceed the recommended simmering temperature — a maximum of 175°F. for citrus juices, 190°F. for other juices. In a hot-water bath the juice is pasteurized and the jar sealed without imparting a cooked flavor to the juice.

Short-Cut Juice

A faster way to make canned juice is to can whole or cut-up fruit in boiling water. The juice will make itself when processed and stored — all you need to do is strain and chill it before serving.

Use fully ripe fruit. Wash, stem, pit, and cut up as necessary,

---

HONEY

In recent years honey has become increasingly popular as a sugar substitute. It is more healthful than sugar but should be used in moderation when substituted for sugar in canning recipes. Substituting half the sugar in a recipe with honey seems to achieve satisfactory results if it is mild flavored, such as clover honey. Buckwheat honeys are typically stronger and will overpower the subtle flavors of fruits in jams and jellies or fruit juices. Old-fashioned recipes, some of which come down from the eighteenth century, when honey was more available than sugar, call for pure honey and no sugar.

Honey in any form should never be given to babies under 1 year of age, as they are apparently susceptible to a particular botulism organism that occurs in honey even when cooked.

depending on the type of fruit. Put 1 to 1½ cups fruit into a hot, sterilized quart jar. Add up to 1 cup of sugar and ¼ teaspoon crystalline ascorbic acid to the less tart fruits. Fill with boiling water, leaving ½ inch headroom. Adjust lids, and process for 10 minutes in a boiling-water bath. This method is particularly successful with grapes and berries.

Do not *squeeze* any juice through the jelly bag if you want it crystal clear, especially for jelly. It should be allowed to just drip for several hours or overnight. For greater quantity and a thicker juice, you can squeeze the bag and re-strain the juice through 4 layers of damp, washed cheesecloth.

APPLE JUICE

Wash and quarter apples that have good flavor. Remove stem and blossom ends and blemishes and bruises. Leave on skins but remove core. Cover with water and simmer until soft (25-30 minutes). Press through jelly bag and re-strain through cheesecloth. Reheat juice to simmering and pour into hot, sterilized jars, leaving ¼ inch headroom. Process in boiling-water bath for 5 minutes.

APPLE CIDER

Wash, crush, and press tart, ripe, juicy apples. Large quantities are most easily done in a cider press, outside on a sunny fall day. Presses can sometimes be borrowed or rented or improvised. Small quantities of apples can be chopped up in a food grinder or juicer, and the cider squeezed through a jelly bag or pressed out with a rolling pin — a messy process!

A cider press may have an attached grinder that chops or grinds up the apples, which go into a cloth bag made of clean muslin, bleached burlap, a sheet or pillowcase. The ground apples are then pressed and the cider flows out, leaving the apple residue, or *pomace*, in the bag. Water can be added to the pomace in order to extract a greater quantity of cider.

Cider-making is a big occasion at our house, attracting lots of kids (and their parents) all wanting to help grind apples and taste the cider. The grinder on the press we use is exposed at the bottom and a great hazard to little fingers, so it is important to supervise the operation closely. Yellow jackets never fail to show up, too, presenting another hazard. Our pony is equally interested in the fragrant apples, and he shares the pomace with the pigs and chickens.

Cider that you make or buy fresh from a cider mill can be canned like apple juice, and since it is pasteurized in the process it will not ferment into "hard" cider. However, if you want the taste of cider and not apple juice, we suggest you freeze it.

SAVING CIDER

"If you bottle and refrigerate cider you can expect it to hold its flavor for about one to two weeks. But there are other ways of preserving cider for longer periods. Freezing is easily accomplished and is a reliable method if you have the space. Or you can pasteurize the juice and keep it just about indefinitely. The traditional method is to store the cider in oak barrels; it is a more complicated procedure, but the time and effort are worthwhile because the result —delicious natural hard cider — is so satisfying."

Judy Raven
Making Apple Cider

Freezing

Pour fresh cider into containers, leaving ample headroom (see page 183). Seal, chill, and freeze.

BERRY JUICES

Wash (if necessary) in cold water and crush fully ripe berries. Simmer briefly until juicy; do not add water. Press through jelly bag, then re-strain juice, without squeezing, through damp cheesecloth. Add sugar if desired, about 1 cup to 9 cups of juice; or for strawberry juice, ⅔-1 cup to 4 cups juice.

Freezing

Pour juice into containers, leaving ample headroom (see page 183). Seal, chill, and freeze.

Canning

Reheat juice to simmering; pour into hot, sterilized jars, leaving ¼ inch headroom. Adjust lids and process in a boiling-water bath:

pints and quarts . . . . 30 minutes

BERRY PURÉES

Wash, sort, and crush fully ripe berries, and press through a sieve or food mill. Then proceed as for Fruit Nectars, page 186.

CHERRIES, RED

Use bright red, tree-ripened cherries, sweet or sour. Stem, sort, and wash thoroughly. Drain, pit, and crush. Heat slightly to start juice flowing, then press through a jelly bag. Let stand overnight or for several hours in refrigerator, and then pour off clear juice. Or else process as is and strain when ready to use. Sweeten sour cherry juice with 1½ to 2 cups sugar to each quart of juice, sweet cherry juice with 1 cup sugar to 9 cups of juice. Juice made from sweet cherries hasn't much zing, so you may want to mix some sour cherry juice with it, either before processing or when ready to use.

Freezing

Pour juice into containers, leaving ample headroom (see page 183). Seal, chill if warm, and freeze.

Headroom Required for Freezing Juices

TYPE OF JAR	SIZE	AMOUNT OF HEADROOM NEEDED
Wide mouth, no shoulder (also plastic containers)	pints quarts	1 inch 1½ inches
Wide mouth, with shoulder	pints and quarts	1½ inches
Regular mouth, with shoulder	pints and quarts	2 inches

Canning

Reheat juice to simmering and pour into hot, sterilized jars, leaving ¼ inch headroom. Adjust lids and process in a boiling-water bath:

> pints and quarts . . . . 30 minutes

CHERRIES, WHITE

Use tree-ripened fruit with good color and flavor. Sort, stem, wash, and drain. Remove pits and crush. Do not heat. Press through a jelly bag. Warm juice to 165°F. in a double boiler or over low heat. Let juice stand overnight in the refrigerator and then pour off clear juice, or process as is and strain before using. Crystalline ascorbic acid may be added, ¼ teaspoon per quart of juice. Sweeten to taste.

Freezing

Pack juice into containers, leaving ample headroom (see page 183). Seal, chill if warm, and freeze.

Canning

Heat juice to simmering and pour into hot, sterilized jars, leaving ¼ inch headroom. Adjust lids and process in a boiling-water bath:

> pints and quarts . . . . 30 minutes

CITRUS FRUITS

Work quickly with small batches of citrus fruits to preserve the natural vitamin C that can be lost from exposure to air and by heating. Use firm, tree-ripened fruit heavy for its size and free from soft spots. The fruit should be at room temperature. Squeeze or ream juice from the fruit using a squeezer that does not press oil from the rind. Strain out seeds and pieces of fruit. Add ¾ teaspoon crystalline ascorbic acid to each gallon of juice.

Freezing

Pour juice into containers, leaving ample headroom (see page 183). Seal, and freeze immediately.

Canning

Heat juice barely to simmering (165°F.). Immediately pour into hot, sterilized jars, leaving ¼ inch headroom. Adjust lids and process in a boiling-water bath:

pints and quarts . . . . 30 minutes

CRANBERRY JUICE

Sort and wash ripe cranberries. Add an equal amount of water and boil for 15 minutes, or until berries burst. Press through a jelly bag and re-strain through damp cheesecloth. Sweeten to taste.

Freezing

Pour juice into containers, leaving ample headroom (see page 183). Seal, chill, and freeze.

Canning

Reheat juice to simmering and pour into hot, sterilized jars, leaving ¼ inch headroom. Adjust lids and process in a boiling-water bath:

pints and quarts . . . . 15 minutes

GRAPE JUICE

Use fully ripe grapes with good flavor and color. Wash, stem, and crush. *Concord grapes:* Add just enough water to cover and simmer gently until soft, about 10 minutes. *White grapes:* Do not heat after crushing. Squeeze through a jelly bag, then let juice stand overnight in refrigerator. Pour off clear juice, being careful not to disturb the sediment that has settled to the bottom. This should remove the crystals of tartaric acid that are a nuisance in grape juice. If crystals are present after processing, re-strain the juice before using.

Freezing

Pour juice into containers, leaving ample headroom (see page 183). Seal, and freeze.

Cherry pitters are really a matter of taste. The large crank type that screws onto a counter is expensive and takes storage space, but if you do quarts of cherries, it might be worthwhile. A small hand pitter is handy and retains the shape of cherries. But a pointed paring knife is adequate.

Canning

Heat juice to simmering, and pour into hot, sterilized jars, leaving ¼ inch headroom. Adjust lids and process in a boiling-water bath:

pints and quarts . . . . 15 minutes

PINEAPPLE JUICE

Use firm, ripe pineapples with full flavor and aroma. Pare, and remove eyes. Chop or grind the pineapple. Add enough water just to cover, and boil for 10 minutes. Press juice through a jelly bag and sweeten to taste.

Freezing

Pour juice into containers, leaving ample headroom (see page 183). Seal, chill, and freeze.

Canning

Reheat juice to simmering and pour into hot, sterilized jars, leaving ¼ inch headroom. Adjust lids and process in a boiling-water bath:

pints and quarts . . . . 30 minutes

PLUMS AND PRUNES

Use firm, tree-ripened fruit with good color. Wash plums and fresh prunes, and simmer for 15 minutes in enough water just to cover. Dried prunes can also be used; they should be soaked overnight in cold water, using 1 quart of water to ½ pound prunes, then simmered in the same water until plump and tender. Turn prepared fruit into a jelly bag and press out juice. Sweeten if desired with ½-1 cup sugar to a quart of juice, or to taste.

Freezing

Pour juice into containers, leaving ample headroom (see page 183). Seal, chill, and freeze.

Canning

Reheat juice to simmering and pour into hot, sterilized jars, leaving ¼ inch headroom. Process in a boiling-water bath:

pints and quarts . . . . 30 minutes

RHUBARB JUICE

Rhubarb comes so early in the season you can use it to practice putting up juice before the real fruits arrive. It can be used all summer as a tart cooler, mixed with other juices or with ginger ale.

Use tender, red stalks with few fibers for the most colorful juice. Wash, trim, and cut into pieces up to 4 inches long. Add 1 quart water to 4 quarts (5 pounds) rhubarb, and bring just to boiling. Press through a jelly bag, then re-strain through damp cheesecloth. Sweeten to taste or with ½ cup sugar to a quart of juice.

Freezing

Pour juice into containers, leaving ample headroom (see page 183). Seal, chill, and freeze.

Canning

Reheat juice to simmering and pour into hot, sterilized jars, leaving ¼ inch headroom. Process in a boiling-water bath:

> pints and quarts . . . . 20 minutes

SYRUPS

Try making syrup from any of the flavorful fruit juices that you make. The process is similar to making jelly except that the cooking time is only long enough to thicken the syrup, not long enough to make it jell. This recipe is particularly adapted to berries and grapes, and it makes one pint of syrup.

> 1¼ cups juice
> 1¾ cups sugar (or 1½ cups sugar and ¼ cup light
>   corn syrup for thicker syrup)
> 1 tablespoon lemon juice (optional)

Heat juice in a large kettle; add sugar and stir to dissolve. Bring to a full rolling boil and boil hard for 1 minute. Remove from heat and skim off foam. Pour into containers and store in refrigerator for immediate use.

Freezing

Let syrup cool, pour into containers, leaving ample headroom (see page 183). Seal, and freeze.

Canning

Pour hot into hot, sterilized half-pint jars, leaving ¼ inch headroom. Adjust lids and process in a boiling-water bath for 20 minutes.

FRUIT NECTARS

Apricots, nectarines, pears, and peaches all can be made into nectars, which are thick pulpy juices to which ice water can be added before drinking. Apricot nectar is the important ingredient of an easily made cake that is a favorite with our family, so we have included the recipe on this page.

To make nectar, use fully ripe fruit. Wash thoroughly, pit, and quarter. With pears, remove stems and blossom ends and quarter. It is not necessary to peel the fruit unless puréeing in a blender. Press raw through a sieve or food mill, or heat for several minutes to the boiling point with a little water to prevent scorching, and then press.

To each quart of nectar, add 1 cup sugar. To help preserve the color and flavor, ¼ teaspoon crystalline ascorbic acid dissolved in ¼ cup water can be added to the nectar just before adding the sugar.

Freezing

Pack the nectar into containers, leaving ample headroom (see page 183). Seal, chill, and freeze.

Canning

Heat the nectar to simmering (185°-210°F.) and pour hot into hot, sterilized jars, leaving ¼ inch headroom. Adjust lids and process in a boiling-water bath:

> pints . . . . . 15 minutes
> quarts. . . . . 25 minutes

APRICOT NECTAR LEMON SUPREME CAKE

1 package Lemon Supreme cake mix
1 cup apricot nectar
¾ cup vegetable oil
½ cup sugar
4 eggs
1 cup confectioner's sugar
juice of 1 lemon

Preheat oven to 350°F. and oil a tube pan. Mix cake mix, nectar, oil, and sugar. Add eggs one at a time, beating thoroughly after each one. Pour into oiled tube pan and bake at 350° for 1 hour or more, until cake springs back at a touch. Cool 10 minutes, turn out upside down onto a plate, and glaze with 1 cup sifted confectioner's sugar, mixed (most easily in a blender) with the juice of 1 lemon.

For variation, try substituting other flavor nectars or juices and a different type cake mix. Orange juice and chocolate cake topped with sifted confectioner's sugar is great!

Other Storey/Garden Way Publishing Books You Will Enjoy

The New Zucchini Cookbook, by Nancy Ralston & Marynor Jordan. At last — wonderful things to do with zucchini. Everything from zucchini marmalade to zucchini raisin pie, with over 250 recipes. 176 pp. Illus. $7.95. Order #589-8.

Garden Way Publishing's Bread Book, by Ellen Johnson. A fabulous collection of 140 original recipes. "Can't fail" instructions for a tasty loaf! 192 pp. Photos & illus. $12.95. Order #139-6.

Down-to-Earth Gardening Know-How for the 90s: Vegetables and Herbs, by Dick Raymond. A treasury of gardening information. Learn how to double, even triple, your yield. 224 pp. Charts, photos & illus. $12.95. Order #649-5.

Fruits and Berries for the Home Garden, by Lewis Hill. Let an expert orchardist guide you to home-grown apples, plums, peaches, blackberries, strawberries, elderberries, nuts, and more. 288 pp. Photos & illus. $10.95. Order #168-X.

Growing & Using Herbs Successfully, by Betty E. M. Jacobs. Easy growing techniques for 64 herbs. Herbs for cooking, teas, dyes, gifts, and medicines. 240 pp. Botanical drawings. $9.95. Order #249-X.

Carrots Love Tomatoes: Secrets of Companion Planting for Successful Gardening, by Louise Riotte. Our strange-but-true book tells what to plant together for best results and why. 240 pp. Illus. $7.95. Order # 064-0.

Saving Seeds, by Marc Rogers. Step-by-step information on raising vegetables and flowers for seed. 176 pp. Illus. $9.95. Order #634-7.

A to Z Hints for the Vegetable Gardener, from the 10,000 members of the Men's Garden Clubs of America. Hundreds of tips, tricks, and suggestions. 128 pp. Photos & illus. $6.95. Order #106-X.

Home Sausage Making, by Charles Reavis. From making to preserving and storing, this book covers brockwurst, frankfurter, cotechino, kielbasa, and salami, etc. 176 pp. Photos & illus. $12.95. Order #477-8.

Pickles & Relishes, by Andrea Chesman. Step-by-step instructions for a variety of pickling methods, and more than 150 recipes, from apples to zucchini. 160 pp. illus. $9.95. Order #321-6.

Peppers, Hot and Sweet, by Beth Dooley. More than 100 inventive pepper recipes, covering a vast range of tastes from classic American to steamy Caribbean, from fiery South American to piquant Asian. 144 pp. $8.95. Order #621-5.

Build an Underground Root Cellar, Bulletin A-76. Complete instructions for building your own cold-storage cellar. 32 pp. illus. $1.95. Order #290-2

These books are available at your bookstore or lawn and garden center, or may be ordered directly from *Storey's Books for Country Living,* Schoolhouse Road, Pownal, VT 05261. Please include $2.75 for postage and handling. Send for our free mail-order catalog.

Index

Page numbers in italics indicate charts, illustrations, or tables.